W9-CAJ-179

To the thousands of students and parents
with whom I have worked over the years,
thank you one and all.

Also by Marjorie Hansen Shaevitz:

So You Want to Go Back to School (with Elinor Lenz)

Making It Together as a Two Career Couple (with Morton H. Shaevitz, PhD)

The Superwoman Syndrome

The Confident Woman

[CONTENTS]

WHO AM I TO BE TELLING YOU WHAT TO DO?

I never intended to be a college admissions coach, develop a website, or write a book about college admissions. That all these have taken place is one of those delightful, unforeseen eventualities that sometimes occur in life.

I have worked at a number of universities including Stanford University and the East West Center at the University of Hawaii. Some years ago, I created a Re-entry Program for adults at University of California, San Diego (UCSD). Over the years, I counseled many adults about going back to school, and often ended up helping their children with college admissions.

Most of my professional life has been spent working as a marriage and family therapist and executive coach with women (and some men), trying to bring some sanity and healthy living practices to their lives. Then a very predictable life event presented itself: my two children entered high school and the buzz about college admissions began leaking into our lives. I wasn't overly concerned about the children's college prospects. They were both very good students and attended a school that had a college counselor who focused on helping students with the admissions process.

However, my sense of calm slowly eroded as I began to see that my children were not getting the information and support they needed. Among other things, the school did not alert my son to sign up for the appropriate subject test after he had completed an AP History class. As it happens, he scored a 5 on the AP test, but by not signing up for the related Subject Test he lost a wonderful opportunity. Another worry was the school outwardly discouraging students from preparing for the SAT I test. Finally, the straw that broke the camel's back occurred when my children, as a sophomore and a junior, began asking questions about college admissions and the college counselor brushed them off by saying that it was much too early to start thinking about such things.

I decided that I was going to cut through all the myths and folklore about college admissions to find out "the truth" about what really happens and what counts. To do so, I read every book written on the subject. I also called many of my admissions friends to get "the skinny" on what was important and not. In the end, I assisted my children in developing college lists that matched their needs and interests, and helped them figure out how to make their applications stand out from those of other applicants. Both were admitted to many different colleges and for their own very different reasons each chose Stanford University for their undergraduate education.

Once they were settled in college, I thought my admissions work was done. However, something very interesting happened. Because of the children's success, my best friend asked me to help her son with his college applications. I couldn't turn her down. Once her son was admitted to Princeton, she then told many of her other friends to get my help with their children's college admissions. Within a year of my children leaving for college, my phone began to ring off the hook with pleas from parents asking for assistance. Soon those phone calls were not just from San Diego where I live, but also from Los Angeles, San Francisco, the East Coast, Pacific Northwest, Mexico City, Tel Aviv, London, Stockholm, Tokyo, and even cities in China and India.

I never dreamed that college admissions coaching would become a full-time job; never once have I advertised or marketed the service. To this day, adMISSION POSSIBLE is totally a word-of-mouth business. I can't keep up with the demand. Who would have thought that helping my children with their college applications would someday evolve into a successful global business, including a coaching service, website, and a series of books and other products.

Because I can't see all the students who want my counsel, and also because there are many people who cannot afford to pay the fees for an independent counselor, I decided that writing a book about college admissions (and developing a website that offers free information and advice) would be a good way to broaden the base of people whom I could help, as well as level the playing field for those who need admissions information, but lack the financial resources to pay for it.

So who am I to be writing a book about college admissions? I bring the following background, experiences, and biases to this work:

* First, I have worked as an admissions counselor for many, many years now, and have coached thousands of students. I consider myself a student advocate. Rather than feel beaten up by the admissions process, my clients feel in control, gain major life skills, and develop confidence in themselves. The students with whom I have worked have been very successful in finding colleges that match their academic backgrounds, as well as their personal needs, wants, and desires. More importantly, they have gained acceptance to the likes of Amherst, Arizona, Babson, Bard, Bowdoin, Brown, Colorado, Cornell, Dartmouth, Duke, Emory, Georgetown, George Washington, Hampshire College, Harvard, Indiana, Loyola Marymount, MIT, Miami of Ohio, Miami, Michigan, Middlebury, NYU, Northwestern, Penn, Pomona College, Princeton, Santa Clara, Sarah Lawrence, Scripps College, Smith, SMU, Stanford, USC, University of San Diego, Vassar, Wake Forest, Washington University, Williams, Yale, the UCs, and many other colleges.

    adMISSION POSSIBLE provides readers with examples of what these successful applicants have done, written, and said. It is also filled with important life-management skills such as decision-making, problem solving, and interviewing techniques, as well as creating an Activities Résumé.

* Second, as a trained marriage and family therapist, I am determined to bring some sanity and calm to this predictably challenging time in a child's and a family's life. It is my hope that in reading this book, students and parents will become informed about admissions, organized, and strategic, thus avoiding the trauma that many people experience during the college admissions process. Even more, I want to redefine the admissions arena so that rather than having it be such a negative event, college admissions becomes a positive one that helps students figure out who they are and what they want to be and do in life.

* Third, as a frequent buyer and reader of admissions books, I have been struck by how difficult it is to find the information I want. To begin with, while most of the current books have a table of contents, often the chapter headings and sub-headings are so obtuse I don't have a clue as to what is in them. Even more

frustrating is the fact that many current books don't have indices. That means I have to read an entire book to see if it contains anything that might answer my questions. Therefore, in writing this book I have tried to be extra-sensitive to the need for readers to find and return to information they deem useful or important.

★ Finally, I am a concerned parent who is alarmed about the feeding frenzy that has developed around college admissions. Having successfully gone through the process with my own children, I know what it's like to experience the pressures and frustrations that occur from beginning to end. I have great empathy for anyone involved with applying to colleges. I want to make things easier for you. What this book represents is all the information and material I wish that I had possessed when I was helping my own kids.

GETTING READY for COLLEGE ADMISSIONS

CHAPTER 1

COURSES, GRADES, AND INTELLECTUAL PURSUITS

What Colleges Look for in Academic Preparation

DEFINITION of ACADEMIC PREPARATION: *Academic preparation refers to all coursework and other scholastic experiences that a student takes on during his or her high school career.*

THE BOTTOM LINE

Along with test scores, admissions officials say that the "rigor of students' coursework" and the grades they receive in those courses are the most important factors in determining their admission to colleges.

ACADEMIC PREPARATION IN HIGH SCHOOL

Many colleges require or recommend that students take academically rich courses, sometimes known as college preparatory or "solids." Solid courses are the most rigorous courses offered by high schools, usually in the fields of English, history, social studies, foreign languages, mathematics, science, and some of the arts.

> **adMISSION POSSIBLE TIP!**
>
> Colleges often look first to excellent grades in English classes and high verbal scores as a predictor of future college success.

To make sure that you meet the college entrance requirements and recommendations for most colleges, here is the high school curriculum that many colleges require or recommend for students:

SUBJECT	REQUIRED AND RECOMMENDED	COURSES
English	4 years	E.g., English 9, English 10, AP English Lit, AP English Language
Math	3 years (4 recommended)	Algebra I, Geometry, Algebra II, Pre-calculus, Calculus
Sciences	2 years including lab (3 recommended)	Biology, Chemistry, and Physics first, then other advanced sciences
Foreign language	2 years (3 recommended)	Some colleges require all language courses be in one language only
History/social sciences	3–4 years	Many schools require one year of Ancient, World, or European History, or Geography, and one year of U.S. History, Civics, and/or U.S. Government
Fine arts	1 year	Some colleges require courses in Dance, Drama, Music, or Visual Art
College prep elective	1 year	I.E. Psychology, Creative Writing, Computer Science, Economics

adMISSION POSSIBLE TIP

For students wishing to apply to the Ivies and other selective colleges, take as many Honors, AP, and IB courses as make sense. A good number of "solids" is twenty by the time you finish your senior year. Students can check the specific requirements of the colleges in which they are interested by consulting the High School Preparation section for each college's website, and also the listings in The College Board's *College Handbook*.

No matter what your college aspirations are, it is a good idea to take college prep courses. This will help keep your options open when admissions time rolls around. **The most rigorous courses offered in high schools today are Honors, AP, and IB courses.**

HONORS, AP, AND IB COURSES

Offered from freshman through senior years in most schools, Honors courses are usually the first level of advanced courses that are available to students in high school. Some schools require students to take certain Honors courses and receive at least B grades as a prerequisite for enrolling in AP or IB courses.

Advanced Placement Program (AP) courses are offered by high schools in a number of content areas (see AP Test list in chapter 4) for which the College Board offers examinations in May of every year. Graded on a scale from 1–5 (5 = the maximum score), students with higher AP test scores are often eligible for college credit and/or advanced placement into some classes at college.

International Baccalaureate (IB) courses are part of a two-year program usually taken during students' junior and senior years, which lead to an IB high school degree. IB tests are also offered at the end of each school year, and scored on a 1–7 scale (7 = the maximum score). Many colleges also accept IB test scores for college credit and/or advanced placement into college classes. AP and IB courses are usually more difficult than Honors courses. Information about the IB program is available on its website: www.ibo.org.

Taking rigorous courses is one thing, but having a balanced life is just as important. As for how many advanced

FAQ #1: Is it better to take a regular class and get an A, or an advanced class and get a B?

ANSWER: In general, it is better to take an advanced course and get a B than to take a regular course and get an A because the advanced or Honors course is an indication to colleges that you are challenging yourself, something admissions officers look for in students.

courses to take, choose as many challenging courses as you can handle well, along with the other things you do. Students with learning disabilities must be especially careful to not take on too much.

Over and over, college admissions people tell students to "take the strongest possible courseload." Many answer the above question by saying that students should take advanced classes and get A's, but the real answer is an individual one, and many different elements should go into the decision-making. What types of colleges are you applying to—most competitive, competitive, or not very competitive—and what do they expect? In what kinds of athletics and/or activities are you involved and how much do they demand? Do you have a learning difference or other disability that might affect how much you can take on or how well you will do? Do what makes sense for you.

Don't fall into the trap of thinking you have to take everything, be everything, and get four hours of sleep every night. That's not healthy for anyone. Sometimes enrolling in a regular class that you've been dying to take is the best choice, especially if this decision results in overall better grades, makes life more enjoyable, and diminishes your stress. However, if you thrive on taking challenging, difficult courses, then go for the advanced.

ACADEMIC PREPARATION OUTSIDE YOUR HIGH SCHOOL

Many admissions officers suggest that the best preparation for college is to be an avid reader and to learn how to write well. Therefore, do everything you can to increase your vocabulary and learn how to write while you are in high school. Among other things:

- **Read books on your own or join a book club**
- **Subscribe to the *New York Times*, *Washington Post*, *Wall Street Journal*, or your local newspaper and read it every day**
- **Ask your English teacher for the names of books to read, and for assistance or coaching if you want to do better in class or learn how to write more effectively**
- **If your parents can afford it, work with a writing tutor**
- **Join a writing club or an online writing group**
- **Take day, weekend, or summer writing courses**

If highly selective colleges are a student's aim, **excellent grades in demanding courses and high test scores are taken for granted.** They also **look for "something else" that separates an applicant from the crowd:**

that is a true love of learning. The exact content of students' intellectual pursuits is not important, only that something fascinates them.

One of the best-kept secrets in college admissions is how much colleges value students' involvement in academic pursuits outside their own school. Especially among the most selective colleges, the phrases most commonly used to describe the kinds of superb students they want are people with "intellectual vitality" (Stanford), a "desire to learn" (Harvard), a "passion for ideas" (Oberlin), "intellectually curious" (Claremont McKenna), or "an intense curiosity about learning for learning's sake" (Reed).

Some years ago, successful applicants could simply make straight A's with a rigorous courseload and get high SAT scores, proof enough for most colleges that they were desirable candidates. Today, the bar has been raised. Developing "academic prowess" is an important part of your preparation for college.

Students can act on their intellectual interests on their own or in organized programs. The following pages offer some suggestions.

1. INDIVIDUAL PURSUITS

* Submit your writing (fiction, nonfiction, poetry, drama) to a newspaper's editorial section, a writing contest, or Web magazine.
* Read everything you can find on a subject or person of interest.
* Do a special research or science project under the supervision of an expert or teacher in the field.
* Put together a special project in one of the arts (art, music, theater).
* Learn about a special interest or learn a language by traveling to a foreign country, working in a special place (such as a farm, cheese factory, outward bound camp), a volunteer setting, in which you think you might like to work (law firm, political office, hospital).
* Because you have exhausted your school's offerings in a particular subject, organize a new, advanced class with the help of a teacher.

Every year, more and more organized opportunities become available to students. They include the following:

2. ORGANIZED OFFERINGS

A. ACADEMIC COMPETITIONS

Are you a science nut, budding engineer, computer buff, artist, writer, history fan, or language person? Whatever your intellectual bent, there is probably a local, state, or national competition that you can enter.

* *Young ARTS, National Foundation for Advancement in the Arts*
* *F.I.R.S.T. Robotics Championships*
* *Canon Envirothon*
* *International Brain Bee*
* *Intel Science Talent Search*
* *National Ocean Sciences Bowl*

- *National Science Bowl, U.S. Department of Energy*
- *International Student Technical Communication Competition*
- *National language tests (French, Spanish, etc.)*
- *USA Biology Olympiad*
- *Young Naturalist Awards, American Museum of Natural History*
- *Young Playwrights National Playwriting Competition*
- *Profile in Courage Essay Contest*

For information about these academic and many other competitions, the Johns Hopkins Center for Talented Youth (CTY) offers a list at www.cty.jhu.edu/imagine/linkb.htm.

B.   REGIONAL AND STATE TALENT SEARCH SUMMER PROGRAMS

Educational programs are offered for academically talented students often beginning in the second grade and all the way through to senior year in high school. The best-known talent search programs are the following, but many states and colleges also offer them as well.

- *Johns Hopkins University's Center for Talented Youth (CTY)*
- *Duke University's Talent Identification Project (TIP)*
- *Northwestern University Center for Talent Development*
- *Vanderbilt University Program for Talented Youth*

Information about these and other programs are also available at the CTY website: www.cty.jhu.edu/imagine/linka.htm.

These students were involved with their respective activities not because they were building up their résumés, but because they loved participating in the activities.

Examples of how adMISSION POSSIBLE students have pursued academic or intellectual interests:

- » Worked for a university professor collecting data for his upcoming book
- » Participated in a college Summer Writing program
- » Took advanced math from Stanford University's Education Program for Gifted Youth (EPGY)
- » Helped a grandfather who is an engineer with the development of inventions such as a new kind of gopher trap
- » Wrote screenplays
- » Attended a Spanish language immersion program at a community college
- » Learned Chinese calligraphy from a grandparent in Taiwan
- » Served as a research intern
- » Took a ten-credit, intensive college course in elementary Arabic during the summer
- » Read every book she could find on James Madison
- » Attended the MIT MITES (minority) program
- » Participated in the California State Summer School for Mathematics and Science (COSMOS) program
- » Participated in the National Latin (French, Spanish) Exam
- » Received permission to attend community college rather than high school classes during her senior year

C. INTERNSHIPS

Internships are a wonderful way to find out more about a subject or cause, or to test whether you want to work in a specific subject area. Here are some of the organizations that provide internships for high school students:

- *Amnesty International Internships*
- *Common Cause Internships*
- *Congressional and Senate Page programs*
- *Project Vote Smart Internships*
- *United Nations Internships*

For information about internships, consult The Princeton Review's The Best 106 Internships and other resources noted in the "Books People Rave About" section of www.admissionpossible.com.

D. ONLINE COURSES AND TUTORIALS

Students can take correspondence courses with instructors by phone, mail, fax, and email in many different subject areas. Some organizations and colleges offering these courses are

- *The Center for Talented Youth (CTY), Johns Hopkins University*
- *Education Program for Gifted Youth (EPGY), Stanford University*
- *Merlyn's Pen Mentors in Writing Program*
- *University of Nebraska Online High School Courses*

Once again, the Johns Hopkins CTY website offers an excellent list of these kinds of programs at www.cty.jhu .edu/imagine/linkd.htm.

E. EARLY COLLEGE ENROLLMENT ACADEMIES DURING THE SCHOOL YEAR

Early college programs allow high school students to enroll as college freshmen in the fall of their junior year, giving them the opportunity to earn college credit, as well as receive their high school diplomas. Some are known as Commuter Programs and allow for students to live in their own homes. Other programs are Residential and offer high school students the opportunity to live in special dorms at the college while attending college classes on campus.

Colleges offering early programs include

- *Bard High School Early College*
- *Mary Baldwin College for the Exceptionally Gifted*
- *University of Washington Early Entrance Program*
- *USC Resident Honors Program*

Information about these programs is also available at the CTY website: http://cty.jhu.edu/imagine/linke.htm.

FAQ #2: **Because my schedule is so tight, I want to take an online course. Do colleges give credit for online courses?**

ANSWER: It's important that you first check with your high school counselor to see if your school will give you credit. Often that depends on who is offering the class. Among the more respected distance learning groups are the Johns Hopkins Center for Talented Youth, Brigham Young University Independent Study, Virtual High School (VHS), and University of California College Prep (UCCP). Many colleges give credit for online courses, particularly if a student's high school has given him or her credit. A few do not give any credit; still others decide on a case-by-case basis. If you know some of the colleges to which you plan to apply, call their respective admissions offices and ask them about their policies (having available, specific information about a course and who is sponsoring it).

F.   PRE-ENRICHMENT PROGRAMS FOR LOW INCOME, FIRST GENERATION, OR UNDERREPRESENTED STUDENTS

Primarily for African American, Hispanic American, and Native American students, these special programs are offered around a variety of subject matters at various colleges during the summer. Some of the better-known programs are

- Arizona State University's Math-Science Honors Program
- The Carleton College Liberal Arts Experience
- Massachusetts Institute of Technology's Minority Introduction to Engineering and Science (MITES)
- Stanford University's Medical Youth Science Program

Information about these programs can be accessed in books such as Robert Mitchell's *The Multicultural Student's Guide to Colleges* and Center for Student Opportunity website: www.csopportunity.org.

G.   SEMESTER, YEAR-LONG, AND SUMMER PROGRAMS ABROAD

Linguistic-immersion or English language programs are offered in countries all over the world, the best known of which are

- Earthwatch Institute (worldwide)
- American Field Service (AFS) (worldwide)
- KEI Study Abroad Programs (China, Germany, Russia)
- Youth for Understanding (YFU) (worldwide)
- Experiment in International Living (worldwide)

A comprehensive list of these and other programs is offered on the CTY website: www.cty.jhu.edu/ imagine/ linka5.htm as well as the Council on Standards for International Educational Travel (CSIET) yearly Advisory List: www.csiet.org.

H.   ATTENDANCE AT A LOCAL COLLEGE DURING THE REGULAR SCHOOL YEAR

High school students often can take regular classes at colleges and universities through concurrent enrollment and open university programs, as well as enrolling in community college classes.

Call your local colleges and universities to see what is available to high school students.

I.   SUMMER COLLEGE PROGRAMS FOR HIGH SCHOOL STUDENTS

Many colleges offer summer programs for high school students that are not only academically rich, but fun as well. The range of courses includes traditional offerings, such as Western civilization and creative writing, as well as career-oriented courses such as the NYU Tisch School Summer High School, Washington University's Architecture Discovery course, and Case Western Reserve University's Equinox Program.

CTY also offers information about other programs at www.cty.jhu.edu/imagine/linka.htm.

FAQ #3: I'm not a real math whiz, so I'm thinking of not taking any math my senior year. How will colleges look at this decision?

ANSWER: The answer to this question depends on the kinds of colleges to which you plan to apply. If your college list is not the most competitive, then not having a fourth year of math might not make much difference. What else are you taking? Will you replace math with another college prep course? Hopefully, the answer is yes because even during senior year colleges want students to push themselves academically. The best way to know for sure is to call the respective admissions offices and ask them this question. They will give you the answer from their own point of view. If you are aiming for the Ivies or Stanford, then NOT having math your senior year is not a good choice. Highly competitive colleges expect students to take math, including any level of calculus, all four years of high school.

FAQ #4: **I'm having difficulty deciding which AP classes to take. Is there such a thing as better or worse AP classes?**

ANSWER: This question brings up something about which many students are unaware: the relative worth college admissions offices give to certain AP classes. As strange as it may seem, the following four courses are considered "AP-Lite" by some colleges: AP Statistics, AP Geography, AP Psychology, and AP Environmental Science. In other words, they are valued less than other AP courses. Bottom line: Any AP course, including "Lite," is probably going to be more impressive than a regular course. However, it is also important that you take courses that you find intellectually interesting and challenging, AP or not.

FAQ #5: **My high school offers both AP and IB courses. Which ones are better for me to take as far as college admissions go?**

ANSWER: College admissions officers say that, course-by-course, there is no preference for either AP or IB courses. However, some also say that having an IB diploma carries a lot of weight in the admissions decision. College admissions officers love to see applicants who have gone beyond the norm to pursue an intellectual interest. Whether your "thing" is math, writing, spacecraft design, marine science, filmmaking, dinosaurs, or anything else, there are probably programs you can attend that will involve you with other students, teachers, and places that share and encourage your passion. Take advantage of one or more of the many, many academic opportunities available to high school students these days. They offer you the opportunity to do something you love, be involved with like-minded people, have a great time, and impress college admissions officers all at the same time!

ENDNOTE

What is available these days to high school students in academic programs is truly amazing. You can learn, travel, meet new people, and have fun all at the same time.

*ad*MISSION POSSIBLE TIP!

Colleges look for grade trends. If you did not do well in a course or two during ninth or tenth grades, it's not the end of the world. Do better in eleventh and twelfth grades.

Timeline for Academic Work

» FRESHMAN YEAR

COURSES

The courses you choose as a freshman set the stage for course selection for the rest of your high school and even college career. For example, if you take French 1 as a freshman, you can take Honors or French 2 as a sophomore, French 3 or AP French Language as a junior, and then AP French or French Literature as a senior.

GRADES

Freshman year can be an important time to establish yourself as a good student. After all, teachers talk among themselves; by having good grades in at least a couple of tough courses your first year, the likelihood of your reputation preceding you is much enhanced.

» SOPHOMORE YEAR

COURSES

This is a good year to "up" the number of challenging courses you take. However, don't take a lot of difficult courses if you are not going to be able to handle them. Talk with your high school counselor or a trusted teacher, as well as with your parents, about how much to take on. Sophomore year is when many good students take their first AP class, although some high schools only allow juniors and seniors to do that.

GRADES

Sophomore year is when good grades become increasingly important.

» JUNIOR YEAR

COURSES

Of all the high school years in which colleges are interested, junior year is at the top. This year is when you should take the most Honors, AP, and IB courses available, and also get the best grades you can. The most competitive students usually take more than two AP/IB classes, but they do this only after carefully assessing what their other commitments are. Generally speaking, whether or not you take three or four advanced classes is not going to keep you out of even the top schools. Nevertheless, junior year should be when you "take the academic plunge"; in other words, go the extra mile on papers and astound teachers with your work.

GRADES

Getting top grades should be a priority in junior year. If any course gives you trouble, talk with the teacher about what you might do as soon as possible. This can also be a good way of developing a relationship with a teacher. Not only will he or she get to know you, but you will also get to know him or her as you ask questions or spend time after class. You never know—you might even become memorable for the turnaround you make. A student who works himself or herself from a C to an A is someone a teacher is not likely to forget.

Some of the other ways that students deal with a class in which they are experiencing difficulty are 1) moving from an advanced class to a regular class and 2) working with a tutor.

Many people are under the impression that only poor students get tutors. In reality, some of the best students get tutoring when courses become problematic for them. Like the best athletes in the country, good students don't settle for getting by; they use outside help to get better at, and excel in, their courses.

» SENIOR YEAR

COURSES AND GRADES

Don't even think about slacking off during your senior year! Colleges pay close attention to students' course selections and grades, including their last semester. If you decide to apply Early Action or Decision, some colleges will even ask to see your first quarter grades. Many college-bound students take a number of AP/IB courses senior year. This is a tremendous workload for most students, especially when they are also filling out college applications. Think about and plan carefully just how much you can take on first semester senior year. And always participate in and do as well as you can in every class.

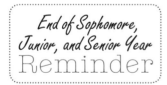
End of Sophomore, Junior, and Senior Year
Reminder

Don't forget to take the Subject Test for any AP courses in which you have been enrolled.

[CHAPTER 2]

EXTRACURRICULAR ACTIVITIES

What You Do with Your Time When You Are Not in Class

DEFINITION of EXTRACURRICULAR ACTIVITIES: *Any involvements beyond a student's regular coursework during high school, including*

- *In-and out-of-school activities*
- *High school sports, as well as outside club, leagues, and individual athletes*
- *Community service and volunteering, work experiences, summer experiences, hobbies, pastimes, and other interests*
- *Intellectual pursuits outside of school*
- *Special talents*

THE BOTTOM LINE Admissions officers usually look first at test scores, the rigor of courses a student takes, and grades in those courses. After that, they are interested in a student's extracurricular activities—that is, how you spend your time outside of class. Colleges really care about the kind of people they admit; therefore, what you do after school, during weekends, and over summers tells them a lot about the kind of person you are, your character, and your personality. When you think about it, you are what you do every day of every month of every year.

Colleges want students who will take full advantage of the academic and other resources offered on their campuses, as well as people who will contribute and give back. They want to admit students who will make a difference during and after college. One of the best ways of predicting what a student will do in college is to see what he or she has done in high school.

DOING WHAT YOU LOVE, OR AT LEAST WHAT YOU'RE INTERESTED IN

Most high school students don't have much control over the courses they take, especially if they are pursuing a rigorous college preparatory schedule. On the other hand, students have a lot of control over what they do outside the classroom. Unfortunately, many students act like robots and sign up for random activity after activity because that's what they think they should do. Some students wait endlessly for something interesting to show up in their lives, and end up doing very little at all. Still others say that they would like to do something, but they don't know what.

Whether it is an extracurricular activity now or later in life, people who do things that they enjoy are much more likely to be happy, healthy people, let alone successful in whatever they pursue. College admissions people often have a sixth sense for when a student pursues an activity about which she or he feels passionate. One's enthusiasm—or lack of it—comes through in applications. Needless to say, lively, energetic descriptions of activities you love are more likely to help with your admissions than simply identifying a long list of "whatevers."

One of the first things you can do to increase the likelihood that you will enjoy extracurricular activities is to pay attention to how you feel when you are doing them. Knowing whether you like something, more importantly knowing when you do not, is very important information. Obviously, there are times when we must do things that we're not really crazy about, e.g., practice an instrument or work out, in order to reach a goal. However, there are many other times when we continue on with activities we dread out of a sense of obligation or guilt, or just because they've become a habit. If the latter is the case, do something to make the activity more interesting, drop it, or move on to an activity that is more rewarding.

> ## adMISSION POSSIBLE TIP!
>
> Before the 1990s, common wisdom was that colleges preferred well-rounded students. Colleges now say they want well-rounded classes; that is, a mix of students in each class who bring a kaleidoscope of backgrounds, talents, interests, and involvements. Admission to a particular college is often more likely for students who are involved in a few select activities or interests in which they demonstrate commitment, achievement, leadership, and passion.

Here are some questions you can ask yourself to increase the chances of your getting involved with the activities that you really like.

» Think back to your childhood for what you always enjoyed. Did you like to draw, help people, write stories, or cook? How can you update or act on these long-term interests?

» What are the activities in which you find yourself losing track of time, when hours seem to fly by?

» What is fun or interesting to you? What gives you energy or leaves you feeling refreshed?

» What do you like learning or reading about? What are your favorite classes?

» What topics or causes do you really care about?

Happy, healthy people do what they really love, and spend time with people about whom they really care. In any and every way you can, consciously choose how you spend your time. You're going to make choices anyway; why not choose what makes you feel good?

FINDING EXTRACURRICULAR ACTIVITIES YOU ENJOY, IF NOT LOVE

If you haven't been able to find things you like to do, here is an exercise you can go through to come up with some ideas.

To start off, go through the following lists and circle anything that you like or attracts you (whether or not you know anything about it), and cross out any that you want to avoid (like it really turns you off). It's just as important to know what you don't like as it is to know what you do like.

SUBJECTS AND TOPICS OF INTEREST

Africa
American domestic issues
Immigration
Legal system
The media
Politics and elections
Asia
Class and race issues
Crime
Drugs
Energy
The entertainment business
Gay, lesbian, bisexual, and transgender issues
Globalization
Global warming, environmental issues
Health issues
The Internet and media
The Middle East
The military

Examples of adMISSION POSSIBLE students' extracurricular pursuits:

» An enthusiastic reader set up a teen reading club at her favorite bookstore.

» Many students have pursued their artistic passions by taking independent art, music, drama, or writing lessons.

» A football player volunteered at a Tijuana, Mexico, orphanage every week after football season, teaching American football.

» A surfer set up the city's first high school surf-athon to raise money for the Juvenile Diabetes Foundation.

» A national chess champion organized a chess club at a homeless school.

» A student took trapeze lessons at the San Francisco Circus Center.

» An outdoor enthusiast moved her way from camper to counselor-in-training to full-time staff member.

» Many students tutor younger or disadvantaged students.

» A talented art student who was also interested in politics became a political cartoonist for her high school newspaper.

» An expert knitter set up a knitting club at high school (half the members were boys).

» A language buff independently studied German, participated in German chat rooms, then took the German AP exam.

» An ardent freedom-of-speech advocate became a programmer for Peacefire, an organization that challenges Internet censorship.

» Many students have worked in their families' businesses, including a car wash, vegetable farm, and landscaping service.

» A trained peer educator went to schools providing sex education about sexually transmitted diseases.

(continued)

(continued)

» A top-notch golfer became assistant coach for the JV golf team at his school.

» A student worked for two years so that she could go to India to study with a sitar expert.

» An animal lover joined an animal rescue group to save animals from California forest fires.

» A soccer player set up a three-week soccer clinic at a disadvantaged school in his town.

» A high school student who lives near a Marine base set up a support group for Marine families whose loved ones are in war zones.

Natural disasters	Sports
Nuclear weapons	Terrorism
Poverty	War and peace
Religion	Women's issues
Social security	Other:_____
South America	

IN-SCHOOL AND OUT-OF-SCHOOL ACTIVITIES

Academic competitions
- Scholars' Bowl
- Science fairs
- Science Olympiad, etc.

Academic clubs
- National Honor Society California
- Scholarship Foundation, etc.

Art activities

Boy and Girl Scouts

Business clubs

Community service

Chess

Computer groups

Dance (drill)

Drama and theater
- Actor
- Stage manager, crew
- Set constructor
- Singer/dancer

Environmental groups

Ethnic groups
- Chinese American, Korean American,

MECHA, etc.

Exchange student

Film activities and groups

Future Business Leaders of America

Future Farmers of America

Journalism
- News website or paper
- Literary magazine

Language clubs
- French, Spanish, German, etc.

Model United Nations

Music
- Choir
- Independent lessons
- Jazz band
- Marching band
- Orchestra

Religious activities and groups

Speech and debate

Spirit activities

Student council

Tutoring

Writing clubs
Yearbook
YMCA, YWCA activities

Young Democrats
Young Republicans

COMMUNITY SERVICE IDEAS

Amnesty International
Animal care center
Beach cleanup
Boys and girls clubs
Cancer camp
Community service board
Disabled services program
Cancer, diabetes, etc.
Habitat for Humanity
Homeless shelter
Hospitals
Hunger Project
Key Club
Kids Korps
Make-A-Wish Foundation

National Charity League
Political campaign
Public library
Red Cross
Retirement and nursing homes
Rummage sales
Students Against Drunk Driving (SADD)
School ambassador
School orientation volunteer
Senior Olympics
Special Olympics
Teens Against Tobacco Use (TATU)
Usher, volunteer arts group
Walks and runs for causes

WORK POSSIBILITIES

Band member
Caddy at golf course
Camp counselor
Cashier
Cat, dog, house sitter
Childcare/babysitter
Computer tech
Fast food preparer, ice cream server
Gardener

Intern (law office, veterinary office, etc.)
Lifeguard
Receptionist
Research assistant
Retail sales person
Sports instructor
Teaching assistant
Tutor
Waiter/waitress

SPORTS ALTERNATIVES

Archery
Badminton
Baseball
Basketball
Biking
Boating
Body boarding
Bowling
Boxing
Canoeing
Cricket
Cross-country
Curling
Deep-sea diving
Equestrian sports
Fencing
Field hockey
Figure skating
Football (flag and regular)
Frisbee golf
Golf
Gymnastics
Hiking
Ice hockey
Kayaking
Lacrosse
Martial arts
Parasailing, paragliding
Racquetball
Rafting

Riflery
Rock climbing
Rodeo
Roller hockey
Rowing
Rugby
Sailing
Scuba diving
Skateboarding
Skiing
Snowboard
Soccer
Softball
Spirit (cheer)
Sports manager
Squash
Surfing
Swimming and diving
Table tennis
Tennis
Track and field
Ultimate Frisbee
Volleyball
Water polo
Water skiing
Weight lifting
Windsurfing
Wrestling
Yoga

SPECIAL SKILLS, TALENTS, AND HOBBIES

Acting	Fishing
Animal care	Flying
Art	Gardening
Backpacking	Hang gliding
Blacksmithing	Juggling
Carpentry	Knitting and sewing
Cattle driving	Leadership
Caving	Lifesaving
Circus arts	Magic
Climbing	Modeling
Clothing designer	Music
Computers	Puppetry
Construction	Outdoor and wilderness skills
Cooking	Quilting
Cross cultural involvements	Robotics
Dance	Rocketry
Film and theater	Writing
First aid	

Now go back to the circled items on the above lists and **rate how interested you are in each one of them on a scale of 1 to 10** (1 = a little interested, 10 = VERY interested). Write down the ten highest numbered items:

1. _____

2. _____

3. _____

4. _____

5. _____

6. _____

7. _____

8. _____

9. _____

10. _____

1. If something jumps out at you immediately, **then just do it, act on it or at least find out how you can learn more about it**.

2. If something sounds interesting, but you're not sure about it or how to get involved, **then talk with other students or your parents and other family members, your high school counselor, a teacher, or perhaps someone who is already doing it, and ask them to help you find out what it's all about or what you might do.**

3. Another way of getting information is to **do an Internet search with Google or Yahoo.**

4. **Go talk to someone who is already doing what you think you might want to do.**

5. Once you find an activity you like, **find a way of learning how to do it, joining it, or getting involved**. If you like it, then hooray for you! If you don't, then go on to something else on your top ten list.

6. It's useful to know that sometimes it takes a while to appreciate and enjoy an activity. The more you get into it, the more enjoyable it becomes. Occasionally, one starts an activity, begins a project, or learns a skill, only to find some tangent of it is what really interests you. **Developing an interest, a talent, or a skill is often a journey**.

GUIDELINES FOR CHOOSING ACTIVITIES

To help you make the most of your time out of class, and eventually provide colleges with an extracurricular list that demonstrates who you are, here are some thoughts about how colleges tend to view extracurricular activities, as well as some guidelines for choosing what you do:

CONTENT OF WHAT YOU DO

When it comes to extracurricular involvements, it doesn't really matter what the content is. Anything from a major research project on DNA to fishing is legitimate for future application grids. No matter the activity, colleges look for the quality of your involvement rather than quantity of activities listed. In other words, it is better to be consistently involved in two, three, or four activities and/or sports over a number of years, than to be superficially involved in eight, ten or twelve for shorter periods of time. Simply said, laundry lists of activities do not impress admissions officers.

You can maximize the time you spend in extracurricular activities by carefully thinking about what you do, and planning for how your activities, academic interests, talents, and skills all come together and make sense to you.

Extracurricular activities are the major way that students can demonstrate how unique they are, and, perhaps, more interesting and better than other student applicants.

QUESTIONS ADMISSIONS OFFICERS ASK WHEN THEY LOOK AT ACTIVITIES LISTS

As they peruse college applications, the following are some questions college admissions people are likely to ask about your extracurricular activities:

A. HAS THE TIME SPENT ON AN INVOLVEMENT BEEN PRODUCTIVE?

* **Have you made a difference** (e.g., doubled the number of students involved in a community service activity)?
* **Have you completed or contributed to a worthwhile end-product** (e.g., created a new website for your school, organized a speaking series around the issues of women and leadership)?
* **Have you learned something or developed a skill or talent** (e.g., became an expert about fireflies, gained fluency in Russian, or became a first-rate improviser)?
* **Have you reached a goal** (e.g., became an Eagle Scout, or after four years of hard work, finally made the varsity team of a sport)?

B. WHAT KIND OF LEADERSHIP OR INITIATIVE HAVE YOU DEMONSTRATED?

* **Are you founder, president, or the "first" of any important organizations** (e.g., founder of a new book club, president of the debate team, the first high school student ever chosen to be a paid staff photographer for a local newspaper)?
* **Are you a captain of an athletic team, member of a championship team, or an individual champion** (e.g., participated in a sport in which you have demonstrated uncommon leadership)?
* **Have you progressively moved from no status to the top position through the course of years** (e.g., starting out as a young camper and after many years moving to head counselor)?
* **Are you a member who has changed the nature of an organization or made it better or more effective** (e.g., organizer of a wildly successful inter-school art exchange, or made the focus of a community service group relevant to a particular disadvantaged group)?
* **Have you gone beyond the norm in contributing to a group, team, or project** (e.g., written a play for your school to perform; performed well enough in a sport to be invited to pre-Olympic competition; as President of your debate team, gathered team members to help create a debate team in a low income school that doesn't have one)?

C. HAVE YOU RECEIVED OUTSIDE RECOGNITION FOR YOUR WORK?

* **Have you received any awards, honors, newspaper accounts, rankings; publication of your work; letters of acknowledgment, thanks, or appreciation?**

D. QUALITIES ADMISSIONS PEOPLE LOOK FOR IN STUDENT INVOLVEMENTS:

* **Competence, effectiveness, high energy level, adventurous spirit, responsibility, curiosity, perseverance, cooperation, sustained commitment, maturity, character, passion, and focus**
* **They also look for how constructively you spend your time;** showing interest in the lives and welfare of others, helping your community; appreciating all that has been given to you.

MAXIMIZING A SKILL, TALENT, OR INTEREST

Admissions officers are often impressed when students take an interest or skill and act on it in any and every way they can. They often look for a pattern of interests.

For example, if **writing** is your "thing," write for your school newspaper or literary journal, or enroll in special off-campus writing programs offered at community colleges or summer sessions at colleges (e.g., Iowa Young Writers' Studio); enter writing contests (e.g., the Scholastic Art and Writing Awards); write an op-ed piece for your local newspaper; volunteer your writing skills to a local organization of interest such as the local historical society; or tutor students in writing at your own school (or perhaps at the local homeless school).

> ## adMISSION POSSIBLE TIP!
>
> With the possible exception of having an extraordinary talent or the skill of a recruited athlete, no single activity will get a student accepted into any particular college. It is the weaving together of a number of interests, involvements, and activities that usually best demonstrates the kind of student and person you are.

If your passion is **cooking**, enter a local, state, or national cooking contest; start a little catering business; provide weekly cooking lessons to children in your school's day care center; offer to be a "celebrity" cook at your school's auction event; take advantage of special English or history projects by doing research and writing papers on some food or cooking topic; attend a cooking school for a short course; work part-time for a company such as Williams-Sonoma.

If you are a **surfing** nut, enter surfing contests; create a surf-a-thon with local high schools to raise money for a charity; teach surfing to disadvantaged kids; take marine science courses at a local college; found a surfing team at your high school; use your surfing skills to become a lifeguard; write a paper on the physics of surfing or the physical and mental health benefits of the sport.

Whatever your interest is, you can find ways of getting better at it, using it, helping others through it, making money doing it, researching or studying it, or being recognized for your talent or skill. This then becomes a demonstration to colleges of your resourcefulness, ingenuity, skill level, initiative, persistence, and leadership. AND it is also a way for you to spend more time doing or sharing what you love.

SOME EXTRACURRICULAR OPTIONS

1. IN-SCHOOL VERSUS OUT-OF-SCHOOL ACTIVITIES

As with academic interests, **colleges are sometimes more impressed when students go outside their own high school's resources to act on their interests.** This is because pursuing out-of-school activities often involves a fair amount of initiative, and takes a lot more effort on your part. Sometimes outside activities and resources are more advanced than what is available at high schools.

2. SPORTS

Hordes of children are now beginning to play sports when they are four, five, and six years old. Every year, boys and girls start out with soccer, often move on to T-ball, and finish up with tennis. If you scratch the surface behind why kids are doing this, many parents might tell you that they have dreams of college sports scholarships or sports "ins" during college admission, even though that may be ten or fifteen years away.

Although not of a varsity caliber, many admissions people have been athletes at one time or another. Therefore, they understand and appreciate the kind of time, energy, and commitment that different sports require. **A high school athlete who is not qualified to be recruited will still be of interest to admissions people because of what his or her involvement represents, both in and out-side of school.**

3. COMMUNITY SERVICE

Many high schools have a minimum community service hours requirement; others don't. Whether or not your school requires community service, you might consider getting involved with some kind of volunteer activity (unless you come from a very low-income family and must use your time outside of school to help support the family).

Colleges pay attention to students' community service or volunteer hours because it is one of the best indicators of student concern for something beyond themselves.

The more advantaged students are, perhaps, the more important it is for them to have community service as a regular part of their lives. Wealth and privilege do not give students an advantage in admissions any more. Sometimes it is just the opposite. It is useful to leave an honest impression of being other- or community-oriented. The last impression you want to give is that you are self-centered or spoiled. Regardless of wealth or privilege, helping others builds character and demonstrates a commitment to selfless endeavors.

On a similar note, it reads better on a college application for a student to give of his or her time—have hands-on experience with a group or cause—than to give or raise a little money. There are exceptions to this rule. One student with whom I worked raised nearly $25,000 for cancer research. Needless to say, colleges were very impressed with that.

As with any other involvement, it behooves you to find a group, service, or cause that taps your natural interests and/or utilizes your inborn talents and skills.

There is absolutely no reason you can't have a good time while you are volunteering. The last impression you want to leave with admissions people is that you have done some community service only because it is a school requirement.

4. WORK EXPERIENCES

Every college application has a space for students to identify what their work experiences have been during high school and summers. **As with other activities, the choice of work doesn't really matter; just about anything from baby-sitting to delivering newspapers to waiting on tables to camp counseling is legitimate. One suggestion is that you try to work in an arena that taps an interest or talent.**

PARENT TIP

Parents need to understand that the actual number of students who end up being recruited athletes at colleges is very low. Even among athletic standouts, there are no guarantees. Therefore, the smart and "right" thing to do about your child's early athletic involvement is to make sure that he or she has a good time, develops some skills, and also learns how to be a part of a team.

adMISSION POSSIBLE TIP

In-depth involvement with one, two, or three community service programs is going to be more impressive to admissions officers than will a long series of individual, one-time events.

FAQ #1: Do colleges look for a magic number of hours spent by a student on community service?

ANSWER: No, there is no "magic number" of hours. However, if it appears that a student has put in volunteer hours because he or she had to rather than wanted to, that will not sit well with admissions people. Colleges want students who give of their time out of the goodness of their hearts.

Also, there are times when the demands of what you are doing in athletics and/or other major activities make it impossible for you to get involved with community service. Colleges appreciate the need for students to have balanced lives; so each student needs to determine what makes sense for him or her.

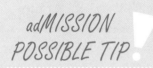

adMISSION POSSIBLE TIP

Any indication that you have done nothing with your summers but watch TV, get a good tan, or hang around at the mall will surely hurt your admission chances, no matter the college. However, don't overload yourself with too much to do, or spend the entire summer working. After all, summers are also a time for you to relax and enjoy yourself so that you can do your best during the regular school year!

For example, if you are really into science, getting a job as a research assistant is consistent with your interests and makes sense. If you want to be a designer, then look for work with an architect, even a furniture store or a builder. If your heart's desire is to be an entrepreneur, then working for any kind of business, significant or not is useful. Let's say you want to be in the entertainment business; having a job as a "gofer" for a production company, as menial as it might be, is an excellent idea.

And it always makes sense for students to identify that they have spent time working in their family businesses whether they are farms, ice cream shops, law firms, or manufacturing plants.

Colleges pay a lot of attention to why you say you work. Some useful reasons include something as simple as "wanting to see what it is like to have a paid job," or "looking for exposure to a possible career," or "wanting to learn something or do something that I have never done before."

5. SUMMER EXPERIENCES

Colleges are very interested in knowing how students spend their summer vacations. In fact, the further along in high school you are, the more interested they are. What you do with the summer before your senior year seems to be especially important to college admissions officers. Once again, the specific activity you choose is not important, but the quality and rationale behind choosing it is. Also know that it doesn't hurt to pursue one interest (such as working in a lab) for more than one summer.

Among the most popular and useful activities students choose are

- *Early College Programs at any number of colleges and universities both in and outside the United States*
- *Career exploration programs, also offered at many colleges*

- *Summer travel with family or as part of an organized group (make sure that you include an element of enrichment or education as opposed to just sitting around in the sun)*
- *Language immersion programs*
- *Special summer programs or camps around an interest such as computers, music, or community services; work or internships; independent study or research*

If the above sound too expensive, some programs offer financial aid for students who need it. Check it out.

6. SPECIAL TALENTS, OFFBEAT HOBBIES, AND INTERESTS

Colleges seem to be especially attracted to students who are superstars in anything from Aboriginal art to zymosan research. They also seem to love students who have interests and hobbies that are rare, even offbeat. Perhaps this comes from the boredom factor of admissions officers having to read hundreds and thousands of very similar applications and essays year after year.

If you are passionate about something, even better if you have become somewhat of an expert, be sure to inform colleges. Likewise, if over the years you have become fascinated by anything unusual (exotic animals, beekeeping, bell-ringing, the start of some quaint business, collections of any sort, uncommon language lessons, the manufacture of new or out-of-the-ordinary products, special environmental concerns, fire fighting, orchid growing, running for local office, skeet shooting, trapeze flying, yodeling, you name it), **don't stop because you think colleges will think it silly.** You never know—this might be the very thing that helps you to stand out from other applicants, and gets you into a school.

There is nothing better than for a college admissions person to notice your talent or hobby and say to the admissions committee something such as, "Yeah, here is that prize winning pastry chef from Texas, or the circus performer from San Francisco, or the kid from Maine who is a waterfall nut."

ACTIVITIES IF YOU WANT TO GO TO ONE OF THE IVIES

These days the competition to get into one of the Ivy League and other competitive schools is absolutely fierce. **Not only are admits expected to be academic powerhouses, but their activities must also be better than best.**

In general, the most selective colleges are looking for students who have achieved state or national recognition in at least some of what they do. Often it is not enough to be a captain of a high school sport, or student body president, or even a National Merit Scholar. Students who get accepted to selective schools are extraordinary in one or more ways: they are nationally ranked sports persons; national chess champions; published authors, playwrights, poets, or prize-winning artists. They are also accomplished musicians or actors, prize-winning scientists or inventors, and founders of new community service organizations.

The most selective colleges want students who are **"movers and shakers," seekers of challenges, risk takers, extraordinary talents, high impact students, exceptional persons, "one of the best (activity or talent) the school has ever had."** In other words, they are people who have worked hard to stand out in the most competitive academic/extracurricular crowd.

FAQ #2: Which activities will impress colleges the most?

ANSWER: Many students (and even more parents) ask what kinds of activities will impress college admissions officers. The answer to this question varies from college to college, and even from year to year. What makes a big splash this year—a top oboe player—may be at the bottom of the list next year.

The best advice about choosing extracurricular activities is what has been said before: participate in what interests you, what you enjoy, and what you love. What really counts for getting into colleges is how you express the meaning of your activity choices on applications, including what you have learned or gained as a result.

Extracurricular activities are a wonderful way of demonstrating the uniqueness of who you are and your interests and/or talents. Don't worry if they are "right" or "appropriate." College admissions people are thrilled with applicants who are passionate about just about anything.

ENDNOTE

The real question is not, "Will an activity get me into college?" but, "Which activities engage me, teach me something, take advantage of my talents, or help me to contribute to society?" Just so you know, extracurricular activities often become what (or part of what) we do for a career.

Timelines for Extracurricular Activities

» FRESHMAN YEAR

Freshman year is when extracurricular activities usually get started. Begin exploring some activities by talking with your high school counselor, dean of students, and teachers about what your interests and talents are and the kinds of activities that might fit you. Also, speak with older students about what they think is really fun, interesting, or meaningful at school. Pay attention to what people who appear to be like you seem to be doing. Don't be afraid to explore. If one activity doesn't meet your needs, then find another that does. Freshman year is the perfect time to taste and discover.

★ **Plan something useful, fun, and/or interesting for the summer before your sophomore year.**

★ **Also, don't forget to keep a record of everything you do, as well as any awards or honors you receive.** Colleges want to know about these things, even as early as your freshman year.

» SOPHOMORE YEAR

Sophomore year is the time to pare down and focus your activities to three or four based on what you really enjoy. See how you might develop each area into something significant. For example, if you are a singer, audition for your school's select singing group. What about taking lessons from the school choir director or a singing teacher outside of school? If your school puts on musical productions, find out how you can become a cast member, maybe even get a role. Check out opportunities outside of school as well. Does your church have a choir? Is there a singing group in the city that you might join? What about attending a special summer music program? If your family takes a trip, be sure to ask them to slip in some musical events. If your school doesn't offer what you like, then create it: found a club; start a team; form a group.

★ **Even as you develop certain activities, keep exploring other interests as possibilities come up.**

★ **Make plans for a useful, fun, and/or interesting summer before your junior year.**

★ **Don't forget to keep a record of everything you do, as well as any awards or honors you get.**

» JUNIOR YEAR

By the time you hit your junior year, you should be well settled in favorite activities. If, however, you haven't done that, it is never too late to get involved.

- ★ **Look for ways to make a difference**—become an officer or leader; go beyond just being a member of a club or activity. Set the stage for reaching the peak of your involvement by your senior year.

- ★ **What you do with the summer before your senior year is of real interest to colleges.** Look for special experiences, jobs, or activities at or by the beginning of second semester, junior year. Many programs have applications and deadlines that come due in March and April.

- ★ **Once again, don't forget to keep a record of everything you do, as well as any awards or honors you get.**

- ★ **This is the time to put together a first draft of your Activities Résumé.** (See chapter 8 on Activities Résumés or the Checklists section of www.admissionpossible.com for how to do that.)

» SENIOR YEAR

Senior year is the time to show the highest development of an activity, skill, or talent. Since going through the college application process will take up a lot of free time, be sure that your extracurricular involvements are those that you really enjoy and are meaningful to you. This might be the time to cut out any that aren't.

CHAPTER 3

TEACHER AND COUNSELOR RELATIONSHIPS

They're More Important than You Might Think

DEFINITION of TEACHER RELATIONSHIPS and the admissions process:
From freshman through senior year, aside from family members and friends, there is no one with whom high school students spend more time than teachers. While some large state universities do not require any teacher recommendations, many colleges ask for at least one, if not two. Therefore, it behooves you to develop good relationships with a number of teachers throughout your high school career.

This is useful not only because teachers might write letters of recommendation for you someday, but also because they are often among a small group of adults who really understand teenagers and their issues. While this will not be true for all teachers, the special place some have in your life ranges from role model to mentor to good friend during, and even after, high school. The better you and a teacher know one another, the greater the likelihood he or she will give you a glowing report on a teacher recommendation form.

{ **THE BOTTOM LINE** } Admissions offices pay a lot of attention to teacher recommendations because no one knows you better as a student.

FAQ #1: How can I find out if a college requires teacher recommendations, and if yes, how many they require?

ANSWER: For colleges that accept the Common Application, usually two Teacher Evaluations are required. To find out if a particular college accepts the Common Application, go to www.commonapp.org. For other colleges, teacher recommendation requirements vary. Some colleges require none; some require one; yet others require two or three recommendations. To find out if a particular school requires recommendations, go straight to the admissions section of their college website.

FAQ #2: I hear that colleges only want recommendations from junior year teachers. What should I do if the teachers I want to ask are from freshman or sophomore year?

ANSWER: Some colleges specify what they want in teacher recommendations, including the year in which a student was in their class (e.g., junior year), the number of recommendations (e.g., one, two, or three), and sometimes the content of the class (e.g., one science class and one social science class). It's important to follow application directions. However, if teachers from your junior year will write recommendations that are less stellar than ones from your sophomore or even freshman years, you might want to politely ignore the directions. Doesn't it make sense to have the best possible, most complimentary letters you can? Simply explain what you have done in a note to the college.

WHAT TEACHERS LOOK FOR IN STUDENTS

If you are unclear about what teachers look for in outstanding students (and about what they might write in a letter of recommendation), here are a few ideas. Teachers look at how students

- ★ Learn to deal with new ideas and concepts; develop their skills, reasoning ability, and analytic power
- ★ Overcome academic challenges in their class
- ★ Interact, contribute, and work with fellow students; assume leadership roles
- ★ Write and express themselves orally
- ★ Go beyond what is expected; put effort into their academic work and extracurricular activities
- ★ Grow over the year(s), including collecting achievements and awards, and developing talents and creativity
- ★ Are academically and personally different from other students
- ★ Will fare in a rigorous college environment and contribute in their own particular ways

> **DEFINITION of COUNSELOR RELATIONSHIPS and the admissions process:** *A school counselor, also called guidance counselor, college adviser, or college counselor, is a person hired by a school to fulfill a variety of functions, ranging from scheduling classes and taking care of disciplinary issues to counseling students about college admissions.*
>
> *Some counselors at large public high schools perform all of those functions and are responsible for as many as 250 to 500 students. Private high schools often have college counselors on their staffs whose sole job is to take care of college admissions.*
>
> *Regardless of their responsibilities, school counselors are the people who complete the part of the college application called the Secondary School Report/School Counselor form, and often write scholarship recommendation letters.*

{ THE BOTTOM LINE } Admissions officers pay close attention to counselor recommendations. More importantly, when they have questions about students and/or their applications, it is the high school counselor whom they call.

ADMISSIONS OFFICERS PAY CLOSE ATTENTION TO COUNSELOR RECOMMENDATIONS

The training, admissions knowledge, and accessibility of college counselors is unbelievably varied. Many public school counselors have been teachers at one time or another, and are required to have a Master's Degree in counseling. However, one of the unknown facts about a Master's in counseling is that there is little or nothing in the curriculum about college admissions. While some information is available through college and/or professional workshops, most people learn about college admissions by simply doing it. Private school college counselors are not required to have a Master's Degree in counseling; some do, but many don't.

The upshot of these varied scenarios is that your college counselor may be someone who has been providing college counseling for a long time, is very knowledgeable about the process, and has wonderful college contacts. However, others might be new to college admissions and have almost no training and little experience. Some college counselors are accessible; others are not. Trained or not, accessible or not, nice or not, it is very important that you develop a good relationship with your assigned college counselor.

adMISSION POSSIBLE TIP

Teachers can choose whether to write a letter of recommendation. It is their decision, not something they are required to do. Remember, teachers don't get paid extra to go beyond their assigned teaching roles to write recommendations. They do this out of the kindness of their hearts.

adMISSION POSSIBLE TIP!

Because counselors often serve large numbers of students, you need to make yourself stand out from the crowd. Because he or she is an important resource to you, it is critical that you begin developing a relationship with the school counselor early in your high school career. By the time you begin sending in college applications, you want this person to be your admissions advocate.

FAQ #3: What do I do if I don't like (or can't stand!) my school counselor?

ANSWER: Some high schools allow students to change counselors; others don't. Some schools have only one counselor. If you cannot change counselors, then it is your job to make friends with the person, no matter how busy, inefficient, annoying, or unpleasant he or she might be. The counselor is very important to your college admissions. Even if you don't feel like it, smile, be polite and respectful, act friendly, and follow through on all that is asked of you. In some ways, this is good preparation for life because there will be many people—a college roommate, a boss, a fellow employee—that you won't like, but with whom you must get along. College counselors do a lot for students. They can mentor, be a resource, open doors to academic competitions, make suggestions about classes, and recommend programs outside of school. At their very best, counselors can also be very good friends.

DEFINITION of INDEPENDENT COUNSELORS and the admissions process: Independent college admissions counselors (sometimes known as educational consultants) are privately paid individuals who provide high school students with admissions information, advice, and coaching. Most private admissions counselors have experience with admissions counseling in a school and/or a college setting. Some have teaching credentials; others have Master's or even Doctorate degrees.

INDEPENDENT COUNSELORS OFFER A NUMBER OF SERVICES:

* Advice about academic and extracurricular choices
* Information and guidance in developing a college list that fits a student's academic and personal needs and wants
* Coaching about how to interact with college admissions officers

* Help in developing an Activities Résumé
* Assistance in dealing with physical or learning disabilities, as well as special talents
* Information about how to make applications "special" and different
* Preparation for how to get the most out of college visits
* Suggestions for how to approach college essays
* Ideas about getting outstanding letters of recommendation
* Techniques for interviewing well
* Information and advice about early applications
* Ways of dealing with deferral, wait lists, and rejection letters
* Advice about making your final college choice

Parents often look to independent counselors when they think that their child is not getting the type of information or advice they need from their public or private school. Frequently this is a result of high schools adding increased counseling loads and/or additional administrative responsibilities to already overwhelmed school counselor job descriptions.

Most professional admissions counselors belong to the National Association for College Admission Counseling (NACAC) or the Independent Educational Consultants Association (IECA).

As with any other personal service, it pays to do your due diligence in selecting an independent counselor. Often the best way to find out who to consider is to ask students and parents who have already gone through the college admissions process. Once you start hearing the same names with glowing reports over and over, that is where you probably should start.

Call the individual or service and find out what they do. Ask what their training, experience, and credentials are in college admissions and counseling. Find out who they work with and what kind of success their clients have had. Ask how much and for what they charge. Get a sense of whether he or she sounds like someone you and your child might like to work with. If you have a few names, take the time to meet each possibility in person. Based on what you see and hear, make your choice. Some independent counselors develop relationships with colleges; others don't.

> ### adMISSION POSSIBLE TIP!
>
> One of your jobs as a senior is to make the college counselor's work easier. Be organized; provide all the materials he or she needs; get forms to him or her before they are due.

ENDNOTE

Your high school counselor and teachers are an important resource for the college admissions process. Use all of your social skills to develop good relationships with them. In the end, college admissions people pay attention to what they say.

Timeline for Developing Teacher Relationships

» FRESHMAN YEAR

This is the opportune time to begin forming good teacher relationships by taking helpful actions:

- **During the first week of class, make a point of introducing yourself to your teachers.**
- **Be polite and treat teachers** (and other students) **with respect.** Always arrive at class on time.
- **Engage in class discussions and speak up** when teachers ask questions, but don't "hog" classroom discussions.
- **Complete homework and papers on time.** To get an A, go the extra mile and complete extra assignments. (The quickest way to get a poor grade is to NOT do homework.)
- **As soon as you find yourself not understanding class material, speak with the teacher.**
- **Let teachers know that you appreciate what they do;** and without any sense of fawning, compliment them on something they do well. Remember to say "thank you."
- If you run into a teacher at a school event or someplace outside school, **make a point to say hello.**

PARENTS

Parents can play a significant role in their child's relationships with teachers by taking helpful actions:

- **Attend any back-to-school night functions.** If the opportunity presents itself, seek out your child's teachers and introduce yourself. Offer to be helpful to the teacher in any way you can.
- **Take advantage of any teacher conferences** that are offered by the school.
- **Be polite and treat teachers with respect.** Always arrive at conferences or meetings on time.
- **Become involved with your child's school** by volunteering for events; become a part of the parents' board; run for trustee of the school. Become a respected, friendly, known quantity.
- **Make sure that all communications between you and teachers are positive;** when a difficult situation arises, be polite, constructive, and helpful. Refrain from being negative, blaming, or destructive.

» SOPHOMORE YEAR

Continue with the freshman suggestions. If a teacher you particularly liked during your freshman year offers a sophomore course, do everything you can to enroll in that class. **For personal and admissions purposes, it is very good to have ongoing, good relationships with certain teachers.**

PARENTS

Continue acting on the freshman year suggestions.

» JUNIOR YEAR

With college admissions just a year ahead, this is a critical year in which to develop and have good teacher relationships.

Before Junior Year Ends

* **Ask favorite teachers if they would write a recommendation** for your college applications in the fall.
* **Let these teachers know what you are doing over the summer** to prepare for admissions. Tell them about any schools in which you are interested. If ready, give them a copy of your Activities Résumé to date.

PARENTS

Continue developing relationships with your child's teachers. If you haven't done it up to this point, do it now!

» SENIOR YEAR

This is the time when good teacher relationships will pay off. Sometimes teachers think so highly of you that they offer to write recommendations even before you have a chance to ask them.

See chapter 13, "Letters of Recommendation" for how to handle every aspect of asking teachers for recs; helping them with the process; and keeping on top of deadlines. One way of really helping teachers is to let them know colleges to which you are applying, and why you want to go to these colleges.

PARENTS

Do everything you can to help your child provide teachers with organized, complete admissions materials. Above all, make sure that all college admissions materials get to teachers on time, preferably long before the deadline.

Timeline for Developing Counselor Relationships

» FRESHMAN YEAR

Unlike teachers, who you see every day, counselors are people with whom you will have to go out of your way to develop a relationship. Even though counselors are very busy and often overwhelmed, take the time to stop by their office during your freshman year. Introduce yourself and ask a question or two (e.g., recommendations for summer programs).

PARENTS

It's not easy to gain access to high school counselors, particularly at large public high schools. Also, be careful about approaching counselors about college admissions issues when your child is a freshman because they might judge you as "helicopter parents." Perhaps the most effective thing you can do is to introduce yourself to the counselor at some school event, and let him or her know that you look forward to knowing them better as your child progresses through high school.

» SOPHOMORE YEAR

* **Continue developing your relationship with the college counselor.**
* **Go out of your way to attend any counselor-planned sophomore college admissions events.**
* **Keep the counselor informed** of any college admissions activities on your part, such as visiting colleges and planning to attend a college's summer program.

PARENTS

Keep introducing yourself to the college counselor at various school functions and identifying who your child is. Because of their caseloads, many counselors are unable to remember the names of all their students, let alone their parents.

* **If you have questions about college admissions, first ask the counselor** whether you should meet in person, communicate by email, or use the phone. Then work out a mode and time that fits both of your schedules.
* **Be sure to attend any school-sponsored college admissions events.**

» JUNIOR YEAR

Junior year is the time to get serious about your relationship with the college counselor. While he or she is going to be preoccupied with current senior admissions in the fall, don't let that deter you from stopping by with a quick smile and hello during that time.

Second Semester, Junior Year

* **This is when the more serious meetings with your college counselor should begin.**
* When you have meetings with the college counselor, **come prepared with specific goals** you want to accomplish, **questions you want to have answered, and information** that will help fill in the counselor's information gaps about you. Share your college list with the counselor and ask him or her for other suggestions.
* **Don't miss any counselor-planned junior year College Nights.**

PARENTS

Junior year is when counselors will become more interested and available to you and your child about college admissions. Be respectful of the counselor's time during the fall because he or she is going to be consumed with current senior admissions.

* ⭐ **Don't miss any counselor-planned junior year College Nights.**
* ⭐ **Be sure to listen to what the counselor has to say,** and even when you hear something with which you disagree, always remain calm and respectful. You don't want to say or do anything that might negatively affect your child.

» SENIOR YEAR

This year your relationship with your school counselor is all about admissions. See chapter 13, "Letters of Recommendation," for specifics on what to do. Before, during, and after the college admissions season, don't forget to thank the counselor for his or her efforts.

Timeline for Developing Independent Counselor Relationships

Students can consult with an independent counselor anytime during their high school years. A few parents have their children begin the process as early as freshman year (although most ninth graders are reluctant to do this). Some students begin counseling during tenth grade (meeting to find out what the process is all about, and to plan courses, extracurricular, and summer activities). Many start in the eleventh grade (a good time to begin developing a college list, visiting colleges, and taking admissions tests). Twelfth grade is a little late to start working with a counselor, especially since most have already filled their schedules. The ideal time to begin working with a counselor is during the fall of eleventh grade, although anytime during junior year is good.

CHAPTER 4

TESTS AND TEST PREPARATION
Which Tests to Take, Why, and When

OVERVIEW OF THE COLLEGE ADMISSIONS TESTS

For people not familiar with college admissions tests, the test names and especially their respective acronyms can be very confusing. Here is a quick overview of what the different tests are:

PSAT AND SAT (COLLEGE BOARD)

TEST NAME	WHEN TO TAKE IT	DURATION	COVERS
Preliminary Scholastic Aptitude Test (PSAT)	Most 11th graders take it in Oct. (some 10th graders take it).	2 hrs, 10 min	Critical Reading, Math, Writing
Scholastic Aptitude Test (SAT)	Preferably taken in 11th grade in Oct., Nov., Dec., Jan., March, May, or June. Can also take fall of 12th grade.	3 hrs, 45 min	Critical Reading, Math, Writing

PLAN AND ACT (AMERICAN COLLEGE TESTING)

TEST NAME	WHEN TO TAKE IT	DURATION	COVERS
Preliminary ACT Test (PLAN)	Usually taken in 10th grade.	1 hr, 55 min	English, Math, Reading, Science
ACT	Preferably taken in 11th grade in Sept., Oct., Dec., Feb., Apr., or June. Can also take fall of 12th grade.	3 hrs, 25 min	English, Math, Reading, Science, optional Writing

SUBJECT TESTS, ALSO KNOWN AS SAT IIS (COLLEGE BOARD)

TEST NAME	WHEN TO TAKE IT	DURATION	COVERS
SAT Subject Tests	10th, 11th, and 12th graders may take it in Oct., Nov., Dec., Jan., May, or June.	On one test date, up to three 1-hr tests	20 subject areas

AP TESTS (COLLEGE BOARD)

TEST NAME	WHEN TO TAKE IT	DURATION	COVERS
Advanced Placement (AP) Tests	May of every year.	2–3 hrs	30 subject areas

Many colleges require one or more standardized tests for admissions, including the SAT or ACT and Subject Tests. Other colleges require none. You need to carefully check the application information for each school on your college list to determine what their respective test requirements are.

PSAT

DEFINITION of PSAT (Preliminary Scholastic Aptitude Test): *The PSAT is a multiple-choice standardized test, offered every October by the College Board and National Merit Scholarship Corporation. The test comprises three sections:* **Critical Reading** *(two twenty-five-minute tests),* **Math** *(two twenty-five-minute tests), and* **Writing Skills** *(one thirty-minute test), which means that the test takes two hours and ten minutes. Each of the sections is scored on a scale from 20 to 80 points, and the sum of the three section scores ranges from 60 to 240. High scores on the PSAT may qualify certain juniors in high school for scholarships from the National Merit Scholarship Corporation and some colleges.*

adMISSION POSSIBLE TIP

If you check "yes" to the Student Search Service question on the PSAT test answer sheet, some colleges will receive your PSAT scores. The College Board also provides colleges with student names and their respective PSAT scores in categories such as (1) students with high scores, (2) students from certain geographic areas, (3) particular ethnic groups, etc. If you check "no," colleges will not receive your PSAT scores unless you give the scores out yourself.

adMISSION POSSIBLE TIP

Neither low nor high PSAT scores affect one's college admissions chances. PSAT scores are not a part of admissions criteria.

{ **THE BOTTOM LINE** } There are no negative consequences for taking the PSAT, and a couple of positive ones if you do take it. By taking the PSAT, you gain some understanding of what the SAT Aptitude Test is all about and how you might score on it. Also, taking the PSAT as a junior might qualify you as a National Merit or other scholarship designee. An hour shorter than the SAT, think of the PSAT as a practice test for the SAT. You have nothing to lose by taking it.

FAQ #1: Should I prepare for the PSAT?

ANSWER: There is no question that preparing for the PSAT can raise your scores, but not many students do it. The people who usually prepare for the PSAT are students who aspire to become National Merit Scholars. Because PSAT scores are not a part of admissions criteria, most students usually wait to do their test preparation for the regular SAT or ACT.

IMPORTANCE OF NATIONAL MERIT STATUS

When I sat in on an admissions session for a very competitive college, much to my great surprise I found that a student's National Merit status was not as big a deal to the admissions committee as I might have guessed. Among the Ivies and other top colleges, it is presumed that one will have top SAT scores, A's in the most rigorous academic schedule, and one or more extraordinary (regional or national) accomplishments, activities, and/or leadership positions.

However, many other colleges pay a lot of attention to National Merit Scholars, and often are willing to offer tuition breaks and scholarships to them. The National Merit Corporation, itself, offers some selected scholars one-time $2,500 scholarships.

adMISSION POSSIBLE TIP

Based on PSAT scores, each year the National Hispanic Recognition Program (NHRP) recognizes five thousand academically talented students of Hispanic/Latino origin. To qualify, a student must be at least a quarter Hispanic/Latino. NHRP does not give scholarships, but provides names of all qualified students to admissions offices to help them recruit talented Hispanic/Latino students.

FAQ #2: What do I do if I am ill on a test day or an emergency comes up?

ANSWER: If a student misses a scheduled College Board or American College Testing test because of illness, emergency, or other extenuating circumstances, he or she should immediately contact the respective customer service people for the test he or she has missed or will miss, explain the circumstances, and request an alternative test date.

SAT

DEFINITION of SAT (Scholastic Aptitude Test or Scholastic Assessment Test):
The SAT Reasoning Test is a multiple choice and writing test that is offered by College Board/Educational Testing Service every school year in October, November, December, January, March, May, and June.

*The test comprises three sections: **Critical Reading** (two twenty-five-minute sections and one twenty-minute section), **Math** (two twenty-five-minute and one twenty-minute section) and **Writing** (one twenty-five-minute essay section and one thirty-five-minute multiple-choice question section on grammar, usage, and word choice) with each section scored from a possible 200 to 800 points. The highest possible score for all three sections is 2400. Every test also includes a twenty-five-minute experimental section that does not count, which means that the total time for the actual SAT is three hours and forty-five minutes, although that does not take into consideration administrative details and breaks.*

{ THE BOTTOM LINE } In spite of everything that you might hear to the contrary, admissions testing is "alive and well." Along with excellent grades in rigorous coursework, many colleges use SAT or ACT scores as a critical first screening device in determining whom they will consider as serious admissions candidates.

TO GET OR NOT TO GET TEST PREPARATION

In spite of some people insisting that test preparation doesn't do any good, there is no question that preparing for the SAT can raise your scores anywhere from 50 to 200 points. Even the best students prepare on their own or receive SAT tutoring. Effective preparation usually takes two to three months.

adMISSION POSSIBLE TIP!

Remember, the SAT I and Subject Tests cannot be taken on the same day.

Think about test tutoring in this way. If you were an athlete and had never played a sport before, wouldn't you want to get some coaching and practice before you actually competed in a tournament? The same is true for taking standardized tests. The best test preparation helps you get the most from the testing experience. It goes without saying that your test score will improve depending on how much time and effort you put into the preparation, and what that preparation is.

Following are a number of test preparation options.

SAT PREPARATION BOOKS

Pros: Inexpensive ($8–$20), convenient, usually contain all the materials you need.

Cons: It takes a very motivated person to stick with working from a book. Also, sometimes a student has poor techniques or keeps making the same mistakes and it's difficult to change these things without feedback from someone who knows what he or she is doing.

SAT COMPUTER SOFTWARE

Pros: Inexpensive ($30+), convenient, and especially for computer buffs, this might do the trick.

Cons: As with books, HIGH motivation and consistent work are absolute musts.

SAT PREPARATION COURSES AT YOUR SCHOOL

These courses are as short as one day or weekend, or as long as a semester.

Pros: Inexpensive (often free), convenient, regularly scheduled, work with other students.

Cons: Often too short to be really effective; quality varies depending on the instructor.

COMMERCIAL SAT PREPARATION COURSES (PRINCETON REVIEW, STANLEY KAPLAN, ETC.)

Pros: Predictable schedule; commercial test companies keep up with the testing trends and changes; small classes with other students can be useful.

Cons: Expensive ($500++); very time-consuming (twenty-five to forty hours plus homework); because the class program is fixed, may spend time on areas where you don't need extra help.

INTERNET SAT PREPARATION RESOURCES

This is a free, award-winning service for SAT and ACT preparation: www.number2.com

Pros: Doesn't cost anything; organized by college professors and graduate students.

Cons: Takes some self-discipline to keep at it.

INDIVIDUAL SAT TUTORING

Pros: Schedule, pace, and often place of meetings based on your needs; often more cost effective than long commercial programs; can focus on weak spots. According to a *Wall Street Journal* article published May 20, 2009, "…the only effective method to prepare for these [admissions tests] is to study with private tutors."

Cons: Expensive ($35–$100 an hour); quality depends on knowledge and skill of tutor that is sometimes difficult to assess.

adMISSION POSSIBLE TIP!

June is the last testing date for any school year. No admissions tests are offered in the summer.

adMISSION POSSIBLE TIP!

One way of utilizing commercial services is to ask for individual tutoring by the most senior and/or best tutor on the staff.

FAQ #3: **Whenever I think about the SAT, I get a big knot in my stomach. What can I do about that?**

ANSWER: Rather than feeling anxious or afraid about the SAT (or ACT), take a positive approach: get prepared for it. The pros and cons of different test prep opportunities are noted above. Perhaps the best way for you to choose one alternative is to ask teachers, an independent counselor, and/or your school counselor for their recommendations.

Another good source of information about which test prep or tutor is best for you is students (and their parents) who have already gone through the experience. And don't just ask one person; talk to three, four, or five. As soon as you begin hearing that one experience is better than others, then you'll know where to go.

A useful way to approach your SAT preparation is to find out where your strengths and weaknesses are on the test and then focus your preparation time on the weaknesses.

GOOD ENOUGH TEST SCORES TO GET INTO COLLEGES

One of the first things students want to know is what test scores are good enough for them to get into the colleges they like. Any student can "guesstimate" the chances of being a good candidate by comparing his or her SAT (or ACT) scores with the scores of previously admitted students.

At this point, some colleges use the combined score of Critical Reading, Math, and Writing, with a possible total of 2400, while other colleges are using just the combined Critical Reading and Math score with a possible total of 1600. Check individual college admissions websites for what scoring system they use.

U.S. News & World Report's America's Best Colleges, hard copy and online versions, provide the Median SAT 25th–75th SAT or ACT percentile scores for combined Math and Critical Reading scores only of admitted students.

adMISSION POSSIBLE TIP!

More than eight hundred colleges and universities in the United States (including the highly respected Sarah Lawrence, Lewis & Clark, Bates and Bowdoin) are test-optional colleges. A list of colleges that no longer require test scores can be found at the FairTest website: www.fairtest.org.

COMPARING YOUR TEST SCORES WITH SUCCESSFUL APPLICANTS

A lot of factors go into admissions decisions besides test scores, including grade point averages, quality of essay writing, the depth and quality of extracurricular activities, counselor school reports, and teacher recommendations, and also how carefully an application has been completed. Test scores offer a good way to estimate your chances of acceptance at different colleges.

To get an idea about how your test scores compare with those of previously accepted students, let's see how that might happen with one college's test scores as an example (see below). According to *U.S. News & World Report's Best Colleges*, 2012 edition the 25th–75th percentile range of admitted students at Tulane University is 1230–1400 (remember, *U.S. News* publishes scores that are a combination of just Math and Critical Reading).

VERY GOOD CHANCE	GOOD CHANCE	NOT VERY GOOD CHANCE
If your SAT scores (or ACT equivalent) are at the high end of Tulane's 25th–75th percentile scores or higher (1400 and over), they are at the top of the Tulane candidate pool. **Your chances for admission are probably very good.**	If your SAT scores (or ACT equivalent) are in the middle of Tulane's 25th–75th percentile range (in the 1300s), **you probably have a good chance of being accepted.**	If your SAT scores (or ACT equivalent) are at the very bottom—and especially if they are below—Tulane's 25th–75th percentile range (1230 or lower), **your chances for acceptance are not very good.**

GOOD ENOUGH TEST SCORES FOR FIFTEEN MAJOR COLLEGES

Here are the 25th–75th percentile scores for fifteen well-known colleges as noted in the *U.S. News & World Report's Best Colleges*, 2012 edition:

COLLEGE	25TH–75TH SAT PERCENTILE RANGE
Massachusetts Institute of Technology	1410–1560
University of Notre Dame	1380–1520
Stanford University	1360–1550
Wellesley College	1270–1480
Kenyon College	1250–1430
Denison University	1220–1340
University of North Carolina, Chapel Hill	1200–1410
Skidmore College	1140–1340
University of Texas, Austin	1100–1370
Juniata College	1060–1280
Iowa State University	1030–1260
Eckerd College	1005–1230
Evergreen State College	970–1230
University of Arizona	970–1230
Cal State University, Fresno	820–1060

FAQ #4: Is there anything I can do to help my child do his or her best on the SAT?

ANSWER: Here are some useful things parents can do: **1)** Become educated about the various tests, and **2)** Don't PANIC about your child taking them. With your child's permission, you can be helpful by **3)** Completing registration forms and reminding your child about deadlines for registration and test dates. You can also offer to **4)** Make sure that test transcripts are sent to the various colleges. **5)** Help with vocabulary lists. **6)** If you are willing to pay for SAT preparation books, CDs, courses, or tutoring, wonderful—that will help as well. Perhaps the most useful thing parents can do is **7)** Provide your child with chauffeur service on the day of a test. This can relieve a lot of the stress from having to drive (often many miles) to a test center and find a parking space where the test is being offered. If you're smart, you and your kid might even make a "dry run" to the test location a day or two before the test to make sure you know where you are going.

adMISSION POSSIBLE TIP!

Even though SAT scores are often a major ingredient in admissions, it is very important to keep SATs in perspective. Both parents and students must remember that a student is not his or her SAT score.

USEFUL INFORMATION ABOUT THE SAT REASONING TEST

- *You can take the SAT as often as you like.* However, taking it more than three or four times might give admissions offices the impression that you are a little compulsive or unsure of yourself.
- *The October test date of your senior year is the last time you can take an SAT test* (or Subject Tests) and have the scores arrive in time for Early Application deadlines.
- *The earlier you sign up for a test, the better the chance you have of getting the test location you prefer.* Signing up late often results in your having to drive miles and miles to a location that is unfamiliar to you. One student I know who lived in Menlo Park, California, signed up so late for an SAT that he had to drive to Monterey, California, eighty-five miles and two hours away from his home.
- *The larger the university, the greater emphasis college admissions officers will place on SAT scores.* This makes sense because these admissions people have to go through thousands of applications and weed out candidates as quickly as they can. SAT scores are a convenient way to preselect. Smaller, liberal arts colleges are much more likely to pay attention to factors in addition to test scores, including who you are as a person as evidenced by your activities list, essays, and recommendations.

- *If after taking an SAT you feel uncomfortable with your performance, you can cancel your test score at the test center by asking the test supervisor for a Request to Cancel Test Scores form. Complete the form and return it to the test supervisor before leaving the room. You can also cancel a score after you leave a test center by writing (but not by email since they require a signature) a request to cancel your scores that is received by the College Board by 11:59 (Eastern time) on the Wednesday after the test date. Directions for doing this can be found at http://sat.collegeboard.com/scores/cancel-sat-scores.*

adMISSION POSSIBLE TIP!

The more competitive a school is, the more important SAT scores are. High SAT scores alone don't get you in, but low scores can keep you out.

PLAN

DEFINITION of PLAN: *Much like the PSAT, PLAN is the pre-ACT test often taken by sophomore students as a way of predicting how they will score on the ACT. The subjects covered are English, Math, Reading, and Science.*

THE BOTTOM LINE

American College Testing describes PLAN as a test that helps students measure their academic development, as well as explore career options. More than anything, it is a pre-ACT test that helps students to see how they might score on the ACT. PLAN is comprised of the following tests:

English (50 items), 30 minutes   **Math** (40 items), 40 minutes
Reading (25 items), 20 minutes   **Science** (30 items), 25 minutes

ACT

DEFINITION of ACT: *A major competitor of the College Board's SAT Reasoning Test, the ACT is divided into four multiple-choice tests, including English, Reading, Math, and Science Reasoning. A writing test is also offered with a score ranging from 2 to 12. Test scores range from 1 to 36. ACT also offers a composite score, which is the average of all four tests. The writing score does not affect the composite score.*

adMISSION POSSIBLE TIP!

One of the real advantages of the ACT is that a student can choose which test sitting he or she wants sent to a college. In other words, if your composite ACT score was higher on a December test date than on a September one, you can ask ACT to ONLY send the December test scores.

{ THE BOTTOM LINE }

ACT scores are accepted in place of and equal to SAT scores by college admissions offices. Some students prefer the ACT and get higher scores on it, while others prefer the SAT and get higher scores on it. The total amount of time for the ACT is 3 hours and 25 minutes. ACT tests are offered in September, October, December, February, April, and June. The ACT is comprised of the following tests:

English (75 questions), 45 minutes
Math (60 questions), 60 minutes
Reading (40 questions), 35 minutes
Science (40 questions), 35 minutes
Optional Writing Test (1 essay), 30 minutes

A COMPARISON OF THE SAT AND ACT TESTS

	SAT	ACT
How often offered	Seven times a year: October, November, December, January, March or early April, May, June	Six times a year: September, October, December, February, April, June
# and content of sections; total time	Ten sections: • 3 Critical Reading • 3 Math • 3 Writing • 1 experimental Total time: 3 hours, 45 minutes	Four sections: • 1 English • 1 Math • 1 Reading • 1 Science • Optional writing section (writing is required for many colleges) Total time: 3 hours, 25 minutes, including optional writing section
English content	No section just on English, although the Reading section focus is on vocabulary, but no grammar. Students with "killer" vocabularies are rewarded.	Stresses English grammar, punctuation, sentence structure. Better for students whose reading skills are stronger than vocabulary skills.
Reading section	Reading comprehension, sentence completion, and paragraph-length critical reading questions that emphasize knowledge of vocabulary.	Four reading comprehension passages that require ability to examine conclusions, make comparisons, interpret significant details, etc. Ten questions per passage.

	SAT	**ACT**
Writing section	Write an essay on one prompt, as well as answer multiple choice questions re improving sentences and paragraphs, and identifying errors. Better for students who like to use illustrative examples rather than arguments.	Write an essay in 25 minutes and answer multiple choice questions.
Science content	None.	Science questions in biology, chemistry, physics, and earth/space requiring analysis and interpretation rather than acquired knowledge. Good science students are rewarded.
Math content	Covers arithmetic, algebra, and geometry. Math accounts for 50 percent of total score.	Covers arithmetic, algebra, geometry, and trigonometry. Math accounts for 25 percent of total score.
Experimental sections	Experimental section masked to look like regular section.	Experimental section clearly experimental; only appears on certain dates.
Scoring	200–800 points for each section for a combined total possible score of 2400. Score of 0–12 for essay. No score choice.	1–36 points for each section, averaged for a total possible highest composite score of 36. Score of 1–12 for optional essay. Score choice.
Test question difficulty	Increasingly more difficult. Students describe test as tricky.	Difficulty of questions is mixed throughout test. Students describe test as more straightforward.
Right, wrong answers	Penalty for wrong answers: ¼ point for each wrong answer on multiple choice but not on student's own answers. Useful to skip difficult questions.	No penalty for wrong answers. No reason not to answer every question.
Test orientation	Emphasis is on critical thinking and problem-solving skills; like an aptitude test. Not all multiple choice; one math section asks for your answer. Good for students who are test savvy.	Emphasis on subject and content based; covers material learned in school. All multiple choice. Good for students who are more content oriented. Feels more like a test you would have in high school.

HOW ACT SCORES COMPARE TO SAT SCORES

Here are the 25th–75th percentile scores for fifteen well-known colleges as noted in a late edition of *U.S. News & World Report's America's Best Colleges*:

ACT	SAT (READING + MATH = 1600)	SAT (READING + MATH = 2400)
36	1600	2400
35	1580	2340
34	1520	2260
33	1470	2190
32	1420	2130
31	1380	2040
30	1340	1980
29	1300	1920
28	1260	1860
27	1220	1820
26	1180	1760
25	1140	1700
24	1110	1650
23	1070	1590
22	1030	1530
21	990	1500
20	950	1410
19	910	1350
18	870	1290
17	830	1210
16	780	1140
15	740	1060
14	680	1000
13	620	900
12	560	780
11	500	750

Extrapolated from information provided on the ACT/SAT tables at EurickaReview.com, UC California, College Board and the South Carolina Department of Education websites.

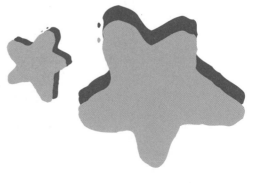

FAQ #5: **How do I know if the ACT or SAT is a better test for me?**

ANSWER: Find out which test better fits your skills and style by taking a practice test with one of the commercial groups, such as Stanley Kaplan or Princeton Review, which often offer this service free to students online or in person at a test center. Test tutors sometimes say that if your strength is in English and writing, then you might want to take the SAT. If your strength is in math and science, then you might decide on the ACT.

FAQ #6: **I have heard that some colleges accept the ACT in lieu of both the SAT Reasoning and Subject Tests?**

ANSWER: You heard right. According to the National Association for College Admission Counseling listserv, the following colleges accept the ACT in lieu of both the SAT Reasoning and Subject Tests: Amherst College, Barnard College, Boston College, Boston University, Brandeis University, Brown University, Bryn Mawr College, Case Western Reserve University, Connecticut College, Davidson College, Duke University, Franklin and Marshall College, Hamilton College, Johns Hopkins University, McGill University (Canada), Middlebury College, Pomona College, Rensselaer Polytechnic Institute, Swarthmore College, Trinity College, Tufts University, Union College, University of Pennsylvania, University of Richmond, Vassar College, Wellesley College, Wesleyan University, Worcester Polytechnic Institute, and Yale University. Check college websites to determine their test practices. You never know when a college will change its policy.

SUBJECT TESTS

DEFINITION of SUBJECT TESTS: *Offered by the College Board, Subject Tests (formerly known as SAT II and Achievement tests) are twenty, one-hour, primarily multiple-choice standardized tests in five general subject areas. Students can take up to three Subject Tests on one single test date. The scores for each Subject Test are reported on a scale from 200 to 800. Some colleges use Subject Test scores for admissions purposes and many others for course placement once a student enrolls at their college.*

(continued)

There are twenty Subject Tests across five content areas, including

ENGLISH

Literature

HISTORY AND SOCIAL STUDIES

U.S. History

World History

MATHEMATICS

Math Level 1

Math Level 2

SCIENCE

Biology (Ecological or Molecular)

Chemistry

Physics

LANGUAGES

Chinese with Listening

French

French with Listening

German

German with Listening

Modern Hebrew

Italian

Japanese with Listening

Korean with Listening

Latin

Spanish

Spanish with Listening

{ THE BOTTOM LINE }
While a number of colleges do not require or recommend Subject Tests, many colleges do. For these schools, Subjects Tests are important. The most Subject Tests any college requires is two.

College admissions websites and the Common Application website are places where you can determine whether and how many Subject Tests are required or recommended.

SCORE CHOICE FOR SAT I AND SUBJECT TESTS

College Board makes it possible for students to choose the SAT scores by test date and Subject scores by individual tests that they want sent to colleges. However, some colleges have their own score policies. Students can check which policy different colleges have when they request that their test scores be sent to different colleges.

FAQ #7: Which Subject Tests should I take?

ANSWER: Most of the time, colleges that require Subject Tests leave it up to the individual student to decide which ones to take. However, some colleges have special requirements, such as specifying two tests in different subject areas. Most students take Subject Tests at the end of their junior year and the beginning of senior year. In general, take Subject Tests in the subjects in which you are particularly strong or have just completed an AP course. Finally, if you plan on being a science or engineering major, take the tests that reflect your math and science knowledge.

FAQ #8: Should I prepare for the Subject Tests?

ANSWER: Yes! Even the College Board people say that preparing for the Subject Tests is a good idea. Because these tests are based on specific content, you really can study for them. More importantly, there is a direct correlation between how much you prepare for Subjects Tests and how high your scores are.

AP COURSES AND TESTS

DEFINITION of AP (Advanced Placement) TESTS: *College Board has developed thirty college-level courses and exams that are offered at high schools in the United States and other parts of the world. Through two- to three-hour AP exams offered in May of every year, students have the possibility of earning college credit or advanced standing at U.S. colleges.*

AP tests are scored on a numerical scale of 1 to 5:

1	**2**	**3**	**4**	**5**
Not Qualified	Possibly Qualified	Qualified	Well Qualified	Extremely Well Qualified

Here is a listing of the current AP courses and exams:

- *Art History*
- *Biology*
- *Calculus AB*
- *Calculus BC*
- *Chemistry*
- *Chinese Language & Culture*
- *Computer Science A*
- *English Language and Composition*
- *English Literature and Composition*
- *Environmental Science*
- *European History*
- *French Language and Culture*
- *German Language and Culture*

- *Government and Politics*
- *Government and Politics, U.S.*
- *Human Geography*
- *Italian Language and Culture*
- *Japanese Language and Culture*
- *Latin Vergil*
- *Macroeconomics*
- *Microeconomics*
- *Music Theory*
- *Physics B*
- *Physics C: Electricity*
- *Physics C: Mechanics*
- *Psychology*

(continued)

- *Spanish Language*
- *Spanish Literature*
- *Statistics*
- *Studio Art, 2D or 3D or drawing*
- *U.S. History*
- *World History*

{ **THE BOTTOM LINE** } Along with test scores, colleges want students to challenge themselves with the strongest possible courseload and best grades throughout their high school career. In addition to Honors and International Baccalaureate (IB) courses, AP courses are regarded as the epitome of the most demanding courses offered in high school.

HOW AP COURSES ARE DIFFERENT FROM REGULAR COURSES

AP courses are usually more demanding than regular courses. What this means is that you may have to read more and write more papers, analyze and evaluate more material, organize ideas and solve more problems. As one student said, "I think AP classes call for more thought, synthesis, and application of material than regular courses, which often demand simple regurgitation of the material presented." The College Board says that most AP classes are "comparable to college courses."

TAKE THE TESTS: Some admissions offices are not happy with students who take AP classes, but don't take the corresponding AP test. Admissions officers might perceive students who do this as either lazy or unprepared.

AP SCHOLAR AWARDS

All colleges, and especially selective colleges and the Ivies, are impressed with any of the following AP Scholar awards given out each fall:

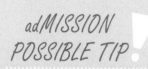

adMISSION POSSIBLE TIP

AP Test scores are not a part of the College Board cumulative test reports. You must request that an AP Score Report be sent separately by calling toll-free (888) 308-0013.

AP SCHOLAR: Given to students who have taken three or more AP exams for which they have received 3 or higher on full-year courses (or the equivalent).

AP SCHOLAR WITH HONOR: Given to students who receive an average grade of at least 3.25 on all AP exams taken, and grades of 3 or higher on four or more of these exams.

AP SCHOLAR WITH DISTINCTION: Given to students who receive an average grade of at least 3.5 on all AP exams taken, and grades of 3 or higher on five or more of these exams.

AP STATE SCHOLAR: Granted to one male and one female student in each of the U.S. states and the District of Columbia with grades of 3 or higher on the greatest number of exams (at least three), and then the highest average grade (at least 3.5) on all AP exams taken.

NATIONAL AP SCHOLAR: Granted to students in the United States who receive an average grade of at least 4 on all AP exams taken, and grades of 4 or higher on eight or more of these exams.

FAQ #9: Can any student sign up for an AP class?

ANSWER: Most high schools have a selection process that determines which of their students are eligible for specific AP classes, based on what kinds of grades and course backgrounds they have. If you are interested in taking an AP course, discuss this with the AP teacher of the course in which you are interested or the school's AP coordinator.

FAQ #10: Since the AP exams are only given once a year, what happens if you are sick on the day of the test?

ANSWER: The College Board provides for late testing on alternative dates under what they call "extreme circumstances" (illness, death in the family, etc.). Contact your AP teacher or AP coordinator for details about how to request and take part in late testing.

TESTING AND INTERNATIONAL STUDENTS

International students must take the same SAT tests as American students. A student can register for the SAT online or by fax. Information about this registration is contained in the SAT Program Registration Bulletin, International Edition, available from your school's high school counselor or at a student's local Overseas Educational Advising Center. For the center closest to you, see Test Centers on the College Board site or write to

College Board SAT Program

P.O. Box 025505

Miami, FL 33102

Fortunately, the College Board has test centers in many countries throughout the world.

TOEFL

In addition to the SATs, international students are also often asked to take an English language test, the most requested of which is Test of English as a Foreign Language (TOEFL), an English proficiency testing for international students planning to study in the United States. TOEFL information is at: www.toefl.org.

FAQ #11: Given that AP tests are not until May of my senior year and colleges will never see my test scores, why should I bother with AP classes?

ANSWER: Clearly, your final test scores on AP tests will not affect your college admissions. However, many colleges use your AP test scores for placement purposes, thus allowing students with high AP scores to skip introductory courses. Some students with a lot of 4 and 5 AP scores begin college with sophomore standing and get college credit for their AP coursework. Your parents will probably like that because this may allow you to graduate early.

And by the way, colleges do pay attention to your second semester grades. In a few cases in which a student has slacked off during the last half of his or her senior year, colleges have been known to rescind their admission.

FAQ #12: What if my high school doesn't offer any AP courses or just a few? Won't that hurt my chances for college admissions?

ANSWER: No. Colleges are pretty savvy about what's going on in high schools throughout the country. They realize that resources at different schools vary, and they take this into account when they evaluate student applications from disadvantaged high schools. They often ask, "Has this student taken advantage of the most demanding coursework and resources available to her or him?" If your high school is one of those that offers few or no advanced courses, let the colleges know; they won't hold it against you.

ENDNOTE

Admissions testing is just one, albeit an important one, of the elements of college admissions. Your goal should be to get the most you can out of each test and that can be accomplished by preparing.

Timeline for Taking the PSAT

» SOPHOMORE YEAR

Since taking the PSAT provides you with an opportunity to gain familiarity with the SAT, as a sophomore consider taking the PSAT as a practice test for the SAT. Students usually sign up through their respective high schools.

» JUNIOR YEAR

Take the PSAT. Remember, it is the PSAT, not the SAT, that determines whether you will be a National Merit Scholar.

Timeline for Taking the PLAN

» SOPHOMORE YEAR

Typically, students take the PLAN during the fall of their sophomore year. Register through your high school.

Timeline for Taking the AP Tests

» SOPHOMORE, JUNIOR, AND SENIOR YEARS

AP exams are offered at high schools during the second and third weeks of every May. The exact time schedule for taking the AP tests can be found at www.collegeboard.com. Students register through their high schools.

Timeline for Taking the Subject Tests

» FRESHMAN AND SOPHOMORE YEAR

JUNE: In June of your freshman and sophomore years, seriously consider taking the Subject Tests for any corresponding AP classes you are completing. If you have taken regular or even honors classes, it usually makes sense to wait until after you have taken AP classes to take the relevant Subject Tests. You can register at www.sat.collegeboard.org/register.

» JUNIOR YEAR

NOVEMBER: November is the only test date in which language with listening tests are offered.

MAY or JUNE: May or June is a good time to take the Subject Test for an AP class you are taking.

» SENIOR YEAR

Seniors Planning to Apply Early Decision or Early Action:

OCTOBER: If you have not taken Subject Tests or the requisite number, the October testing date is the last time you can take the tests and make the early application deadlines.

Seniors Applying Regular Decision:
If you have not taken Subject Tests in your junior year, you still have three chances to take them as a senior: October, November, and December.

Timeline for Taking the SAT and/or the ACT

» JUNIOR YEAR

Because fall of your senior year is unusually crowded with classes, activities and completing college applications, seriously consider taking the SAT or ACT test before the end of your junior year. If you are not satisfied with your scores, you can always retake it as a senior in October, November, or December (SAT only). You can register at www.sat.collegeboard.com/register.

You can register for the ACT at www.actstudent.org/regist/index.html.

» SENIOR YEAR

Seniors Planning to Apply Early Decision or Early Action: Because the deadlines for Early Decision and Early Action applications are often the first of November, the latest a student can take the SAT or ACT is October of his or her senior year.

Seniors Applying Regular Decision: If you have not taken the SAT or ACT in your junior year, you still have time to take it as a senior in October, November, and December (SAT only). The sooner you are prepared and get the SAT or ACT out of the way, though, the better it is. For regular decision applications, take the SAT or ACT no later than the December testing date in your senior year.

Remember, June is the last testing date of any school year. No tests are offered in the summer.

FINDING COLLEGES YOU LOVE

[CHAPTER 5]

YOUR COLLEGE LIST
Finding and Choosing Colleges that You're Going to Love

Deciding where you want to apply to college is the first important admission decision you will make. Fortunately, this is one part of the college admissions process over which you have a lot of control; it really is up to you.

> **DEFINITION of COLLEGE LIST:** *A list of between eight and twelve colleges that is consistent with your GPA and test scores, and also matches your intellectual, personal, social, financial, and spiritual needs, as well as future career goals. More than anything else, you want to find colleges where you feel at home.*

THE BOTTOM LINE
The college selection process should begin and end with who you are as a student and person and what you want from an undergraduate college experience. The better you are at finding colleges that match you, the more likely it is you will be accepted by these colleges.

The goal in creating a college list is to identify colleges that are "best" for you, which may or may not be the "best" according to other people's judgments or to the *U.S. News & World Report* rankings. Don't fall into the trap of thinking that you should attend the most prestigious school you can get into.

A college's high ranking does not mean that its educational opportunities and lifestyle are right for you. This is not to say that high-ranking schools are bad choices for students. However, there are many, many distinctive, high-quality colleges and universities with lesser rankings to which high school students apply, get accepted, and end up loving.

In a nutshell, coming up with a college list involves

★ Research about you, i.e., what you need and want in a college

★ Research about colleges, i.e., what they offer you

★ Bringing the two pieces of research together to find colleges that are a good match for you

adMISSION POSSIBLE TIP!

Not only is your list of preferred college characteristics critical to your putting together a good college list, it will also be very useful to you when answering college application or interview questions, such as "Why do you want to attend X college?"

IDENTIFYING WHAT YOU NEED AND WANT IN A COLLEGE

Many students say they have no idea about what they want in a college. That's understandable since very few high school students know what to take into account when they begin the college selection process.

To help you begin thinking about what you want, go to the checklist section of www.admissionpossible.com for a downloadable copy of the College Selection Questionnaire, and fill it out. Don't worry if you don't know exactly how to answer the questions; write down the best answers you can.

The questionnaire should take you about five to seven minutes. When you are done, summarize your responses on the following summary form:

SUMMARY OF WHAT I WANT IN A COLLEGE

1. *Geographic location* (e.g., either region or individual states):

2. *Landscape/environment and kind of weather* (e.g., near the ocean, in the mountains or desert, sunny, four seasons, hot, cold, or moderate weather):

3 *Nearby community* (e.g., city, town, college town, etc.):

4. *Cities you would like to be in or near* (e.g. New York, Boston, Chicago, San Francisco, etc.):

5. **How far from home** (e.g. close, moderately close, far away, doesn't matter):

6. **Religious affiliation of and/or ethnic makeup of student body** (e.g. Christian, Catholic, Muslim, Jewish, Hispanic, African American, Native American, Asian, Arab, etc.):

7. **Kinds of colleges or universities** (e.g., small, liberal arts college, Ivy League, public state university, science and engineering college, art or drama school, private university, etc.):

8. **Size of undergraduate student body** (e.g., 1,000, 5,000, 10,000, or 30,000+):

9. **Campus personality, atmosphere** (e.g., intellectually oriented, outdoorsy, big on sports, techie, party school, artsy, like a family, etc.):

10. **Type of curriculum** (e.g., lots of course requirements, some course requirements, no requirements, etc.):

11. **Academic climate** (e.g., competitive or cooperative academic climate, large or small classes, available or unavailable professors, supportive or not supportive of undergraduates, etc.):

12. **Types of students** *(e.g., smart, liberal, moderate, or conservative; diverse; supportive of LGBT; preppy; techies; free spirited; etc.):*

13. **Campus environment and facilities** *(e.g., beautiful, well-kept campus; fast, moderate, or quiet pace of life; good dining halls; nice housing; safe, cool neighborhood; etc.):*

14. **Athletics** *(e.g., good workout facilities, Div I, II, III sports, etc.):*

15. **Anything else** *(e.g., a special major or program you want, anything you want to avoid, etc.):*

The above list of characteristics should help you to begin researching colleges. As you read guidebooks, visit colleges, and talk with college contacts, you will become aware of other things you want or don't want in a college experience.

ANNIE BECK—HOW A TYPICAL STUDENT DEVELOPED HER COLLEGE LIST

To help you develop your college list, we're going to follow Annie Beck (not her real name) as she developed her college list a year or so ago. Annie was a senior at a public high school in California, with a GPA of 3.75 and SAT combined test score of 1350 (Critical Reading + Math).

From now on, anything in orange font will be about Annie.

SUMMARY OF WHAT ANNIE BECK WANTED IN A COLLEGE

After completing the College Selection Questionnaire, Annie came up with this summary of her preferences:

a. **Physical location** (landscape and weather): West and Northeast, (like beaches, mountains, lakes, and rivers, NO DESERT, moderate and cool weather.)

b. **Cities, nearby communities, kind of college:** Small- to medium-sized liberal arts or single-sex college in or near San Francisco, Portland, Boston, or in a small town, rural area OK

c. **Student body size:** Size range of about 2,000–5,000; want to avoid huge campuses

d. **General campus atmosphere and personality:** Intellectually oriented, collaborative, outdoorsy, down-to-earth, friendly people, tight-knit community of students, artsy

e. **Curriculum and academics:** Not competitive academic climate, small classes, supportive professors, excellent record for students getting into grad school

f. **Students:** Ethnically diverse student body, supportive of LGBT, liberal, health and fitness conscious

g. **Campus environment and facilities:** Very safe, beautiful campus, quiet, moderately paced lifestyle, most students live on campus, nice neighborhood

---

THE SEVEN STEPS OF RESEARCHING COLLEGES AND DEVELOPING A GOOD COLLEGE LIST

1. Begin your college list with a brainstorming session
2. Confer with trusted people to add more colleges to your list
3. Make use of Internet college searches to identify other colleges
4. Research the colleges
5. Determine your chances for acceptance
6. Put your list into "Reach," "Good Chance," and "Pretty Sure Thing" categories
7. Refine and settle on a final college list

---

1. BEGIN YOUR COLLEGE LIST WITH A BRAINSTORMING SESSION

Your first college list should be a brainstorming list, containing whatever colleges you come up with, whether or not you know much about them. There are no rights and wrongs on this list, just ideas for schools to research and explore.

COLLEGES ON ANNIE'S BRAINSTORM LIST:

Pomona College	University of Vermont
Wellesley College	Southern Oregon University
Scripps College	Lewis & Clark College
UC Santa Cruz	

Here's a space for you to brainstorm some colleges for your list:

COLLEGES IN WHICH I'M INTERESTED:

2. CONFER WITH TRUSTED PEOPLE TO ADD MORE COLLEGES TO YOUR LIST

Share your list of preferred characteristics and preliminary college choices with people whose opinions you respect. Ask for recommendations about colleges they think would be a good fit for you. People to consult include

- Your parents, grandparents, or older siblings
- Your high school counselor
- High school teachers
- An independent admissions counselor
- Family friends

3. MAKE USE OF INTERNET COLLEGE SEARCHES TO IDENTIFY OTHER COLLEGES

Some better known Internet college search programs are:

College Board	College Navigator, U.S.	Peterson's
www.collegeboard.com	Department of Education	www.petersons.com
	www.nces.ed.gov/collegenavigator	

These and other search programs will come up with college names based on hard data such as your test scores and GPA, geographic location, college costs, and possibly availability of certain majors, but their lists won't tell you if colleges match who you are as a student and person. Don't worry; you can find that information on your own when you research the different colleges.

Annie spoke with her parents, counselor, and a teacher, and also consulted the College Navigator search tool. When she was done, she added a number of new colleges to her old list.

ANNIE'S FIRST COLLEGE LIST

Carleton College	Occidental College	University of Vermont
Grinnell College	Pomona College	UC Santa Cruz
Kenyon College	Scripps College	Vassar College
Lewis & Clark College	Smith College	Wellesley College
Middlebury College	Southern Oregon University	Whitman College
Oberlin College	St. Olaf College	

After consulting your college counselor, parents, and others, put together your first college list.

MY FIRST COLLEGE LIST

FAQ #1: How many colleges should I apply to?

ANSWER: In theory, there is no limit to the number of colleges to which you can apply. We suggest about eight to twelve divided into the different acceptance categories of Reach, Good Chance, and Pretty Sure Thing. However, some public and private high schools have policies that limit the number of college applications students can submit. Be sure to find out what your high school's policy is.

4. RESEARCH THE COLLEGES

The goal of researching colleges is to learn as much as you can about what colleges offer students in general, and also what individual colleges offer you specifically. Some ways to research colleges:

A. College Admissions Guides

A good place to start your college research is with one or more books about colleges and college admissions.

* **Subjective Admissions Guides**

    Subjective admissions guides are the most useful of all the books. They offer written reviews of colleges by students and/or other knowledgeable people. You can get a real feeling for colleges if you read *The Fiske Guide to Colleges*, *The Insider's Guide to the Colleges*, or *Colleges That Change Lives*.

* A creative use of the subjective guides is to go to the colleges that interest you and **highlight in one color things you like, and in another color things that you don't like**. You will soon see that some colleges will have a lot more of one or the other color. The pages filled with highlights of things you like are the colleges to keep on your list. You will soon be able to use the highlighted information when you answer the college application questions about why you want to attend a certain college.

* **Objective Admissions Guides**

    These guides provide objective data about colleges in the United States, such as high school preparation, college costs, majors offered, etc. The best known of these books are The College Board's *The College Handbook* and its *Book of Majors*.

* **College, Program, and Major Rankings**

    These guides offer rankings of either individual colleges, or specific kinds of programs or majors at colleges. Among the ranking publications on the market are *U.S. News & World Report's America's Best Colleges* and *The College Finder*.

* **Special Interest Guides**

If you are an athlete, a student with learning or other disabilities, an international student, a member of a minority or religious group, or someone who wants a special college summer program, there is a special admissions book written just for you. Important, specific information is available ranging from unique admissions criteria to names of staff people and coaches. Some of the most helpful books in this category are *College Access & Opportunity Guide*, *International Student Handbook*, *The College Sourcebook for Students with Learning and Developmental Differences*.

> ## adMISSION POSSIBLE TIP!
>
> You can find admissions books in local bookstores, online, in public libraries, and in high school guidance and career centers.

B. Knowledgeable Individuals

Another way of researching colleges is to speak with people who are very familiar with different colleges.

* **Current College Students**

    No one knows a college better than a current student.

* **College Alumni**

    Alumni are also good resources, particularly those who graduated from college in the last five to ten years.

* **High School Faculty and Counselors**

    Your teachers and high school counselors are also valuable sources of information. Each has attended a college and taught or counseled thousands of students who have gone on to college. They usually have a real sense for which colleges make good matches for different students.

* **Independent Counselors**

    Just as your high school counselor has worked with a multitude of students, so too have independent counselors. Year after year, they see who applies to which schools, who gets in, and who is happy.

C. College Visits

A particularly effective form of research is visiting colleges. When you're physically at a campus, you can use all five senses to check it out. You can see what the campus environment, surrounding community, students, and faculty look like. You can hear the clamor of university life—or sometimes the lack of it—and decide if that's what you want. You can taste the food in the dorms or cafes and judge whether it pleases you. You can "smell" the energy of the student body and note if it matches your own. Finally, you can touch the books at the bookstore and library, the benches and grass on the quads, the overstuffed chairs and room decorations in the student center, and determine your comfort with them. Use your "sixth sense," or gut feelings, to assess whether a particular college is one that feels like home. (For more information on visiting colleges, go to chapter 6.)

D. College Websites and Other Internet Resources

★ **College Websites**

College websites provide prospective students with maps to the campus, course descriptions, professor bios and email addresses, activity lists, athletic team information and schedules, information about health, disability, and other support services—you name it.

Every college website has a section devoted just to admissions, where prospective applicants can see what the school's admissions requirements are, request an application, get application and financial aid deadlines, and download applications.

★ **Other Internet Resources**

Almost every day new college admissions blogs, websites, and webinars seem to pop up. Social networking sites around admissions issues are out there too. If you want information about admissions, Google a term or a question and many resources usually show up.

E. Informational Materials Sent to You by Colleges

Have you ever wondered why you're suddenly getting mail from colleges? The answer is, if you have taken the PSAT, made a phone or website inquiry, or attended a college fair, college marketing departments follow up with letters, brochures, view books, and videos. These materials often contain useful information even though they are usually from marketing offices.

F. High School Guidance and Career Centers

Both public and private high schools have counseling offices in which materials from colleges are collected and put on display. These offices are often a good place to do some research.

G. College Rep Information Sessions and College Fairs

Every year, particularly during the fall, college representatives visit high schools throughout the country. These visits are usually open to seniors, and sometimes to juniors. As noted in chapter 7 on developing relationships with colleges, these visits are special opportunities to meet and develop relationships with different college reps, as well as gain insights into the colleges. Don't pass them up.

Sometimes college reps also hold open meetings at alumni homes, local hotels, or large high schools in cities and towns. These are further opportunities to find out about colleges.

> **adMISSION POSSIBLE TIP!**
>
> Many happy college students say that it was their first gut reaction that led them to know whether a particular college was a top candidate for them. Within minutes of arriving on a campus, they report thinking, "I love this place, the people, the town...just everything!" They liken the experience to falling in love. Pay attention to your immediate first reaction to a college; it usually lasts.

Attending a regional college fair that is scheduled in different cities throughout the United States is another way of gathering information about colleges and meeting reps. To find out when a fair is being offered in your area, go to the Events/Training area of the National Association of College Admissions Counselors' (NACAC) website: www.nacacnet.org.

Annie took a college trip during her junior year, visiting Midwest colleges during spring break. She visited West Coast colleges during two long weekends. She attended every informational session at her school offered by colleges on her list.

Annie also bought *The Fiske Guide* and *Colleges That Change Lives* and highlighted what she liked and didn't like about the colleges. One of the things she liked best in *Fiske* was the list of overlap colleges at the end of each college's description. With those recommendations, she found other colleges similar to ones that she knew she liked.

As a result, she added Kalamazoo, Macalester, and Goucher to her college list.

5. DETERMINE YOUR CHANCES FOR ACCEPTANCE

The first part of this chapter has been about how you can find colleges that match who you are as a person. Here's how you can find colleges that match you as a student.

Many factors go into whether you are admitted to a college, including

- ★ Your academic record, including your GPA, rigor of classes, and class rank
- ★ Test scores, such as the SAT, ACT, and Subject Tests
- ★ Extracurricular experiences
- ★ How well your application is completed—especially the essays
- ★ Letters of recommendation
- ★ Occasionally just plain luck

Sometimes other factors are taken into account, such as whether you are a recruited athlete, a legacy, or come from a disadvantaged background.

It's nearly impossible to know how admissions people will assess your applications, but as you put together a college list, you need some idea about which colleges are in your admissions ballpark.

Three pieces of information—**A) the GPA of previously accepted students, B) the test scores of previously accepted students, and C) the acceptance rates of colleges**—will help you guesstimate your chances of getting into different colleges.

A. Grade Point Average (GPA)

Colleges are very interested in both your GPA and the rigor of the classes you have taken. In assessing your chances for acceptance, you need to see if your GPA is at the high end, in the middle, or at the low end of a college's previously accepted students. Every college website, as well as guides such as *The Fiske Guide*, provides the mean GPA of successful applicants.

B. Test Scores of Previously Accepted Students

The test scores of previously accepted students can be either SAT or ACT scores. (See chapter 4 for a list of comparable ACT/SAT scores.)

When it comes to reporting their test scores, most colleges offer the "Middle 50 Percent Test Scores" of the previous year's accepted applicants. Other terminology for Middle 50 Percent Test Scores, includes

Middle 50 Percent Test Scores (used by *College Board, The Insider's Guide*, and many colleges)
SAT/ACT 25th–75th Percentile (used by *U.S. News & World Report's Best Colleges*)
SAT Range and ACT Range (used by *The Fiske Guide* and others)

What do "Middle 50 Percent Test Scores" and the other terms mean? If you put all of last year's accepted student test scores in one basket, they will come out in a bell-shaped curve as follows:

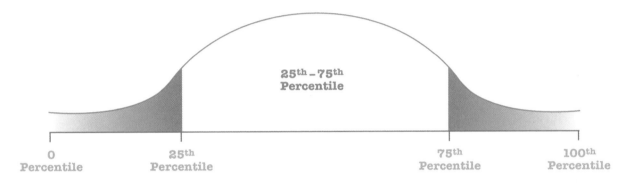

★ One out of four students (25 percent) will have scores in the 0 to 25th percentile range.
★ One out of two students (50 percent) will have scores in the 25th to 75th percentile range. This is the Middle 50 Percent Test Scores.
★ One out of four students (25 percent) will have scores in the 75th to 100th percentile range.

To help you understand how this information can be used, let's take one of Annie's colleges as an example. Oberlin College's 25th–75th Percentile Test Scores are 1310–1470.

What this means is that

★ 25 percent of the freshman class scored below 1310
★ 50 percent scored between 1310 and 1470
★ 25 percent scored above 1470

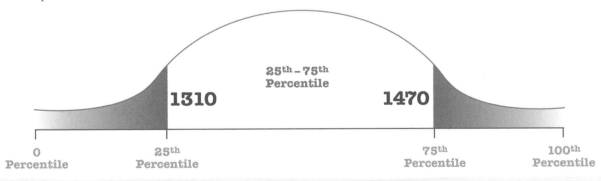

While you can go directly to individual college admissions sites (specifically the Freshman Profile Information section) to get test score information, a more efficient method is to use one source that provides test scores for most colleges. Some of those resources are *U.S. News & World Report's Best Colleges* (hard copy or online), *The College Board's College Handbooks* or College Board online.

Having said all this about test scores, remember that a growing number of colleges don't use standardized test scores at all or make test score use optional. The website www.fairtest.org lists the more than eight hundred four-year colleges that follow this practice, including Bard College, Bowdoin College, Sarah Lawrence College, and Wake Forest University.

C. Acceptance Rates For Each College

Acceptance rate (or percentage of acceptances) is the ratio of students who are admitted to a college compared to the number of students who apply.

Regardless of your test scores and GPA, the lower a college's acceptance rate, the more difficult it is for you to be admitted. However, there are more than 3,800 accredited colleges and universities in the United States, and about 100 colleges have acceptance rates of 35 percent or lower.

The good news is that 3,700 schools have acceptance rates of 35 percent or higher. Surely, there are a number of colleges whose test scores and acceptance rates fit you, AND also offer what you want in a college.

Acceptance rates for colleges can be found on individual college admissions websites, but also in the latest hard copy and online editions of *U.S. News & World Reports Best Colleges*, on the U.S. Department of Education's College Navigator website, in *The College Handbook* or www.collegeboard.com, or in different college guides.

This is what Annie's college list looked like with the Median 25th–75th SAT Test Scores and acceptance rates for the schools on her college list.

ANNIE'S COLLEGE LIST WITH TEST SCORES AND ACCEPTANCE RATES

COLLEGE	SAT/ACT 25th–75th PERCENTILE TEST SCORES	COLLEGE ACCEPTANCE RATES
Carleton College	1300–1500	31%
Grinnell College	1220–1470	43%
Kenyon College	1250–1430	39%
Lewis & Clark College	Test optional	68%
Middlebury College	1290–1480	17%
Oberlin College	1310–1470	31%
Occidental College	1200–1380	42%
Pomona College	1380–1560	15%
Southern Oregon University	890–1130	93%
St. Olaf College	1180–1380	57%

Scripps College	1270–1450	39%
University of California, Santa Cruz	1020–1270	65%
Smith College	1190–1420	47%
Vassar College	1310–1460	24%
University of Vermont	1085–1280	71%
Wellesley College	1270–1480	34%
Whitman College	1220–1440	47%

MY COLLEGE LIST WITH TEST SCORES AND ACCEPTANCE RATES

COLLEGE	SAT/ACT 25th–75th PERCENTILE TEST SCORES	COLLEGE ACCEPTANCE RATES

6. ORGANIZE YOUR LIST INTO CATEGORIES

As you compare test scores, GPA, and acceptance rates of colleges to your own data, place colleges on your list in one of the following categories:

DEFINITION of REACH (aka Long Shot): *These are colleges at which you have a 25 percent or less chance of being admitted because your GPA and test scores are less than applicants who have been admitted in the past. To be a Reach,*

- *Your **test scores** are near or are in the bottom 25 percent of accepted students (Just so you know, students who are accepted in the 25 percent and less range are often athletes or other kinds of special admit.)*
- ***The acceptance rate** is 35 percent or less*
- *Acceptance is possible, but not probable*

adMISSION POSSIBLE TIP !

The most selective colleges tend to admit students with SAT combined Math and Reading scores in the 1500+s or 34+ on the ACT. But even superstar students should consider as Reaches any Ivy League schools, the top tech schools such as Cal Tech and MIT, and other highly selective colleges and universities. No one can count on being accepted.

DEFINITION of GOOD CHANCE (aka Target, Good Match, Possible): *These are colleges at which you have a 50 percent or better chance of being admitted because your GPA and test scores are in the middle 50 percent of the range of applicants who have been admitted in the past. To be a Good Chance,*

- *Your **test scores** fall in the 25th to 75th percentile range of accepted students (The closer you are to the 75th percentile score, the better your chances are for admission.)*
- *The **acceptance rate** is over 35 percent, and usually closer to 50 percent*
- *You have a decent to good chance of being accepted*

DEFINITION of PRETTY SURE THING (aka Safety, Good-Bet): *These are colleges at which you have a 75 percent or better chance of being admitted because your GPA and test scores meet or exceed applicants who have been admitted in the past. To be a Pretty Sure Thing,*

- *Your **test scores** are near or in the top 25 percent of accepted students*
- *The **acceptance rate** is above the 50th percentile*
- *You are reasonably sure you will be admitted*

It's very important that you are more than willing to attend any Pretty Sure Thing school if for some reason you should not be accepted to your Good Chance and Reach schools.

So far this chapter has been about finding colleges that are good for you and becoming aware of how test scores and acceptance rates affect your chances of being admitted. Now let's get down to the business of your coming up with a selection of schools that are an appropriate mix of Reaches, Good Chances, and Pretty Sure Things. We suggest that you have two to four Reaches, three to five Good Chances, and two to four Pretty Sure Thing schools on your college list.

A. If you haven't already, write down your college list, and identify the 25th–75th Percentile Test Scores and Percentage of Acceptance for each of the colleges.

B. Now rank order the list by those Median Test Scores, highest scores first, all the way down to the lowest scores.

With the addition of Kalamazoo, Macalester, and Goucher, here is Annie's college list ordered from highest to lowest test scores:

ANNIE'S COLLEGE LIST ORDERED BY HIGHEST TO LOWEST TEST SCORES

COLLEGE	SAT/ACT 25th–75th PERCENTILE TEST SCORES	COLLEGE ACCEPTANCE RATES
Pomona College	1380–1560	15%
Oberlin College	1310–1470	31%
Vassar College	1310–1460	24%
Carleton College	1300–1500	31%
Middlebury College	1290–1480	17%
Wellesley College	1270–1480	34%
Scripps College	1270–1450	39%
Macalester College	1260–1450	43%
Kenyon College	1250–1430	39%
Grinnell College	1220–1470	43%
Whitman College	1220–1440	47%
Occidental College	1200–1380	42%
Smith College	1190–1420	47%
St. Olaf College	1180–1380	57%
Lewis & Clark	Test optional	68%
Kalamazoo College	1110–1340	75%
University of Vermont	1085–1280	71%
Goucher College	Test optional	73%
UC, Santa Cruz	1020–1270	65%
Southern Oregon University	890–1130	93%

Little Known Fact

If you are a highly qualified student, don't treat Pretty Sure Thing schools as slam dunks. Some colleges and universities reject or wait-list highly qualified applicants because they predict that these students are likely to attend a higher ranking, more prestigious college. In other words, colleges don't want to be anyone's "safety school." Therefore, it's very important for you to treat every college, especially Pretty Sure Thing schools, as serious considerations. Go out of your way to give them the same demonstrated interest (see chapter 7 on relationships with colleges), same effort in the applications, same college visits, etc. as Good Chance and Reach schools. Also make sure that you provide good reasons for your interest in their colleges, e.g., their Honors or other special programs.

MY COLLEGE LIST ORDERED BY HIGHEST TO LOWEST TEST SCORES

COLLEGE	SAT/ACT 25th-75th PERCENTILE TEST SCORES	COLLEGE ACCEPTANCE RATES

C. Based on the definitions of Reach, Good Chance, and Pretty Sure Thing categories, arrange your college list:

Annie's Reach Schools

Since Annie's combined Critical Reading and Math test score is 1350, and the lower end of Pomona's 25th–75th percentile test scores is 1380, she put Pomona into the Reach category. She also added Oberlin, Vassar, Carleton, Middlebury, and Wellesley to the Reach category because their acceptance rates are less than 35 percent.

Annie's Good Chance Schools

Annie put Scripps, Macalester, Kenyon, Grinnell, Whitman, Occidental, Smith, and St. Olaf in her Good Chance category because her combined test score of 1350 fell into the 25th–75th percentile range of accepted students at those schools.

  Also, their acceptance rates are at least 35 percent, and some close to 50 percent.

Annie's Pretty Sure Thing Schools

Because the highest end of their respective 25th–75th Percentile Test Scores were lower than her combined Critical Reading and Math test score of 1350 and/or their acceptance rates were above 50 percent, Annie put Lewis & Clark, Kalamazoo, University of Vermont, Goucher College, University of California, Santa Cruz, and Southern Oregon University into the Pretty Sure Thing Category.

Here is Annie's college list divided into Reach, Good Chance, and Pretty Sure Thing categories:

ANNIE'S FULL COLLEGE LIST DIVIDED INTO REACH, GOOD CHANCE, AND PRETTY SURE THING CATEGORIES

COLLEGE	SAT/ACT 25th–75th PERCENTILE TEST SCORES	COLLEGE ACCEPTANCE RATES
REACHES		
Pomona College	1380–1560	15%
Oberlin College	1310–1470	31%
Vassar College	1310–1460	24%
Carleton College	1300–1500	31%
Middlebury College	1290–1480	17%
Wellesley College	1270–1480	34%
GOOD CHANCES		
Scripps College	1270–1450	39%
Macalester College	1260–1450	43%
Kenyon College	1250–1430	39%
Grinnell College	1220–1470	43%
Whitman College	1220–1440	47%
Occidental College	1200–1380	42%
Smith College	1190–1420	47%
St. Olaf College	1180–1380	57%
PRETTY SURE THINGS		
Lewis & Clark College	Test optional	68%
Kalamazoo College	1110–1340	75%
University of Vermont	1085–1280	71%
Goucher College	Test optional	73%
University of California, Santa Cruz	1020–1270	65%
Southern Oregon University	890–1130	93%

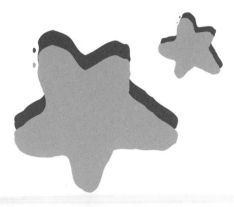

MY COLLEGE LIST DIVIDED INTO REACH,
GOOD CHANCE, AND PRETTY SURE THING CATEGORIES

COLLEGE	SAT/ACT 25th-75th PERCENTILE TEST SCORES	COLLEGE ACCEPTANCE RATES
REACH		
GOOD CHANCE		
PRETTY SURE THING		

D. Having put your college list into Reach, Good Chance, and Pretty Sure Thing categories, ask your high school counselor for feedback on your chances for admission at different colleges based on your high school's college acceptance record.

Your counselor has the high school's College Class Profile (which shows where graduating seniors from previous years were accepted, and their corresponding GPA and SAT/ACT scores) with which you can compare your academic background and college list with previous graduates.

If your school uses Naviance, a software program that manages the college admissions process, it can also provide a comparison of your GPA, test scores, and college list with previous students who have graduated from your school.

Annie took her college list to her high school counselor who confirmed that her potential for acceptance categories were right on the button.

7. REFINE AND SETTLE ON A FINAL COLLEGE LIST

A. Add and subtract colleges on your list as you become more knowledgeable about colleges and yourself.
Your college list (as well as the criteria for selecting colleges for it) should be open to change, not cast in stone.
For example, after visiting a school you might decide that the location of a college is a lot more important than
you thought, or that a large college is inconsistent with your wanting small discussion classes and close relationships with professors.

B. The summer before your senior year is a good time to finalize your college list. Here are some things to
consider in coming up with that list:

* ★ **Each college on your final list should meet many of the criteria you established in filling out the
  College Selection Questionnaire.** The list should contain colleges that you really like and want to attend,
  regardless of whether they are Reaches, Good Chances, or Pretty Sure Things.
* ★ **Try not to fall in love with one single college.** It's natural for students to find that they like some schools
  better than others, even one school better than the rest. But in today's admission climate, no student is
  guaranteed admittance to any college, even if he or she offers "the best" of everything.

Here is Annie's final college list:

ANNIE'S FINAL COLLEGE LIST

COLLEGE	SAT/ACT 25th–75th PERCENTILE TEST SCORES	COLLEGE ACCEPTANCE RATES
REACHES		
Oberlin College	1310–1470	31%
Vassar College	1310–1460	24%
Carleton College	1300–1500	31%
GOOD CHANCES		
Scripps College	1270–1450	39%
Kenyon College	1250–1430	39%
Whitman College	1220–1440	47%
Occidental College	1200–1380	42%
Smith College	1190–1420	47%
PRETTY SURE THINGS		
Lewis & Clark College	Test optional	68%
Kalamazoo College	1110–1340	75%
Goucher College	Test optional	73%

Annie decided that the most important characteristics for her were to attend a small, liberal arts college (with all that this means) with 2,000 to 5,000 students, in an intellectual atmosphere with friendly, down-to-earth people and a very safe, beautiful, well-kept campus.

Just so you know, Annie was accepted to two Reach colleges, four Good Chance colleges, and two Pretty Sure Thing schools. She ended up very happily at Whitman College, her first choice college that happened to be a Good Chance school. You just never know!

MY FINAL COLLEGE LIST

COLLEGE	SAT/ACT 25th–75th PERCENTILE TEST SCORES	COLLEGE ACCEPTANCE RATES
REACH		
GOOD CHANCE		
PRETTY SURE THING		

adMISSION POSSIBLE TIP

If you have trouble deciding which colleges to keep on your list, go through your list and evaluate each college on a scale from 1-10 (1 = not interested, 10 = most interested). What you should end up with is a list of schools that are at the top of your list.

ENDNOTE

There is nothing more important in the college admissions process than putting together a college list that matches your academic background, needs, and wants. Hopefully this guide will help you do this. As we said before, we want you to love the school you decide to attend.

Timeline for Developing Your College List

» FRESHMAN AND SOPHOMORE YEAR

It's never too early to begin thinking about colleges, but during ninth and tenth grades, do it in a lighthearted, unhurried way.

As you hear college students or their parents rave about different colleges, make a note of the names of the colleges and what is said. If so inclined, also read articles about colleges in newspapers, magazines, and on the Internet.

PARENTS

Freshman or sophomore year is a good time to create a special file for college materials. Frequently, parents do this because students simply aren't ready to think about colleges.

Parents can plan college "drive-throughs" as a part of vacation trips. (See chapter 6, "College Visits," to learn how.)

» JUNIOR YEAR

FALL SEMESTER

★ **This is a good time to complete the College Selection Questionnaire.** (Go to the Checklists section of www.admissionpossible.com for a down-loadable copy.) Once you have identified your preferences, wants, and needs, you can begin looking for colleges that match those characteristics. This will help you put together a first college list, which is important if you plan to visit colleges during spring semester and other breaks.

SPRING SEMESTER

★ **Continue researching colleges and gathering information** about what you like and don't like. (If you haven't already, put together your first college list or update what you have.)

★ As you visit colleges, **update your college list.**

★ Before the end of the school year, **take your college list to your high school counselor for feedback.**

SUMMER AFTER JUNIOR YEAR

★ **This is the time to complete your college list.** At the latest, have it done before you start senior year.

★ While it's useful to visit colleges during the school year, **visiting colleges in the summer is better than not visiting them at all.**

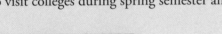

PARENT TIP!

If your freshman or sophomore is resistant to thinking about college, don't worry; many students feel this way. That doesn't mean that you can't begin gathering information, but in an unobtrusive way.

PARENTS

★ **Avoid the temptation to take over your student's college admissions process.** Do everything you can to maintain a good relationship with your son or daughter. He or she really needs your help and support right now.

» SENIOR YEAR

FALL SEMESTER

★ **If you haven't already, put together your college list.** It's never too late to do a good job.

PARENTS

★ **Parents need to help their children deal with the financial aid** section of college applications.

SPRING SEMESTER

★ **This is when all of your college research really pays off.** Your final choice about where to go to college will be much easier having identified what you want.

PARENTS

★ **Remember that your child's college list should represent his or her needs and desires, not yours.** Your son or daughter, not you, will be spending four years at some college or university. It's in everybody's interest that a student chooses and attends a school that he or she loves. Do everything you can to make that happen.

SAMPLE COLLEGE LISTS

SAMPLE COLLEGE LIST 1

Learning disabled student from Texas, with SAT I combined score of 950 (Critical Reading and Math), GPA of 3.2, two AP courses, and active in community service activities. Student decided to attend the University of Arizona.

COLLEGE	SAT 25th–75th PERCENTILE TEST SCORES	COLLEGE ACCEPTANCE RATES
REACHES		
Southwestern University (TX)	1100–1330	67%
Birmingham–Southern College (AL)	1100–1300	61%
Texas Christian University	1050–1280	53%
GOOD CHANCES		
University of Arizona (SALT program)	970–1230	75%
Arizona State University	970–1220	87%
Northern Arizona University	950–1170	65%
PRETTY SURE THINGS		
University of New Mexico	910–1140	66%
University of Northern Colorado	910–1140	88%
Prescott College (AZ)	990–1240	99%

SAMPLE COLLEGE LIST 2

Student from Massachusetts, with SAT I combined score of 1100 (Critical Reading and Math), GPA of 3.3, one AP course, and active in the arts and the environment. Student decided to attend the College of the Atlantic.

COLLEGE	SAT 25th-75th PERCENTILE TEST SCORES	COLLEGE ACCEPTANCE RATES
REACHES		
Boston University	1180–1370	58%
College of the Atlantic (ME)	Test optional	64%
GOOD CHANCES		
Hampshire College (MA)	Test optional	71%
University of Vermont	1085–1280	71%
University of Massachusetts, Amherst	1060–1260	68%
PRETTY SURE THINGS		
Massachusetts College of Art & Design	970–1180	NA
University of Maine	960–1190	78%
Green Mountain College (VT)	Test optional	96%

SAMPLE COLLEGE LIST 3

Student from Washington, D.C., with SAT I combined score of 1200, GPA of 3.5, three AP courses, and active as a dancer. Student decided to attend Skidmore College.

COLLEGE	SAT 25th–75th PERCENTILE TEST SCORES	COLLEGE ACCEPTANCE RATES
REACHES		
Barnard College (NY)	1250–1440	28%
Connecticut College	Test optional	32%
Skidmore College	1140–1340	47%
GOOD CHANCES		
Muhlenberg College (PA)	Test optional	49%
Fordham University (NY)	1160–1340	51%
PRETTY SURE THINGS		
Hobart & William Smith College (NY)	Test optional	62%
University of Illinois	1180–1380	67%
Hollins University (VA)	970–1230	89%
Goucher College (MD)	Test optional	73%
Marymount Manhattan College (NY)	960–1170	81%

SAMPLE COLLEGE LIST 4

Student from Oregon, with ACT composite score of 29 (SAT equivalent of 1300), GPA of 4.0, five AP courses, and interested in science. Student decided to attend UC Santa Barbara

COLLEGE	SAT 25th–75th PERCENTILE TEST SCORES	COLLEGE ACCEPTANCE RATES
REACHES		
University of Southern California	1270–1470	24%
Colorado College	1260–1430	33%
GOOD CHANCES		
Whitman College	1220–1440	47%
Occidental College	1200–1380	42%
UC Santa Barbara	1110–1340	46%
UC Davis	1100–1340	45%
PRETTY SURE THINGS		
Lewis & Clark College	Test optional	68%
University of Portland	1080–1300	45%

SAMPLE COLLEGE LIST 5

Student from California, with SAT I combined score of 1480, GPA of 4.2, five AP classes, editor of school newspaper, and interested in English/Journalism. Student decided to attend Duke University.

COLLEGE	SAT 25th–75th PERCENTILE TEST SCORES	COLLEGE ACCEPTANCE RATES
SUPER-REACHES		
Princeton University (NJ)	1400–1580	9%
Dartmouth College (NH)	1360–1570	12%
Stanford University (CA)	1360–1550	7%
REACHES		
Duke University (NC)	1350–1530	16%
Emory University (GA)	1310–1500	29%
Georgetown University (VA)	1300–1490	20%
GOOD CHANCES		
University of Rochester (NY)	1230–1420	38%
University of Michigan	1220–1380	24%
PRETTY SURE THINGS		
George Washington University (NY)	1210–1390	32%
University of Wisconsin	1180–1340	55%

SAMPLE COLLEGE LIST 6

Student from Kansas, with SAT I combined score of 1530, GPA of 4.4, seven AP classes, involved in and winner of academic competitions, congressional intern, and involved in politics. Student decided to attend Williams College.

COLLEGE	SAT 25th–75th PERCENTILE TEST SCORES	COLLEGE ACCEPTANCE RATES
REACHES		
Yale University (CN)	1410–1590	8%
Harvard University (MA)	1390–1590	7%
Amherst College (MA)	1340–1540	15%
Williams College (MA)	1310–1530	19%
GOOD CHANCES		
Carnegie Mellon University (PA)	1300–1500	33%
Macalester College (MN)	1260–1450	43%
Grinnell College (IA)	1220–1470	43%
PRETTY SURE THINGS		
University of Michigan	1220–1380	51%

CHAPTER 6

COLLEGE VISITS

The Best Way of Finding Out What You Want in a College

DEFINITION of COLLEGE VISIT: *A college visit is the best way to truly get to know a school. Time spent on a campus can include*

- *Visiting the college admissions office and/or attending an admissions office presentation*
- *Taking a campus tour, organized by the college or on your own*
- *Sitting in on a class or two*
- *Meeting a professor in your field of academic interest*
- *Meeting and talking to one or more current students*
- *Looking into your extracurricular, athletic, or special service interests*
- *Walking or driving through the adjacent college community or town*

{ THE BOTTOM LINE #1 } Visiting colleges is a critical part of developing a good college list and also making a wise, final college choice. College visits also offer one of the best opportunities to develop relationships with college admissions personnel. Although not guaranteed, having frequent personal contact with a college's admissions office can be a tip factor in your being admitted to a school. (Read chapter 7, "Relationships with Colleges," for more about this.)

When you see a college for the first time, what may be most important is your "gut feeling" about it. The author, Malcolm Gladwell, calls this the "blink" factor. That is, if you like (or don't like) the look and feel of a school during the first few minutes, you will probably feel the same from that point on.

Ask yourself these questions:

- ★ Am I turned on by the look of the campus?
- ★ As I walk around, do I find myself smiling and feeling comfortable with what I see?
- ★ Is the campus attractive and well cared for?
- ★ Do the students I see seem to be the kind of people I want to know and spend time with?
- ★ Is the atmosphere friendly and inviting?
- ★ Do I feel excited about the prospect of spending four years here?

THE BOTTOM LINE #2

While the remainder of this chapter is about what to do on a college visit, feel free to pick and choose among the many ideas. Your life is probably already filled with enough stress and hassle, so whatever you do, don't make any college visit into an ordeal.

Rather, take it easy and enjoy yourself. Stop in the middle of your visit and have a bite to eat at the student union or a soft drink at one of the campus cafes. Approach the campus with a light-hearted attitude, as if you are spending a few hours at a favorite destination filled with interesting things to do. Make your college visits fun experiences.

adMISSION POSSIBLE TIP

Many freshmen and sophomores are not ready for serious campus visits. If that's the case with your son or daughter, don't push them. Just driving through a campus on your way to some other destination is a good first introduction.

WHEN AND HOW MUCH TIME TO SPEND AT COLLEGES

To get a real feel for a college, it is better to visit it when school is in session, not during vacations or final exams. Needless to say, visiting a campus when classes and activities are in full swing provides you with a much better picture of what life is really like. Try to be on campus during a weekday when classes are running, and if you are serious about a campus, on a weekend day or night when many other activities take place. This is possible if you put together a Friday-Saturday or Sunday-Monday visit.

Often student or parent schedules don't mesh with college schedules. **Visiting campuses during summer or during winter/spring breaks or even during finals is preferable to not visiting a campus at all.**

If you end up visiting a campus during an "off time," keep in mind that "what you see is not exactly what you may get" under normal campus conditions. Empty campuses (during vacations or summers) or stressed-out students (during final exams) may not represent actual campus life. Talk with students about what you see and find out from them if this is the usual scene. In other words, be cautious about forming a wrong impression of a campus based on the particular time you are there.

The amount of time students and their families spend at one college campus varies from a fifteen minute drive-through by car (on your way to some other place), to a couple of hours, to a half-day, all day, or even a full weekend.

★ **A good amount of time to spend for a first visit is a half-day per campus.**

THINGS TO SEE AND DO WHEN VISITING A COLLEGE

A college visit can be made up of many parts. It is up to you to decide how much you want to see and do at any given campus, as well as the pace in which you do them. What you do is often determined by whether this is a first campus visit, a repeat visit, an interview visit, or a final visit after you have been admitted to the school. Once on campus, here are a variety of things you can do:

1. VISIT THE COLLEGE ADMISSIONS OFFICE

Colleges sometimes give admissions preference to students who "demonstrate interest" in their colleges. One of the strongest demonstrations is a visit to their campus. Just visiting a college is not enough; **you need to document a visit by signing in at the admissions office.** Whether you are a freshman or a senior, you might also try to introduce yourself to the admissions representative assigned to your high school. If that person is not available, then from the front desk people get his or her business card and email address.

GROUP INFORMATION SESSIONS

Many college admissions offices offer group information sessions, a time when a staff person gives a formal presentation about admissions at his or her college and answers questions from the audience. Some colleges do not offer on-campus personal interviews, so a group information session becomes the only opportunity to have firsthand contact with an admissions officer. If you attend one of these sessions, be sure to go up to the college rep after the session is over, introduce yourself, ask a question or two, and also find out if he or she might be visiting your high school in the near future.

IF THE ADMISSIONS OFFICE IS CLOSED

If you happen to visit a campus when the admissions office is closed, then it is useful to let the admissions people know that you have been on campus. Email a note to the admissions representative assigned to your school. If you don't know who the college rep is or his or her email address, when you get home simply call the admissions office at the college or look it up in the Admissions section of the college website.

2. TAKE A CAMPUS TOUR

Admissions offices usually offer free campus tours during weekdays (and sometimes weekends). Phone the office to see what days and times are available and sign up. Undergraduates at colleges usually lead these tours and the quality varies; some are very good and some are not.

Whether you go on a guided tour or on your own, here are some places to visit to get a sense of what a campus is like:

- ★ College bookstore
- ★ Student center
- ★ Student hangouts such as coffeehouses, snack bars, and dining halls
- ★ Residence halls
- ★ The college library, especially the study areas
- ★ Athletic playing fields

adMISSION POSSIBLE TIP

While your first gut reaction to a college is often "right on," don't let first impressions of any one admissions officer, tour guide, student, or professor dictate your overall feelings about a college.

3. SIT IN ON A CLASS

One way to get a picture of student-professor relationships at a college is to sit in on a class. The college admissions office often arranges this. Also, if you know a student at a college, ask her or him to take you to a class. If possible, attend a freshman survey course and/or a class in your major field of interest.

If you attend a class, consider going up to the professor before or after class and introducing yourself. Give your name and say that you are a student from X high school visiting the campus. You might tell the professor that you enjoyed the class, and ask a question or two. Get a business card before you leave the classroom and when you get home, send him or her a thank you email.

4. MEET A PROFESSOR IN YOUR FIELD OF INTEREST

Some students know exactly what they want to major in when they go to college (most students don't). **If you have a future major in mind, you might try to talk with a professor in the department of your field of interest.**

Appointments with professors can often be arranged through the admissions office. If not, call the department office. Professor names, biographies, and contact information are usually available in the Academics section of the college website. If you are uncertain about what to talk with a professor about, here are some ideas about what to say, as well as a few questions to ask:

- ★ First, **introduce yourself and tell the professor which high school you attend.**
- ★ Second, **tell the professor about your interest in his or her specialty.** You might give him or her some examples of how that interest has played out in high school courses or activities (e.g., you have taken AP courses, gone to special summer programs, written papers, etc.).
- ★ Third, **here are some questions you can ask:**

QUESTIONS FOR A PROFESSOR

- *How many students are in this major?*
- *Who and what are the "special" professors and courses in the department?*
- *What kinds of undergraduate research opportunities are there?*
- *Can you give me some suggestions about books, courses, or experiences that will prepare me for a major in the subject?*
- *How do you like teaching at X college? Why did you decide to teach here?*
- *If you had to do it all over again, to which colleges would you apply?*

5. TALK WITH CURRENT STUDENTS

One of the best ways of really "getting" what a college is all about is to talk with current students. Chat with students you already know at the college. Also, get names of current students at a college from teachers, counselors, friends, and family.

Admissions offices are good sources for names of college students who are willing to speak with prospective students. Of course, you can always strike up a conversation with random students as you walk around campus. Here are a few questions you might ask:

QUESTIONS FOR STUDENTS

- *What do you like best (least) about this college?*
- *How is the social life? What do students do during the week and weekends for fun?*
- *Where do students live? What are those places like? Which are the best living arrangements?*
- *How are the support services on campus (academic advising, internship or career counseling)?*
- *How accessible are the instructors to undergraduate students?*
- *What are some of the best and worst classes and who are some of the best and worst professors?*
- *What kinds of students are most compatible with this college's academic and social environment?*
- *Why did you decide to attend this college?*
- *If you had to do it all over again, would you choose this college? If no, where would you go?*

6. LOOK INTO EXTRACURRICULAR/ATHLETIC INTERESTS OR SPECIAL STUDENT SERVICES

If you are into **acting**, go to the drama department and speak with professors and students. Ask if you can attend a dramatic production or rehearsal.

If you are an **athlete**, speak with a coach in your sport; also talk with student athletes. Attend a practice or a game. Check out the athletic facilities.

If **volunteering** is an interest, visit the community service center on campus and speak with someone about the opportunities they offer students. Check out volunteer prospects as noted on bulletin boards, meeting notices, etc. Ask about activities in areas in which you are already interested (Habitat for Humanity, MADD, tutoring, etc.).

If you are **religious or have a strongly felt ethnic background**, find out how you might act on either of those affiliations on campus (e.g., ask to visit the college Hillel organization if you are Jewish or meet with the Hispanic student group sponsor if you are Latino, etc.).

If you are interested in **studying abroad**, go to the study abroad office. Ask when, where, and for how long most students go on programs.

If you are **learning or physically disabled**, make an appointment with the head of the disabled services center. Whatever your special concerns are, see how they are addressed on campus.

If you think you will be applying for **financial aid**, make an appointment with a financial aid officer. Often, this is more comfortable for parents to do than students.

Find out about activities that will take place while you are on campus, including athletic events, concerts, rallies, special lectures or events, student productions, and anything else that interests you. Sources of information include bulletin boards, activities kiosks, the campus newspaper, and students.

7. CHECK OUT HOUSING ARRANGEMENTS

If a dorm visit is not a part of your college tour, **ask the admissions office about visiting one or two housing situations.** Most colleges offer a variety of residence facilities, including freshman, co-ed, single sex, theme, and all-class dorms, as well as campus apartments, fraternity/sorority houses, small independent houses, and cooperatives.

Check out different student rooms (singles, doubles, triples, suites), study coves, lounge areas, bathrooms, and, of course, the dining hall.

Also ask the admissions office to arrange for you to have a meal while you are visiting a residence. Because of security concerns, most nonresidents cannot just walk into a dorm and have a meal. You will need to get permission to do this.

adMISSION POSSIBLE TIP!

Some colleges have special guest rooms in dorms set aside for prospective students. This might be a perfect way to stay overnight, combining access with privacy and a good night's sleep! Ask the college admissions office if such rooms are available. Do this early on because these rooms are often booked far in advance.

FAQ #1: What do I do if I want to spend the night at a college?

ANSWER: College sleepovers are often arranged with friends or friends of friends at colleges. If you don't know anyone on campus, then admissions offices often make overnight arrangements. Spending the night in a college residence hall is a great way to see a college, but how and when should be thought through carefully. If, for example, you are visiting just one college, then spending the night is probably a good idea. However, if you are traveling to seven colleges in seven days as a part of a whirlwind tour, then sleepovers at every college are probably a bad idea. Many high school students are not aware that sleep is a rare commodity in college dorms. Dorm meetings and activities often take place at midnight and later. If you are on a tight schedule and only getting a couple of hours or no sleep at all, you're going to be too exhausted to take full advantage of your college trip.

8. READ THE CAMPUS NEWSPAPER

One of the best sources of information about any campus is the college newspaper. By reading it, you can get a flavor for who students are, what they are interested in, and what happens on campus. Some colleges have daily newspapers; others have weekly. You can usually get a current copy at the student center, in dorms, or on newsstands located throughout the campus. While you may not have time to read the paper when you are on campus, be sure to read it later. It is an invaluable source of information.

9. WALK OR DRIVE THROUGH THE ADJACENT TOWN

When you go away to college for four years, you're not only moving to a college campus, but also to the town and area surrounding the college. Before you leave for home, take a walk or drive through what is around the college. Look at the stores, cafes, bookstores, retail establishments, and entertainment centers.

QUESTIONS TO ASK ABOUT THE ADJACENT TOWN AND COMMUNITY

- *Do I feel comfortable here?*
- *Do I feel safe?*
- *Look at the people walking the streets. Do I like what I see?*
- *Can I see myself shopping for clothes and other things here?*
- *If there is a residential area nearby, does it please me?*
- *Are there good places close by to run or cycle?*
- *Can I see myself having this as my "home away from home" for the next four years?*

10. GO BACK TO THE "BLINK" CONCEPT: SIMPLY VISIT A COLLEGE, SPEND AS MUCH TIME AS YOU WANT, AND JUST HAVE FUN!

FAQ #2: Should I go on a college tour with my parents, with friends, or on my own?

ANSWER: There are positives and negatives for each choice. You and your parents need to decide which choice is best for you.

Parents: If you go with your parents, they can help take care of a lot of the hassles, such as transportation, motels or bed and breakfast reservations, parking, and paying for different things. Students who get along with their parents are likely to enjoy sharing college trips with Mom and Dad, including their different impressions.

Some students fear that their parents will be "too visible" during tours, information sessions, and the like. If you decide to visit a college with one or both parents, it's probably a good idea to talk about expectations and also decide in advance what you will do on your own and with one another.

Know that college interviews are for students only.

Friends Sans Their Families: Going with a friend or a few friends on a college trip sounds great. Sometimes it is, but sometimes it's not, depending on who your friends are. If you are very compatible with a friend or two and have traveled with them before, then you will probably know if they will be good college visit companions.

A college trip is different from a vacation. It is very important that you work out from the beginning what your expectations are. For example, each person should articulate how much time he or she wants to spend at a college. Determine what exactly each of you wants to do while you're on campus. Will you spend all of your time together or have time for individual pursuits? How do you want to spend your evenings? Does one of you want to spend time with students talking about ideas while the other wants to party? These are important questions to discuss in advance because your goals may be very different from your friends'.

On Your Own: Some students prefer to visit colleges on their own. They are usually people who are accustomed to traveling and doing things independently. One important part of planning a trip on your own is to make arrangements for who to meet up with while at a college. Friends, friends of the family, friends of friends, former students at your school, or strangers that the admissions office introduces you to are a few of the options. Just because you travel alone doesn't mean you have to be alone while visiting a college.

FAQ #3: My parents' work schedules make it impossible for them to take me on college trips. What should I do?

ANSWER: There are **commercial groups** that take students on college tours. One of the better-known groups is College Visits (www.college-visits.com).

You might ask your **friends** if their families are planning college tours. Perhaps you can join one of them.

Some high schools offer their own college tours, although they tend to restrict the people taking them to their own students.

Some local and national organizations **such as YMCA and YWCA** groups offer college tours.

Probably the best sources for information regarding college visits are high school counselors or current and previous students at your high school who have already been through the college visit process.

ENDNOTE

In summary, visiting a campus is the very best way of knowing whether it is where you want to go to college. It can also be an adventure and a way of having a great time. Thinking through what you want to do while visiting a college is the best way of ensuring that you have a good experience.

If you cannot actually visit colleges, then take some virtual tours with the likes of www.unigo.com or www.collegeprowler.com.

adMISSION POSSIBLE TIP

Prospective and accepted students for whom faraway college visits are financially difficult should speak with admissions offices about financial assistance to help with travel and other expenses. These are called "fly-in" programs and take place both in the fall when students are considering schools and in the spring after students have been accepted.

Timelines for Visiting Colleges

» FRESHMAN AND SOPHOMORE YEAR AND PARENTS

* Ninth and tenth grades are a good time to begin driving by or briefly stopping at college campuses as you visit cities in your home state or other parts of the United States. **It doesn't really matter if you know anything about the colleges. Simply getting exposed to a wide array of college types**—different geographic areas, big and little schools, private and public colleges, colleges in cities, college towns, and in rural settings—**will give you very useful information for when you begin to develop your college list.**

* **Visit colleges in your own hometown.** Even though you might want to attend college in another city, getting exposed to different kinds of colleges is very useful. Pay particular attention to what you like and don't.

adMISSION POSSIBLE TIP!

A good rule of thumb is to never decide to attend a college that you have not seen personally.

» JUNIOR YEAR AND PARENTS

* **Junior year is the time to get serious about college visits.** Plan family vacations around colleges that interest you. **Or take trips for the sole purpose of visiting colleges.**
* If you haven't already, during school days off or on weekends, **visit colleges in your own hometown.**
* **Take day trips to visit colleges that are within driving range** of where you live.
* **Take notes about your impressions** of colleges.

» SENIOR YEAR AND PARENTS

FALL SEMESTER

* **If you can, visit every college on your college list.**
* **Begin planning college interview meetings the summer before your senior year.** Interview time slots fill up fast, so make appointments as soon as you know when you will be at a specific campus. (See chapter 14, "Admissions Interviews: Knowing Exactly What to Say and Do.")

SPRING SEMESTER

* The middle of March to the beginning of April is when most colleges inform students about regular admissions decisions. **If you are unsure about where you want to go to school, then visiting the colleges is absolutely critical.**

CHAPTER 7

RELATIONSHIPS WITH COLLEGES

How to Make College Contacts a "Tip Factor" in Your College Admissions

DEFINITION of RELATIONSHIPS WITH COLLEGES: *Relationships with colleges come in many forms. It is as simple as*

- *Phoning or emailing a college admissions office*
- *Returning a postcard from a college marketing piece*
- *Signing up to be on a college's mailing list*
- *Having an on-campus interview with an admissions officer, or*

- *Attending an on-campus group information session with someone from the admissions office*
- *Meeting with admissions people at a college fair or a local college reception*
- *Interacting with an admissions officer during their visit to your school*
- *Stopping by an admissions office for a quick hello and sign-in during your visit*
- *Having an off-campus interview with an alum from your hometown*

Relationships with colleges also include appointments with coaches, meetings with art professors to show them your portfolio, or auditioning for places in music or theater departments.

Contact you make with colleges can be an important piece of your college admissions. Sometimes it can even make the difference between your being accepted, wait-listed, or rejected.

{ THE BOTTOM LINE }

At a recent National Association for College Admissions Counseling convention, counselors from all over the country reported that colleges are turning down some of their otherwise qualified students, often for no other reason than the student had little or no contact with them. Daniel Golden, a journalist who received the Pulitzer Prize for his articles on admissions, has noted that "…*all things being equal, colleges tend to favor strong applicants who make the most contacts with the school—interviews, campus overnight visits, college fairs, and the like.*" Moreover, some admissions deans have described student contact as a "tip factor" in admissions.

Common sense says that a good student whose name and face are recognizable to an admissions office may have a better chance of being admitted than someone who is simply a name and an application. If there are two students, each with high SAT scores and equally good grades, whom do you think will be chosen: A student who has taken the time to make contact with an admissions office or one who hasn't? You know the answer. Bottom line: contact with an admissions office before filing your application may help you and no contact could possibly hurt you.

CONTACT WITH COLLEGES (AKA DEMONSTRATED INTEREST)

Student contact with colleges has become a big issue in the past few years. Mostly used by private colleges, the term **"demonstrated interest" is defined as both the quantity and quality of contact students have with colleges, contact that indicates students'** *perceived likelihood to enroll* **should they be offered admission to a college.**

Obviously, the ultimate in "demonstrated interest" is applying Restrictive Early Action or Early Decision to a college.

In the old days, colleges simply admitted the best applicants they could, irrespective of any contact the students had with them. Turns out that many admitted students turned down less competitive schools for so-called more desirable, competitive ones. That wasn't such a big deal even a few years back, but in today's competitive world, it is. Being turned down by students is becoming increasingly unacceptable to colleges because it affects their "yield rate" (the percentage of accepted applicants who actually enroll in a college compared to the number of acceptances offered). **So a new trend among less competitive colleges is to turn down some of the best applicants they get—particularly if they have not bothered to "demonstrate interest"—for less qualified students who the colleges think will likely accept their bid to enroll.**

adMISSION POSSIBLE TIP

There is great variety in how colleges keep track of student contact. While larger, public universities cannot afford the time and effort it takes to note when and how often students contact them, other colleges can. Many, but not all, private colleges have computer programs to keep track of each student's contact with their respective admissions offices.

THE DEAL ABOUT ADMISSIONS YIELD RATES

Yield rates are used by colleges 1) as important statistics they report to college ranking groups; 2) as highly touted statistics appearing in public relations pieces in their college guidebooks and alumni bulletins, or to share with Boards of Trustees; and 3) as a recruitment tool to attract new faculty and administrators. Even bond-rating agencies pay attention to yield rates when making decisions as to how good an investment a college is. That's why colleges care about yield rates.

WHO YOUR HIGH SCHOOL'S COLLEGE ADMISSIONS REPS ARE AND WHY YOU SHOULD CARE

Did you know that every four-year college in the United States has a representative from their admissions office assigned to every high school in the United States? **Yes, even your high school has an admissions officer assigned to it by the different colleges.** College admissions offices usually divide responsibility for high schools by geographic region. In other words, an admissions office might assign New York City and its boroughs to one officer, Southern California to another, and the states of Idaho, Montana, Wyoming, and South and North Dakota to another.

> **adMISSION POSSIBLE TIP!**
>
> You want your top choices to know that they are top choices. Some kind of contact with every college to which you apply is a good idea.

A part of the job description for every representative is spending time (usually in the fall) in their assigned geographic areas, meeting high school counselors and getting to know the schools, holding admissions meetings for students at individual schools, or offering larger meetings for students from many high schools at a hotel or large high school auditorium.

Admissions reps also participate in joint admissions meetings with other colleges. An example is the "Eight of the Best Colleges" Reception involving Claremont McKenna College, Colorado College, Connecticut College, Grinnell College, Haverford College, Kenyon College, Macalester College, and Sarah Lawrence College.

Of greatest relevance to students, though, is the role these college reps play during the admissions process. While every college has its own selection process, often it is the admissions rep assigned to your high school who first reads your application, rating it according to some prescribed set of characteristics and making a summary comment. Sometimes the application goes on to other readers, sometimes to a committee, and sometimes to the Dean of Admission for the final decision of Admit, Deny, or Wait list.

In the best of all worlds, that admissions rep becomes an advocate for you, arguing your case in selection meetings. If the representative has

★ **communicated back and forth with you by email, or**
★ **met you at your school or at a larger group meeting, or**
★ **had an interview with you, or**
★ **come to know you, like you, and develop a relationship with you,**

then he or she may have a very positive effect on your admissions possibilities.

FAQ #1: If a college representative comes to my school and holds a meeting at the same time I'm scheduled to take a test, what do I do?

ANSWER: **No college rep wants to feel that he or she has been snubbed or forgotten by a student who is applying to his or her college.** If a college meeting takes place during a class, ask your teacher to be excused to visit the college rep. (Many teachers require twenty-four-hour advance notice.)

It's always nice for college admissions people to meet students who are excited about their college. They also like when students seem to understand what the college is all about, and why they (the students) and the college are a good match.

If you are unable to attend a college meeting (a teacher won't excuse you, you have a test), try to find a way to explain the reason why you cannot be at the meeting. You might say something such as

Hi, I'm Debby Lange. ***Thanks so much for visiting our school. I'm really excited about the possibility of coming to your college.*** *I would love to hear what you have to say in the meeting, but my AP (name of class) teacher has told me that I have to be in class today.*

If you can't do that, it is both a wise move and a courteous response IN ADVANCE of the meeting to let your high school college counselor and the college rep know why you won't be at the meeting.

If you can attend a college meeting, be sure to get the business card of the individual(s) from the college and send a thank-you note or email.

FAQ #2: Is there such a thing as too much contact between a student and the admissions office?

ANSWER: Absolutely. Excessive calling, particularly when admissions officers are reading the current applications, is both annoying and nonproductive. Don't become a pain. Also, admissions people are quick to complain about phone calls that involve questions easily answered by looking carefully at the application or reading the school's guidebook. Polite, clear questions are almost always welcomed. Calling to make sure that the college has received various parts of your application is also fine. Common sense says that all inquiries should be a model of politeness, patience, and appreciation.

FAQ #3: **How do admissions offices feel about parents calling them on behalf of their son or daughter?**

ANSWER: Again, using common sense is the best way to answer this question. Colleges usually prefer to speak with students, but sometimes that's just not possible. So if a parent calls, it's useful to explain that your son or daughter is not available to ask the question because of his or her current schedule (in school all day, or involved with after-school activities until late, or away at a summer experience in Argentina, or whatever the circumstances might be). Whether it is a student or a parent, it's still a good idea to get the name of the person with whom you speak so that you can ask to talk with this person the next time you call (particularly if that individual has been unusually helpful or nice to you).

WHAT TO SAY AND DO WHEN YOU STOP BY AN ADMISSIONS OFFICE

As you visit college campuses, stop by the admissions office to introduce yourself and say hello to whomever is there. Be sure to sign in or fill out a visitor card. If you don't, your visit may go unnoticed. Here is what you might say and do:

Go to the desk or counter where there is a receptionist. Say something such as

You: "Hi, I'm (your name) from (your high school) in (your town) ."

Explanation: Who will be manning the admissions desk is always an unknown. You never know who it will be, especially at a small college. It might be a student or even the Dean of Admissions. So be on your toes: walk in with a smile on your face, act interested, and be polite.

Admissions Person: (Welcomes you to the campus. Some kind of reply.)

You: "Can you tell me the name of the admissions rep for (your high school) ? If she or he is here today, I'd really love to meet her or him."

Admissions Person: (Some kind of reply.) If the rep is not there, then ask for his or her business card.

Explanation: If your admissions rep is available and comes out to meet you, introduce yourself and then be prepared to ask a few questions. For example,

You: "Hi, I'm (your name) from (name of your high school) in (your town) ."

> * We are spending just a short amount of time on campus; is there anything you can recommend that we do or see?
> * Are you planning a visit to (your high school or city) in the next year?
> * Well, we have to be on our way. Thank you so much for coming out to say hello. Please let me know if you will be coming to (your high school) or (your town) . By the way, may I have your card?"

Congratulations; you have just made a college contact.

COLLEGE FAIRS

College Fairs held in your hometown or nearby towns are a very convenient way of meeting admissions representatives. They are usually offered by the likes of National Association for College Admissions Counseling (NACAC) and the Colleges That Change Lives organization (CTCL). See the Cool Web Links section of www.admissionpossible.com for links to these groups.

Once you hear about an upcoming fair, go online to the sponsoring organization's website and register for it. Note the date, time, and location on your calendar. When the time comes, be prepared

1. Before you go, **identify the colleges you want to visit.** Or once you arrive at the college fair venue, get a list of the colleges and circle the ones you want to visit.

2. **Bring a copy of *The Fiske Guide* (or another guide) to write down notes about what you find out from the rep** on the college page of each school you visit.

    Hint: It will also be very useful to have highlighted in one color what you like and in another color what you don't like about each school so that you have some knowledge about each school and what to say should the college rep ask you why you are interested in his or her school.

3. As you approach a booth or table, say something such as this:

> **You:** "Hi, I'm (your name) and I am a junior (or sophomore) at (your school) . As I have researched colleges, I found that I am very interested in your school. I'm wondering if you have a minute to answer a few questions."

4. **Ask questions that you really want to have answered.** Here are some possibilities:
   * Can you tell me something about the campus atmosphere at your school? What happens during the day, evenings, (during the week and weekends)?
   * What kinds of students tend to go to your school (serious academics, athletes, techies, party-goers, environmentally conscious people, preppies, funky/unconventional people)?
   * Do most students live on campus? If no, where do they live?
   * What are the dorms like?

* What do students like most about your college? What do students tend to complain about?
* What is the usual class size? How accessible are professors?
* Ask for a list of majors that you can look at when you get home. If you have a particular major you are interested in, ask about it.
* If you have a particular activity you're interested in, ask about it.
* If you have a learning disability, ask what kind of learning disability services the college offers.
* Ask anything else about which you want to know.

5. When you feel like you're done, **thank the rep before you leave his or her booth.** Ask for his or her business card and make sure that you have signed the guest book.

6. When you get home, **send a thank-you note to each of the reps you met.** It might say something such as

> Dear Ms. (or Mr.) (name) :
>
> Just a note to thank you so much for taking the time to talk with me at the (name of town) College Fair. I so enjoyed hearing about (name of college) and especially about (say something specific you heard from the rep) .
>
> I am very interested in (name of college) and look forward to sending in my application next fall. Please let me know if/when you plan a return visit to (your town) .
>
> Sincerely,
>
> (your name) ,
> (your school)

FAQ #4: When is it too late to show your interest in a college?

ANSWER: Never. Having said that, however, know that the earlier you show interest in a college, the longer the contact record you will have. Letting colleges know that you're interested in them (even as late as the fall of your senior year) is always a good idea.

ENDNOTE

Ultimately, contact with colleges is something you do to

* Become educated about campuses and the kinds of experiences their respective students have there
* Personalize a process that often seems cold and impersonal
* Create advocates for yourself within admissions offices

It's just common sense that the better they know you, the more likely it is that they will choose you to be a student at their college.

Timeline for Contact with Colleges

» FRESHMAN YEAR

Unless a student is very motivated, freshman year is pretty early to begin making contact with colleges; nevertheless, it does happen. For example, as a freshman, one student I know began looking for colleges that were well known for dance programs. In her search, she found an East Coast college that was exceptionally good, so on her own (and without her parents' or my knowledge), she sent the dance department chair/professor an email, to which the chair replied. Over the course of four years, the student and professor emailed one another back and forth. By the time the girl applied to the college as a senior, she and the dance chair were friends and the chair wrote a recommendation letter for the girl. The girl applied Early Decision to the school and—no surprise—she was accepted. Serendipitously, sometimes college contact comes early and really pays off.

PARENTS

Starting when children are quite young, some parents make college visits a part of any visit to a vacation town or city, simply because they are cool places to go. Student centers and bookstores always have something of interest to children and the campus, itself, often offers a park-like setting. What this does is introduce children to the notion that colleges are neat places.

» SOPHOMORE YEAR

If as a sophomore you are curious about colleges and are interested in making contact with them, here are some things you can do:

- ★ On your way to different destinations away from your home or while on a family vacation, **have your parents take a few minutes to make a quick stop at a college or two.** Find the college admissions office and sign in. This is one way of showing your early interest in a college and also gets you on their mailing list.
- ★ **Sign up for and attend college fairs held in your hometown** (see below for what to do and say).
- ★ If there is an opportunity to **meet a college rep in a school in which you are interested**, you might want to consider taking advantage of it.

PARENTS

Sophomore year, some high school students begin showing interest in colleges; however, many more don't. Parents should pay attention to where their children are in their interests and not push them. Tenth grade is still very early in the admissions process.

» JUNIOR YEAR

This is the year for getting serious about making college contacts. As soon as you know that you are interested in a college, make a point of letting them know. Here is what to do:

- **Go to the college website and click on the Admissions section.** Complete whatever form is available to indicate your interest (e.g., "Add Me to the Mailing List," Register for Events," "Contact this College").
- If there is no online sign-up mechanism, then simply **call the admissions office and let them know of your interest.** The phone number is usually listed in the Contact section of the website Admissions section.
- More importantly, **find out who the college rep is assigned to your high school** and his or her email address. Some colleges make this very easy by having a section in the Admissions section of their website called something like "Find Your Admission Counselor."

Other colleges don't list that information on their websites, so you will have to call the admissions office and ask for the name and email address. Once you have the rep's name and email address, then send an email such as this:

> Dear Ms. (or Mr.) (name) :
> My name is _____ and I am a junior at _____ High School in _____.
> As I have been reading about your college in guidebooks and on the Internet, I have become very interested in learning more about your college. Will you be coming to my high school _____ sometime in the next few months? If yes, I would love to have the opportunity of meeting you and hearing about _____.
> Sincerely,
> Name
> High School

- **Sign up for and attend college fairs held in your hometown.**
- **If a college rep comes to your high school, try to meet that person.**

PARENTS

Junior year is the best time to take your child on college visits. While interviews are not usually available to juniors, everything else is—from college tours to sitting in on a class to spending some leisure time just people-watching. (See chapter 6, "Visiting Colleges," for more.)

» SENIOR YEAR

Contact with college admissions offices during fall semester senior year is inevitable. Not only will you be sending them your applications, but also making arrangements for personal interviews and calling them with any questions you have. To make your contact count, do some or all of the following:

* If you haven't already, **let colleges know that you are interested in them by getting yourself on their mailing list** (online or through a phone call).
* If you haven't already, **find out who the college rep is assigned to your high school and his or her email address and make contact.**
* **Arrange for a personal interview** on campus with your college rep or another admissions officer.
* **Arrange for an off-campus interview** in your hometown.
* **If a college rep comes to your high school, go out of your way to meet that person.** Ask your high school counselor for a list of dates and times when college reps will be visiting your high school. If there is no printed list, find out where a list is posted so that you can consult it and add the dates and times to your calendar. Also ask the counselor if you need an official excuse from a teacher to leave a class for the meeting.

PARENTS

More than any other time during the admissions process, senior year is when you can be a real help to your child. Help your student plan and make college trips where they can make contact with different campus people, including admissions reps, students, faculty, and others. Be supportive of their meetings with college representatives at their high school, at local meetings, or on college campuses. You can be a means of transportation, as well as a companion and support person, remembering that "This is my kid's college process, not mine."

Regardless of ranking, prestige, the football team's record, or anything else, what's important is what colleges your child wants and likes.

GATHERING APPLICATION AMMUNITION

[CHAPTER 8]

YOUR ACTIVITIES RÉSUMÉ
Helping Colleges "Get" Who You Are

Many students feel reluctant to write or talk about themselves for fear of being seen as a show-off. While the instinct for not coming across as a braggart is "right on," students need to have a means for conveying how they spend their time in and out of school. An Activities Résumé is an excellent tool for doing that.

> **DEFINITION of ACTIVITIES RÉSUMÉ:** *A cornerstone of the adMISSION POSSIBLE process, an Activities Résumé is a one- to four-page written picture of your academic, extracurricular, sports, and other interests and involvements that focuses on high school years, but also ties in long-term interests and activities that may go back to when you were a young child.*

{ THE BOTTOM LINE } After test scores and grades, admissions officers look for how and where you spend time, including the quality, depth, and length of involvement. Developing an Activities Résumé is not only a way to provide colleges with information about who you are, but also a way for you to learn about yourself.

As students gather information about activities they have engaged in over the years, they often gain a new perspective of how interesting and "one-of-a-kind" they are. Seeing everything you have done written down is altogether different from having faint memories of past activities (or no memory of them at all). As you look over your résumé, themes and patterns of interests often pop out. Sometimes you realize that what you are doing now is connected to something you did when you were four years old. These insights are useful for you to have and for admissions people to know.

An Activities Résumé is one of adMISSION POSSIBLE's secret weapons, because of its power to help others "get" who you are. Few students take the trouble to put together an Activities Résumé, let alone do it very well.

ADVICE ABOUT THE CHOICE OF ACTIVITIES

Chapter 2, "Extracurricular Activities," discusses in length how to choose involvements that are both good for you as a person and will look good on your college applications. Here are a few things to remember about choosing your activities:

* Many students think that the more activities they have on their résumés, the more desirable they will be as an admissions candidate. This is a myth. In fact, colleges prefer students who are deeply involved in a few activities that demonstrate uncommon leadership, accomplishment, or talent. **Colleges want a well-rounded student body, not necessarily well-rounded students.**

* **The content of your activities does not matter, although it doesn't hurt if some of your interests are considered "unusual" or different.** For example, if you're about to choose **a sport** and you're not sure which one, why not look into less popular sports such as rowing, pole vaulting, or fencing? These sports might be easier for you to enter and eventually stand out.

  If you're a guy who loves **to cook**, look for ways to excel in this endeavor. Start a little cooking business, attend cooking classes that focus on your favorite foods, enter (and possibly win) a cooking contest.

  If you're a girl who is looking for something interesting to do, **pursue areas that are not typically female**, such as learning how to fly-fish, or taking trapeze lessons, or focusing on a hard science such as physics. Let your imagination run loose. **BUT...don't do any one of the above unless you are really interested in it.**

> ### adMISSION POSSIBLE TIP!
>
> If you are a student who must work to help support your family or has major family commitments such as child or elder care, be sure to list these things on your Activities Résumé. They are legitimate and important ways of spending your time. More importantly, college admissions people want to know about them.

* Want to learn to make goat cheese, take up mountain climbing, learn to speak a Middle Eastern language, play an unusual instrument, become an expert about orchids (or another flower species), breed and raise snakes, trace your family genealogy back five hundred years? But do these things only if you're dying to.

* If you are a student who aspires for a place in an **Ivy League** or other very competitive college, to say that they look for "depth and quality" in your activities and accomplishments is an understatement. **Students who are admitted to the most competitive colleges**
  * **demonstrate "extraordinary commitment" to community service or other activities with regional or national recognition**
  * **show "unusual accomplishment" in a sport or talent**
  * **display significant leadership in activities that they have founded or made a real difference in**

- **win significant academic competitions or prizes**
- **demonstrate unusual intellectual depth**

Of course, these activities take place in the midst of your being a good student.

Having said all of the above, it's also important that you try to keep some kind of balance in your life. You don't want to burn yourself out before you get to college.

WHY AND HOW TO USE AN ACTIVITIES RÉSUMÉ

Having a well thought-out Activities Résumé makes filling out your college applications much easier. First, it **helps organize the many pieces of information** you will need for various parts of the college applications, in particular the activities grids.

Second, it enhances your ability to **find a theme or focus for the applications**, which in turn helps you choose good topics for the application essays.

Third, any person whom you ask to write a letter of recommendation should be given an Activities Résumé, including

- ★ Your high school counselor
- ★ Teachers who are completing Teacher Evaluation forms
- ★ Other people who write letters on your behalf

High school counselors and teachers have dozens of recommendations to write. Because they are responsive to so many students, even at smaller, private schools it is difficult for them to know details about students or know about your activities during all four years of school. Therefore, anything you can do to make their job easier—including providing them with a résumé—will be greatly appreciated. Presenting recommenders with an impressive, well-organized, easy-to-read résumé can only have a positive effect on what they say in their recommendation forms and letters.

An Activities Résumé can help you in other ways too:

- ★ **As a supplement to the activities grid on a college application.** Virtually all colleges ask you to fill out an activities grid. This is a critical part of the application. While an Activities Résumé should never be used as a replacement for completing a grid, unless told otherwise, you can use it as an addendum. Some students use the Additional Information space on the Common Application for this purpose. Other students ask one of their recommenders to include a copy of their résumé as a part of the recommender package.

- ★ **As a giveaway to a college admissions person interviewing you.** What better way of "breaking the ice" with an interviewer than to arrive with an impressive Activities Résumé. Not only will this give you something to talk about, but the résumé will help you to leave a lasting positive impression on the person.

> **adMISSION POSSIBLE TIP!**
>
> Some college applications indicate exactly what they want in a résumé. Be sure to follow their directions carefully. As mentioned many times before, admissions offices don't like when you fail to follow their instructions.

★ **As an attachment to a thank-you note after a meeting or interview with an admissions officer, college coach, or other college person.** Whether you meet an admissions officer at your school or at a large gathering in a hotel off-campus, it is always useful to get his or her name and email address so that you can send a follow-up thank-you note. Attaching your résumé is a perfect way of reminding the person who you are and what you have done.

FAQ #1: My high school counselor tells me that I don't need to have an Activities Résumé. Why do you suggest that I have one?

ANSWER: In over twenty years of working in the admissions arena, I have found nothing more helpful to the admissions process than an Activities Résumé. Because of the uses noted above—1) an organizing mechanism, 2) a starting place for finding a focus for your applications, 3) a source for coming up with essay topics, 4) a resource for people writing recommendations, 5) an addendum for applications, 6) an interview handout, and 7) an attachment for a thank-you note to a college contact—I strongly recommend that you put together a résumé. No matter what other people say, **having a compelling Activities Résumé during the application process sets you up as "just a little different and just a little better" than the competition.**

It is true that a few colleges and universities, such as the UC system and Stanford University, ask you NOT to submit a résumé, but there are many schools that allow and even encourage you to include one.

FAQ #2: Can I use the Activities Résumé for things other than college admissions?

ANSWER: Absolutely. Many **students use their Activities Résumé as part of a scholarship application.** They also use it **for special programs applications while they are still in high school** (e.g., Girls' and Boys' State, various special summer academic programs such as that offered at the Brandeis Institute), as well as **for jobs during the school year and summer.**

Once in college, students continue to use their résumés, updated, of course, for their present circumstances. Many college students report going back to their old high school résumé to develop a new one when they begin applying to graduate school.

Here is a model for what an Activities Résumé can look like and contain. At the end of this chapter are real-life examples of résumés for students from different academic and personal backgrounds. Even more résumé examples can be found in the Checklists section of www.admissionpossible.com.

Full Name
Current Mailing Address
Telephone Number / Fax Number / Email Address

SCHOOL(S) ATTENDED

Dates: Name of School(s):
Address: Tel:
College Board School Code: **Cumulative High School GPA:**

TEST SCORES

SAT Score Combined:	_____	and/or ACT Composite:	_____	Subject Test Scores:
Critical Reading:	_____	English:	_____	Test/Score:_____
Math:	_____	Math:	_____	Test/Score:_____
Writing:	_____	Reading:	_____	Test/Score:_____
		Science:	_____	Test/Score:_____

ADVANCED PLACEMENT, INTERNATIONAL BACCALAUREATE, AND HONORS COURSES

Senior Year   Junior Year
Sophomore Year   Freshman Year

HONORS AND AWARDS (in and out of school)

Senior Year   Junior Year
Sophomore Year   Freshman Year

SPECIAL INTERESTS, TALENTS

(e.g., art, music, drama.) (For each year, also identify summer activities.)
Senior Year   Junior Year
Sophomore Year   Freshman Year

ACTIVITIES AND SPORTS IN HIGH SCHOOL

(For each year, also identify summer activities.)
Senior Year   Junior Year
Sophomore Year   Freshman Year

COMMUNITY SERVICE AND OTHER INTERESTS OUTSIDE OF HIGH SCHOOL

(For each year, also identify summer activities.)
Senior Year   Junior Year
Sophomore Year   Freshman Year

EMPLOYMENT

(during school year and summers) (For each year, also identify summer activities.)
Senior Year   Junior Year
Sophomore Year   Freshman Year

TRAVEL _____

While the above appears to be a one-page résumé, in fact it is an outline of what a typical résumé might include. Depending on your particular involvements, you can adapt it in any way you want to fit your own background.

MAKING THE MOST OF YOUR RÉSUMÉ

Here are some suggestions for making your résumé effective:

* **Not only should you identify activities and awards, but also explain what they are, what positions you held, and what you did or accomplished.** (See Ways of Describing Activities in the checklists section of www.admissionpossible.com.)

* Note that the résumé is **organized in reverse chronological order: list the most recent activities and awards first. Also, begin each section with the most important activities**, followed by less important ones.

* After page 1, **make sure that for each subsequent page you include the page number and your name.**

* **Since admissions readers will probably give your résumé about thirty seconds, it must be organized and formatted so that is very easy to read.** Your résumé must help a reader "get who you are" very quickly.

* Some colleges call for a one-page résumé, and others give directions for no more than two pages. If a school to which you apply requests a short résumé, it is useful to start out with a long version and then cut it down. No matter what, follow the application directions, whatever they are.

ENDNOTE

An Activities Résumé is not only a way of providing colleges with information about who you are, it is also a powerful means for learning about yourself.

SAMPLE RÉSUMÉS

A. AVERAGE STUDENT FROM A PUBLIC HIGH SCHOOL WHO NOW ATTENDS A FOUR-YEAR PUBLIC UNIVERSITY IN THE SOUTH

John Adam Doe
1234 Main Street, Anytown, U.S. 00000
Tel: (123) 555-1234 **Cell:** (123) 555-1234 **Email:** jdoe@anyurl.com

---

SCHOOL ATTENDED

2009–present	ABCD High School
	123 Main Street Anytown, U.S. 00001
	Tel: (123) 555-1234 **Fax:** (123) 555-1234
	Cumulative GPA: 2.7

HONORS AND AP COURSES

Senior Year	**Junior Year**
AP Government	Honors Intermediate Algebra
Sophomore Year	**Freshman Year**
Honors Geometry	Honors Algebra

TEST SCORES

SAT I	**SUBJECT TESTS**
Combined: 1590	U.S. History: 590
Math: 580	Math II: 600
Critical Reading: 530	
Writing: 480	

HONORS AND AWARDS
Junior Year
- Men's Soccer All League (city, states)
  - Only student chosen from school

Sophomore Year
- Most Valuable Player, Boy's Varsity Soccer team, ABCD High School

Freshman Year
- Math Departmental Award, ABCD High School

SPECIAL INTERESTS
Soccer
Sports have been a big part of my life, something that I have done since I was six years old. For many years, I played on community soccer teams. As a teenager, I began playing Club soccer, as well as Varsity soccer for my school. I play both midfield and forward positions on community and school teams.

(continued)

ACTIVITIES, VOLUNTEER/OTHER WORK, SPORTS (continued)

Senior Year
- Captain, Varsity Soccer team, ABCD High School
- Midfielder, Forward, Premier Club Soccer team (Anytown, GA)
- Volunteer tutor, ABCD Elementary School (Anytown, GA)
  - Help students with homework in all subject areas, particularly math
- Independent math tutor for high school student
- Babysitter to little sister, cousins

Summer 2009
- Employee, XYZ Construction Company (Anytown, GA)
  - Worked as a carpenter

Junior Year
- Captain, Varsity Soccer team, ABCD High School
- Midfielder, Forward, AAA Club Soccer (Anytown, GA)
- Midfielder, Forward, Soccer League (Anytown, GA)
  - Community soccer
- Volunteer tutor, ABCD Elementary School (Anytown, GA)
- Babysitter to little sister, cousins

Summer 2008
- Employee, XYZ Construction Company (Anytown, GA)
  - Worked as a "gofer"

Sophomore Year
- Letterman, Varsity Soccer team, ABCD High School
- Midfielder, Forward, Soccer League (Anytown, GA)
  - Community soccer
- Volunteer tutor, ABCD Elementary School (Anytown, GA)
- Babysitter to little sister, cousins

Summer 2007
- Student, Summer School, ABCD High School
  - Took English class

Freshman Year
- Member, Junior Varsity Soccer team, ABCD High School
- Midfielder, Forward, Soccer League (Anytown, GA)
  - Community soccer
- Babysitter to little sister, cousins

LANGUAGES

I am fluent in both Spanish and English.

TRAVEL

Every year, my family and I travel back to Mexico to visit my grandparents and other family members.

B. A BETTER THAN AVERAGE PRIVATE SCHOOL STUDENT WHO ATTENDS A MIDDLE-SIZED PRIVATE UNIVERSITY IN A MID-ATLANTIC STATE

Jane Anne Doe
1234 Main Street, Anytown, U.S. 00000
Tel: (123) 555-1234 **Cell:** (123) 555-1234 **Email:** jdoe@anyurl.com

EDUCATION

2009–present	ABCD High School
	123 Main Street Anytown, U.S. 00001
	Tel: (123) 555-1234 **Fax:** (123) 555-1234
	College Board School Code: xxxxx
	Cumulative GPA: 3.43

AP AND HONORS COURSES

Senior Year
AP U.S. History
AP Art

Sophomore Year
AP Biology: 3

Junior Year
AP Art History: 4
AP Spanish Language: 4

TEST SCORES

SAT I
Combined: 1920
Writing: 650
Critical Reading: 640
Math: 630

SUBJECT TESTS
Biology: 620
Spanish with Listening: 650

SPECIAL EXPERIENCE

Exchange Student, Experiment in International Living, Madrid, Spain
In 2007, I spent the summer living with a Spanish host family, studying Spanish at a language school and visiting a variety of cultural and historical sites.

HONORS AND AWARDS

Junior Year
- Volunteer of the Month, ABCD School
  This award is given to students who perform an extraordinary amount of community service during a particular month.
- Honor Roll, ABCD School

Sophomore Year
- Volunteer of the Month, ABCD School
- The Yellow Rose Award, National Charity League, 2006
  This award is given to the girls in NCL who perform at least one hundred hours of community service.
- Honor Roll

(continued)

HONORS AND AWARDS (continued)

Freshman Year

- Outstanding Community Service Award, ABCD School

    This award is given to students who throughout the year have performed an exceptional amount of community service.
- The Yellow Rosebud Bouquet Award, National Charity League, 2005

    This award is given to the girls in NCL who perform at least fifty hours of community service.

ACTIVITIES, COMMUNITY SERVICE, SPORTS, AND WORK

COMMUNITY SERVICE

Since 2006, I have been a volunteer at the ABCD Day School, a school for children who have learning disabilities. I have also been involved with the National Charity League, a nonprofit national organization of mothers and daughters who join together in community involvement within local chapters throughout the United States. Its goal is to foster a sense of community responsibility in girls, as well as strengthen the mother-daughter relationship. The daughters participate in a six-year program of community service work, educational activities, and cultural events.

VIOLIN

I began taking violin lessons in the fifth grade and have continued playing it and participating in competitions.

Senior Year

- Volunteer, ABCD School

    ABCD School offers a holistic approach to teaching day, after-school, and summer programs for children with learning and other disabilities.
    - Serve as a mentor and tutor
- Vice President, Community Service Club, ABCD School

    The major community service group at school that focuses on world issues.
    - Raise funds for philanthropic organizations around the world
    - Participate in special projects such as a school in Darfur
- Member, National Charity League
    - Work in the adoptions department of a local animal shelter
- Independent violin student and performer

Summer, 2008

- Exchange Student, Experiment in International Living, Madrid, Spain

Junior Year

- Member, Community Service Club, ABCD School
- Volunteer, ABCD School
- Member, National Charity League
    - Volunteer, Mothers Against Drunk Driving (MADD)
    - Volunteer, XYZ Retirement Home
    - Usher for city chamber orchestra
    - Usher for city symphony orchestra
- Independent violin student and performer

ACTIVITIES, COMMUNITY SERVICE, SPORTS, AND WORK (continued)　　　　　　　**Doe - 3**

Summer, 2007
- Participant, ABCD University Tennis Camp
- Counselor, ABCD School Summer Camp

Sophomore Year
- Member, Community Service Club, ABCD School
- Member, National Charity League
    - Volunteer, Special Olympics, tennis division
    - Volunteer, XYZ Retirement Home
    - Monthly volunteer for city parks and beaches cleanup
- Independent violin student and performer

Summer, 2006
- Student , XYZ Violin Camp

Freshman Year
- Member, National Charity League
    - Volunteer, Special Olympics, tennis division
    - Volunteer, XYZ Retirement Home
    - Volunteer, Animal Care Center
- Independent violin student and performer

EMPLOYMENT

Freshman Year - Junior Year
- Dog sitter, cat sitter, house sitter
- Frequent babysitter

C. A SUPERSTAR PUBLIC SCHOOL STUDENT WHO NOW ATTENDS A VERY COMPETITIVE COLLEGE IN THE EAST

John Barry Doe
1234 Main Street, Anytown, U.S. 00000
Tel: (123) 555-1234 **Cell:** (123) 555-1234 **Email:** jdoe@anyurl.com

---

EDUCATION
2009 - present   **ABCD High School**
                     123 Main Street Anytown, U.S. 00001
                     Tel: (123) 555-1234 **Fax:** (123) 555-1234
                     College Board School Code: xxxx
                     Cumulative GPA: 4.5

AP AND HONORS COURSES
Senior Year

AP Physics	AP Art
AP English	AP Computer Science
	AP Calculus, BC

Other Years

AP Biology: 5	AP Government and Politics: 5
AP Chemistry: 5	AP European History: 5
AP U.S. History: 5	AP Spanish: 4

TEST SCORES

ACT	**SUBJECT TESTS**
COMPOSITE: 35	Math II: 800
English: 34	Biology: 780
Math: 36	Spanish: 780
Reading: 35	American History: 760
Science: 35	

SPECIAL EDUCATIONAL EXPERIENCES
JOHNS HOPKINS UNIVERSITY, CENTER FOR TALENTED YOUTH
As early as seventh grade, individuals are selected to become a part of the Center for Talented Youth program by scoring higher than average college-bound seniors on the College Board's SAT.

College Level Courses Taken:
2009: Tutorial College in Creative Writing
   - Grade: A

High School Level Courses Taken:
2008: Fast-Paced High School Chemistry
   - Grade: A
2007: Individually Paced Mathematics
   - Grade: A

ACADEMIC HONORS AND AWARDS

Senior Year
- National Merit Scholarship Semifinalist
- AP Scholar with Distinction

Junior Year
- Stanford University Book Award
- Inductee, Cum Laude Society
- Departmental Award in English
- 2nd Place, National Spanish IV Exam
- Finalist, Rotary Club Speech Competition
- Inductee, Sociedad Honoraria Hispánica
- Academic High Honor Roll

Sophomore Year
- 1st Place, National Spanish III Exam
- AP Scholar
- Departmental Award in Social Science
- Finalist, Rotary Club Speech Competition
- 1st Place team, San Diego County High School Math Field Day
- Academic High Honor Roll ABCD

Freshman Year
- 1st Place, National Science Olympiad State Finals
- 1st Place, Junior High Math Field Day
- Academic High Honor Roll, LJCDS

SCHOOL AND COMMUNITY ACTIVITIES

Senior Year
- Editor, school newspaper
- Editor, school literary magazine
- Guest teacher, AP European History class
- Reporter, community newspaper
    - Write weekly article for paper

Summer, 2008
- Volunteer teacher's assistant, ABCD Elementary School

Junior Year
- Editor, school newspaper
- Editor, school literary magazine
- Captain, Academic League Varsity team
- Selected Member, Madrigal singing group
- Lead role, school musical
- Volunteer teacher's assistant, ABCD Elementary School

Summer, 2007
- Student, Center for Talented Youth, Johns Hopkins University

(continued)

SCHOOL AND COMMUNITY ACTIVITIES (continued)

Sophomore Year

- Editor, school newspaper
- Assistant Editor, school literary magazine
- Co-Captain, Academic League Junior Varsity team
- Selected Member, Madrigal singing group
- Lead role, school musical
- Volunteer teacher's assistant, ABCD Elementary School

Summer, 2007

- Student, Center for Talented Youth, Johns Hopkins University

Freshman Year

- Staff Reporter, school newspaper
- Assistant Editor, school literary magazine
- Co-Captain, Academic League Novice team
- Selected Member, Madrigal singing group
- Volunteer teacher's assistant, ABCD Elementary School

TRAVEL

I am very fortunate that my parents must travel for their business. Therefore, I have traveled to England, Austria, Italy, Holland, Spain, Hungary, Peru, Chile, Costa Rica, Guatemala, and Mexico.

Timeline for Putting Together an Activities Résumé

» FRESHMAN YEAR

Ninth grade is not too early to begin keeping a record of your various activities, awards, sports, and other involvements, regardless of how important or unimportant they may seem. You are likely to forget some (or a lot) of what you do if you don't write it down. Keep a record of your activities and awards, how much time they took, and note any leadership, honors, and special accomplishments involved. After all, what starts out as insignificant in your freshman year may become significant in your junior or senior years. Colleges are very impressed with students who choose an activity, stay with it, and develop it over a period of years.

» SOPHOMORE YEAR

Continue writing down everything you do.

» JUNIOR YEAR

Your junior year is the time to put together your first résumé. You will have any number of uses for it this year.

» SENIOR YEAR

Finalize your résumé with information regarding your current and projected senior year activities.

[CHAPTER 9]

COLLECTING PERSONAL STORIES AND ANECDOTES
Secret Weapons in Writing Application Essays

> **DEFINITION of PERSONAL STORIES AND ANECDOTES:** *Every family has stories about children that get told over and over. Some are inconsequential in the beginning, but then take on almost legendary qualities. Some are apocryphal; still others are nothing more than cute little episodes or favorite moments. Life is filled with little and big events that are potential fodder for college essays. Often told stories begin right after children are born, like the one about a six-week-old baby who literally crooned when he was fed ice cream for the first time in his life (as an adult, he became a well-known chef). As children get older, the number and pace of stories usually pick up, like the story of a one-year-old who at Thanksgiving suddenly decided that it was time to walk (and he's been running ever since).* **Personal stories and anecdotes are important because they are pregnant with messages about who a person is and what he or she is all about.**

BRAINSTORMING IDEAS

The one aspect of college admissions that puts shudders down the spines of high school students is having to write college application essays. There is nothing that students fear, fret about, or procrastinate over more. What should I write about? What do admissions people look for or want? How can I hit a "home run" with my essay? How can I make my essay different from everybody else's?

Long before the time when application essays are due, you can do something to lay the groundwork for essay topics and content that are one-of-a-kind-you. What is this, you ask? Nothing more than identifying and writing down personal stories and anecdotes about yourself.

adMISSION POSSIBLE TIP

If you are a senior and you need the stories right away, ask your family to take a few family dinner hours to brainstorm ideas. You might be surprised at the number of stories—especially the humor—that comes out.

{ THE BOTTOM LINE }

As soon as you finish reading this chapter, you can begin writing down your own stories. If you are a parent, you can help your child by doing the same. It can be as simple as noting a phrase or two such as, "The time I got lost in the forest." You can also write a story in elaborate detail. Whatever you do, when a story pops into your head, keep a written record of your thoughts in a journal, on a computer, or on your cell phone. These written recordings will pay off come college essay time.

DEFINITION of BRAINSTORMING: *Brainstorming is a technique used by one or more persons for coming up with as many ideas as can be generated about a topic within a certain amount of time. Anything that pops into a person's mind is said, and written down, regardless of the idea's merit or relevance. In a brainstorming session, no idea is bad; all ideas are good.*

---

adMISSION POSSIBLE TIP

Personal stories are not just useful for essays; they can also be given to people who write letters of recommendation as examples of personal characteristics. Admissions people appreciate reading about real-life examples as opposed to just words, words, words. When you have a college interview, you can also sprinkle some of your answers with personal stories and anecdotes. If you do, you'll be seen as a much more interesting person (if not a more desirable candidate).

Here are some topic areas students (on their own or with parents and other family members) can use to brainstorm ideas for personal anecdotes and stories:

1. *Favorite toys, games, activities, hobbies, and passions*
2. *Personality characteristics*
3. *Special talents*
4. *Special people*
5. *Interesting summer activities, trips, holiday events*
6. *The best, worst, or most amazing experiences in a student's life*
7. *Accomplishments, triumphs, victories*
8. *Moments that brought a change in a student's life*
9. *Cute or amusing sayings*
10. *Individual or family idiosyncrasies, traditions, or rituals*

REAL EXAMPLES OF STORIES AND ANECDOTES AND HOW STUDENTS USED THEM

Over the years, adMISSION POSSIBLE has encouraged students and their parents to collect personal stories and anecdotes. Here are some examples and how they came to be used:

STORY #1: When he was nine years old, a young boy saw that his school was littered with all kinds of paper lunch bags, milk cartons, and trash. He was so upset by the mess that he decided to do something about it. On his own, he designed, got manufactured, and then sold recyclable lunch bags, with the profits going back to his school.

How story was used: To answer an application essay question about how a student's unique interests would contribute to a university's community.

Messages of story:
The student has been a "doer" since he was a little boy. He is resourceful, community oriented, hard-working, and environmentally sensitive. Even as a young boy, he found ways to make a difference in his community.

STORY #2: As a twelve-year-old, a Mexican American girl was selected by her family to give a testimonial speech for her grandfather in English and Spanish before five hundred people in Mexico City.

How story was used: To answer an application question about first experiences being a defining moment in a student's life.

Messages of story:
The writer is bilingual, a good speaker (of all the adults and children in the family, she was the one chosen to speak), comfortable in front of large audiences, very family oriented, and proud of her Mexican heritage.

STORY #3: A foodie student applied to and was selected for a yearlong student exchange program in France. She couldn't wait to live the French way of life, especially to eat wonderful French cuisine three meals a day for nine months. Among many other BIG surprises, her French family ended up serving canned and packaged foods, fish sticks, frozen pizza, and the like.

How story was used: To answer an application essay question about how a student faced a major challenge in his or her life.

Messages of story:
With a heavy emphasis on humor, this writer showed how she could roll with the punches, be flexible, and make the best out of any challenging situation. Also, her essay was a demonstration of her positive outlook on life.

STORY #4: A word-loving nine-year-old used to stay up until midnight waiting for the Sunday *New York Times* to be delivered so that he could read William Safire's column on words.

How story was used: A teacher used this story as part of the student's letters of recommendation.

Messages of story: The student has been a "word guy" since he was a little boy. He is precocious, intellectual, curious, and very, very smart.

STORY #5: A description of the journey a boy took on the way to becoming a national chess champion. This story started with his receiving a small, inexpensive chess set when he was five years old. Because he couldn't read, he asked his mother to read chess moves to him instead of bedtime stories. The story ended with a grueling chess match in which he won a national championship.

How story was used: As an answer to an application essay question about what outside interest has been particularly meaningful to the student.

Messages of story: The student is a true competitor; he has it in his blood. He has enormous powers of concentration and is resolved and persistent. It goes without saying that chess players tend to be very smart.

STORY #6: When a student began driving, her parents found that she became inordinately distracted. This worried them, so they took her to an educational therapist for testing. Turned out she had Attention Deficit Disorder. She was relieved by the news, because this explained why she seemed to have difficulty concentrating in school and completing homework and why tests, especially the SAT, were difficult for her, meaning she had to study more than most of her friends.

How story was used: The student's college counselor used the story to explain why the student's grades and scores were lower than they might be, and how when she began to take medication, many things improved (including her driving).

Messages of story: Academic deficits sometimes are a result of situations about which students are unaware, such as having a learning disorder. A diagnosis often explains the disparity between a student's apparent intelligence and her less than stellar grades and test scores. Once a student finds out what his or her problem is, he or she often can do something about it.

STORY #7: A boy described how he had been curious all of his life. For example, when he was very young, he was always touching, poking, even tasting anything he could get his hands on. Then one day when he was five years old, his curiosity took him to a hole in a tree in his backyard. Out of curiosity, he poked the hole with a stick and a swarm of hornets came out and covered his entire body. His parents rushed him to a hospital, where it took hours to take out the hornet stingers. He then described all the other ways/places that his curiosity took him over the years.

How story was used: In answer to an application essay question that was merely a request for a topic of the student's choice.

Messages of story: This student has always been curious, a characteristic colleges are always on the lookout for.

STORY #8: A student wrote about how passionate he was about the game of basketball, but also how he was the worst basketball player on his championship team. He freely admitted that he couldn't dribble, pass, shoot, or run but nevertheless adored the game and was always at practices and games long before he needed to be. On the bench, he was a cheerleader and often strategist for other players. In the end, because of the kind of person he was (and not because of his basketball talents), the team voted him Most Valuable Player.

How story was used: The coach of the basketball team wrote a letter to the admissions office about what a pleasure it had been to have this "worst" player on his team and what his special contributions had been.

Messages of story: Attitude is very important. Even if you're not very good at something, let alone a champion, you can offer something and do your best. As a result, you can gain the respect of others and yourself.

STORY #9: A student wrote about how his grandmother had been married seven times to six different men. What he learned was, "If at first you don't succeed, then try, try, try, try, try, try, try again."

How story was used: In answer to an application essay question that asked about an influential person in a student's life.

Messages of story: The student has a great sense of humor, is witty, and is very down-to-earth. Also, there is a lot one can learn from grandparents, sometimes in the strangest, most mysterious ways.

STORY #10: A girl explained how in a speech class, her fellow classmates described her as like the "tip of a pin" because she was so unbelievably focused.

How story was used: A teacher used this story to explain how much concentration the student brought to her work, thus explaining why she was so accomplished. The teacher also gave the example of when the student was studying for the AP French exam, she did not speak English for two weeks—at home (watched only French movies, listened to French music, spoke to her brother in French) and at school (spoke English only when she had to).

Messages of story: The student is like a laser with regard to her studies, very hard-working, persistent, and focused. She is the best student in her class.

STORY #11: A girl born in Taiwan told the story of how she was adopted by her American uncle and aunt, and spent much of her life dreaming of returning to her birth parents. The student also described the trauma of leaving her home and parents, but also how she converted her sadness and longing to strength and confidence, ending up at Yale, an option that would never have been available to her had she remained in Taiwan.

How story was used: To answer an application essay question about writing a personal essay that helps the college get to know you better.

Messages of story: Facing major hurdles, this writer was able to become determined, mature, focused, and very accomplished.

STORY #12: Born with a profound hearing impairment since birth, a student wrote about all the things he could do (a list of more than one hundred) and only mentioned one that he couldn't (talk on the phone without the assistance of a TDD). He described how he chose to use his strengths to overcome his disability, specifically choosing to study and use computers, a focus that eliminates any hearing bias.

How story was used: To answer an application essay question about what the college should know about the student.

Messages of story: Clearly, this is a "when life gives you lemons, make lemonade" story. The writer describes what it's like to be a hearing-impaired person, and why admissions people should not worry about his being successful at college.

STORY #13: A boy wrote in English and Spanish about a harrowing night in Zaragoza, Spain, when he got lost, forgot how to get back to his host family's home, and after many hours of walking the streets, returned to an angry host father at 3 a.m.

How story was used: To answer an application essay question about any challenge a student has overcome.

Messages of story: The student is a great storyteller, can write well, is fluent in Spanish and English, is a good problem-solver, and is good at human relations as he dealt with an irate host father.

STORY #14: The student wrote about a C student who was terribly disorganized, always late to class, forgot or lost homework, didn't prepare for tests or quizzes, and was always in the nurse's office for random illnesses. Then he wrote about another student who had a burning passion to learn, sought out the most difficult classes, was always ahead in homework, and got straight A's in Honors and AP classes. He revealed at the end of the essay that he was both students.

How story was used: To answer an application essay question about writing a story either creative or personal.

Messages of story: The student is clever (writing about a before-and-after situation and giving the reader a surprising ending), resourceful, and insightful. The deaths of his grandmother and best friend turn his head around in terms of what is important in life.

STORY #15: A girl wrote about what she learned from working at her father's car-wash business.

How story was used: To answer an application essay question asking applicants to reflect on their family's personal circumstances and to tell about anything that is not already revealed or explained in the application.

Messages of story: The student learns many lessons from watching her father create and manage his car-wash business. As a result, she is very sensitive to others, including employees and customers of the car wash, and has developed a maturity and business savvy way beyond her years.

STORY #16: A "computer nerd" wrote down what he thought his Dell computer would say about him should the computer be able to think and write.

How story was used: To answer the Common Application Topic of Choice essay question.

Messages of story: Not only is the student adept at using, programming, fixing, and setting up computers for himself, family, friends, and even teachers, he is very creative in finding a way to describe his talents and abilities.

STORY #17: A student wrote about her Chinese grandfather, and how in spite of being orphaned at an early age, he taught himself how to be an artist by reading art books and sketching.

How story was used: To answer the Common Application essay question about a person who has had a significant influence on you and to describe that influence.

Messages of story: The student is an accomplished artist herself, very creative, and aware of what older people have to offer in wisdom, maturity, and insight.

STORY #18: A boy reflects on how he started to cook when he was four years old, and how cooking has led him to learn a whole lot more about the world than the food he eats.

How story was used: To answer an application essay question about evaluating a significant experience or achievement you have had in your life and the impact it has had on you.

Messages of story: Not only is the student a prize-winning cook, but he has used his thirst for knowledge about the topic as a way of learning about nutrition, different cultures, history, even the physics of food. In addition, he is creative, curious, sophisticated, and has a wonderful sense of humor.

STORY #19: A high school student described how he used surfing as a way to handle his Tourette's syndrome. (In case you don't know, Tourette's is a neurological disorder in which a person displays multiple physical, vocal, and other tics.)

How story was used: A high school teacher used this story to not only identify that the student suffers from Tourette's, but how creative he has been to use surfing every morning as a way to relax and calm himself before he goes to school.

Messages of story: The student is resourceful, doesn't let his Tourette's get in the way of academic or social involvements, and is likely to do the same in college.

STORY #20: A boy described his fascination with bugs since he could barely walk or talk, and how this interest has developed into a concern about endangered species in the animal world.

How story was used: To answer an application question about what led the student to choose the area of academic interest that he listed on his application.

Messages of story: The writer has had myriad experiences (reading, researching, working, volunteering) in school, at museums, and with organizations learning about and working with animals. This has led him to his choice of biology as a major, a natural progression of his long-held passion for learning.

ENDNOTE

In Chapter 12, "Writing Admissions Essays," I show you how to use your stories as a major theme or part of your college essays.

Timeline for Collecting Stories and Anecdotes

» FRESHMAN, SOPHOMORE, AND JUNIOR YEAR AND PARENTS

Any time you (or your parent) remembers a story or anecdote is a good time to write it down. The earlier you start, the more stories you will have from which to choose.

The ideal time to have family brainstorming sessions for essay topics or content is junior year and the summer before a student's senior year.

» SENIOR YEAR

By this time, you will have some of the essay questions you will need to answer. If you haven't done it before, begin brainstorming ideas for the questions on your own and with family members. Dinner times are a perfect time to do this.

Remember, it is never too late to generate personal stories and anecdotes. You can even do it a few minutes before you begin writing a college essay.

CHAPTER 10

TO DO OR NOT TO DO THE EARLIES

Early Action, Restricted Early Action,
and Early Decision

DEFINITION of EARLY APPLICATIONS: *Only a few public universities, such as the University of Michigan, offer an early application program, but many private colleges offer such plans. While a few colleges offer both Early Action and Early Decision, most colleges offer just one of those options.*

Early applications include

Early Action (EA)

*In this **non-binding** application program, students apply by the November 1st (or for some schools, by November 15th) and receive their admission decision by the middle of December. If accepted, students can immediately commit to the college, but **are not obligated** to commit until the usual May 1st response deadline.*

This means that you can wait to accept or decline an admission offer until you know the results of other early or regular admissions applications, as well as financial aid offers. In addition to being accepted, Early Action applicants may also be denied or deferred. EA colleges do not place any restrictions on the number of other early applications you submit.

Restricted Early Action (REA—aka Early Action, Single Choice)

*A non-binding early admission option for freshman applicants offered by such universities as Stanford and Yale, in which a student may **not** apply to any other early program, except to public colleges and universities Early or Rolling applications. Along with their parents and high school counselor, applicants are asked to sign a statement stipulating that they agree to file only one early application. Students are **not** obligated to accept an invitation to attend a college until the usual May 1 deadline. In addition to being accepted, Early Action applicants may also be denied or deferred.*

Early Decision (ED)

In this binding contract application program, students apply by the November 1st (for some schools, by November 15th) and receive their admission decision by the middle of December. **If accepted, students are obligated to say yes or no by a certain date.** *In addition to being accepted, students may also be denied or deferred. If a student applies ED to a college, he or she may **not** apply Early Decision to any other schools, but may apply to EA schools.*

Early Decision II (EDII)

*A few colleges offer a second round of Early Decision, with due dates at the end of December or first part of January and notification within six weeks. These are also **binding contract** programs.*

Rolling Admission

*Some colleges offer freshman applicants an application program in which applications are accepted, evaluated, and decided upon as they are received (from as early as September until a final deadline sometimes as late as the summer). If accepted, students can immediately commit to attending the college, but **are not obligated** to commit until the usual May 1st response deadline. Students may apply to other colleges without restriction. In this type of program, a student may be accepted, denied, or wait-listed.*

When it comes to early applications, you have three decisions to make:

1. Whether to apply early

2. To which college(s) you want to apply early

3. Whether you are ready to commit to the school if applying Early Decision

Applying early can increase your chances of getting accepted at your chosen college if you are a top candidate who has put together a stellar application.

WHY COLLEGES OFFER EARLY ADMISSION

Most students and parents focus on the advantage early admissions gives to students, often not realizing that it is colleges that stand to benefit the most. Therefore, it is important to understand the reasons colleges like early programs. They not only tell you something about the early admissions game, but whether or not you want to play it.

Colleges are committed to their early programs for a number of reasons

1. By admitting more freshmen under an Early Decision plan, a college can improve its yield rate (the percentage of students admitted who actually attend the college), which often means a higher number of future applicants to the school, more alumni donations, and overall higher prestige. A lower yield rate can mean the loss of all those factors, plus increased recruiting costs.

2. Early Decision programs **help colleges choose a good foundation for their upcoming freshman class because they know these students will definitely attend their school.** ED programs also help colleges control the composition of a class (including such factors as the number of students from various geographic regions, from individual high schools, with specific intended majors or athletic backgrounds, etc.). This is also a way to minimize the chances of having either too many or too few students in the fall.

3. Early Decision programs provide colleges with an **opportunity to lock in special, top candidates,** thereby preventing competitor colleges from having them.

4. Early Decision programs tend to **attract more upper-middle class students who don't need financial aid.** Spending less on financial aid during the early admission phase leaves more money available to spend on students in the regular one, although wealthy, need-blind schools don't abide by this practice.

5. Because colleges want **students on their campuses who are thrilled about being there,** the likelihood of this happening is much enhanced by accepting a large number of applicants who have applied early because the school is their top choice.

> **ad*MISSION* POSSIBLE TIP!**
>
> If you will need financial aid to help pay for your college education, Early Decision is probably not the best application program to use. Exception: the generous, need-blind schools such as Stanford, MIT, Harvard, Cal Tech, Yale, Princeton, Dartmouth, and Williams.

USEFUL INFORMATION ABOUT EARLY PROGRAMS

1. AS MANY AS FIVE HUNDRED COLLEGES AND UNIVERSITIES OFFER ONE OR MORE OF THE EARLY APPLICATION OPTIONS.

Fewer colleges offer Early Action than Early Decision programs, and year-to-year some colleges change which type of early program they offer. **Check with individual college admissions offices and/or their websites, the Common Application,** U.S. News & World Report's America's Best Colleges, **or the** College Handbook **to determine which kind of program they offer.**

www.admissionpossible.com also provides lists of colleges that offer EA, REA, and ED programs.

2. NOT EVERYONE WHO APPLIES TO COLLEGE SHOULD APPLY EARLY.

The circumstances of whether a student should choose to apply to an EA, REA, or ED program vary. Applying early will not help you if you are not a competitive applicant. If you are a C or even B student, while most of the school's admitted students were A students in high school, your chances for admission are slim, early or regular admission.

adMISSION POSSIBLE TIP!

Especially for the most selective colleges, admission rates for early, qualified applicants tend to be higher than for regular applicants.

3. "HOOKED" IS A TERM APPLIED BY ADMISSIONS OFFICES TO SOME APPLICANTS.

Hooked students may have a substantial admissions edge at colleges if they apply early or during the regular admissions cycle. Depending on the school, hooked students may include

* Recruited athletes
* Applicants with distinct talents
* Under-represented minorities (African Americans, Hispanics, American Indians)
* High potential disadvantaged students
* Students with development connections (children of donors to the college)
* Legacies (children of at least one alumni parent)
* Children of famous parents (celebrities, wealthy executives, politicians, and the like)
* Faculty children

FAQ #1: Does applying early really increase my chances for admission to a college?

ANSWER: It depends on the college to which you are applying and whether or not you are a serious candidate for the school. To get a handle on that, find out how your grades and test scores compare to previously admitted students to your favorite colleges. First, will your application stand out from other students' applications? Second, are you a hooked student?

Many selective colleges admit 25–50 percent of their freshman class from the early application pool. College admissions websites usually provide information about how many students a college admits from the early admissions versus the regular pool. From those websites, you can also find out what the GPA and test score averages are for admitted students, both early and regular admission.

ADVANTAGES AND DISADVANTAGES OF EARLY APPLICATIONS

There are advantages and disadvantages for applying through an early application program. In some cases they apply both to Early Action and Early Decision; in other cases they apply to just one.

ADVANTAGES	DISADVANTAGES
1. For both Early Action and Early Decision programs, often there are higher acceptance rates compared with regular admission rates.	1. There is no guarantee of acceptance for early applications.
2. You find out much earlier whether or not you have been accepted to a school. You don't have to wait until March or April to get your college admissions results.	2. If you are deferred in an early application program, the chances of acceptance during regular admission are not high, but aren't much worse than regular admission.
3. If you are accepted to a college, the rest of your senior year is often more relaxed and enjoyable.	3. Early rejection or deferral is difficult for many students to deal with.
4. Applying early potentially shortens the admissions process and eliminates the necessity for filling out multiple applications and writing a number of essays. Usually, you spend less time and money on multiple applications. If you apply early and don't get accepted, you can probably adapt some of the essays you wrote for the early application to new ones.	4. A few students develop "senioritis" when they know that they have been admitted to a school early. This can be dangerous because slacking off during second semester might lead to lower grades and the possibility of having your college admission rescinded at the end of the school year.
5. Applying early is a strong indication of your interest in a college. It is a form of demonstrated interest.	5. Your first choice college in November may not be your first choice later in the spring.
6. Even negative outcomes from early applications are useful. Among other things, you might decide to apply to less selective colleges, and identify and rectify weaknesses in your application.	6. If you are rejected or deferred, unless you have planned ahead for this, you may end up scrambling to get applications out during Christmas vacation.
7. Applying early can help in clarify your thinking about what you want in a college.	7. You might not be ready to make a commitment to one school in the fall.
	8. Early Decision admits can't compare financial aid offers from a number of schools.

WHETHER TO APPLY EARLY

Whether or not to apply early is an important decision. Here are some questions to ask yourself to help you make up your mind:

1. WHICH COLLEGES AM I MOST INTERESTED IN?

Consult your college list to determine which colleges most interest you. If you have difficulty coming up with real favorites, that in itself is important information for you. Perhaps you are not ready to apply for early admission.

2. OF THE COLLEGES THAT ARE MY TOP CHOICES, DO ANY OFFER AN EA, REA, OR ED OPTION?

Check individual college websites, the Common Application website, or the College Board website.

3. WHAT ARE MY CHANCES FOR GETTING ACCEPTED TO MY TOP CHOICE COLLEGE?

There are no surefire ways for determining your chances of getting accepted to any one college. However, you can get some idea by doing the following:

★ Consult your school counselor for his or her read on your chances. Ask for a comparison of your GPA, SAT I or ACT, and Subject Test scores with previous graduates from your high school who were accepted at your top choice colleges.

★ Compare your test scores with those of successful previous applicants at colleges that interest you. Go to college admissions websites or to the *U.S. News & World Report's America's Best Colleges* website for this information.

adMISSION POSSIBLE TIP!

For students planning to apply to the Ivies, Stanford, or other very competitive colleges and universities, a large percentage of accepted early applicants have test scores of 34 on the ACT, 2260 on the SAT I, or over 1500 for the combined Reading and Math scores on the SAT I.

4. ASK YOUR COLLEGE COUNSELOR IF OTHER STUDENTS FROM YOUR HIGH SCHOOL ARE APPLYING EARLY DECISION TO YOUR TOP COLLEGE CHOICE

The counselor will not divulge the names of students, but might be willing to give a general answer.

Try to assess how you compare with other students from your school who are applying ED. You may not be able to get this information, but it is worth a try. Is your application likely to be significantly better, about the same, or not as good? If it is better or about the same, then consider applying ED. If it is not as good, you should probably think twice about applying.

5. IF APPLYING EARLY DECISION, AM I READY TO COMMIT MYSELF TO THIS ONE SCHOOL?

You should apply Early Decision to a school only if it is your top choice.

FAQ #2: **If I want to apply Early Decision to a school, does its binding agreement bar me from applying to the University of California schools?**

ANSWER: No. Because you must submit the UC application between November 1 and November 30 and this deadline is before you will hear the decision from an ED school, you are allowed to apply to the UCs. If you should be accepted to the ED school, then you must immediately notify the UC campuses to which you applied that you are withdrawing your application.

A SUMMARY OF EARLY APPLICATION OPTIONS

	EARLY ACTION	RESTRICTED EARLY ACTION	EARLY DECISION	ROLLING ADMISSION
Apply to other colleges?	Yes	Yes if to public institutions. No to private.	Yes to EA schools, EA II, EDH, and Rolling.	Yes
A binding contract?	No	No	Yes	No
Deadline for committing to the college?	May 1	May 1	A stated date, usually a few weeks after receiving the acceptance letter.	May 1

THE OUTCOME OF EARLY APPLICATIONS

The outcome of early applications, whether Early Action, Restricted Early Action, Early Decision, or Rolling Admissions is the same:

* **Acceptance**
* **Denial**
* **Deferral**

As noted earlier, if you are accepted to a Rolling Admissions, Early Action, or Restricted Early Action program, you can accept the admission offer or wait until May 1 to respond to the acceptance.

If you are **accepted** to an Early Decision program, you must respond yes or no to the school by their designated date.

If you are **denied** admission to any of the programs, that application process is over. There is nothing more to do.

However, if you are **deferred** from any one of the above programs, there is a lot for you to do.

> **DEFINITION of DEFERRAL:** *Deferral is an action taken by colleges for both Early Action, Restricted Early Action, and Early Decision applications in which a college admissions office postpones making an admissions decision about a student's application until the regular admission cycle.*
>
> *Getting deferred is not bad news because of the obvious fact that you were not rejected. If deferred, your application is good enough to be considered in the next round of admissions. Who gets off the deferral list and onto the acceptance list varies a lot from college to college. Whether you are accepted or not often depends on what additional information and materials you provide the admissions office.*

WHAT TO DO IF YOU GET DEFERRED

To have a chance of getting off a deferral list and onto the accepted one, you must become very proactive. Here are some steps to take:

1. RETURN THE DEFERRAL CARD

Immediately return any card that comes with your deferral letter.

Be sure to follow any directions the college gives you for being considered in the regular admissions cycle. Some colleges have very specific directions about what they want. Be sure to follow them to the "T." To find out what they want, look at any communications you receive from the college admissions office, through their website, email, or phone messages.

2. CHOOSE ONE COLLEGE TO ACTIVELY WORK ON

If you have been deferred by a number of Early Action programs, **choose one to actively work on.** As you will see, there is a lot of work to do in turning around a deferral.

3. SEND AN EMAIL OR SHORT NOTE TO THE SCHOOL

Immediately send an email or short note to the Dean of Admissions (or the college representative assigned to your school), expressing your sadness about not being accepted to his or her school, but also your relief at not being denied admission. Indicate your continuing strong interest in the school. Be very positive, polite, and respectful. Never complain or make reference to other students in your school who have been accepted.

4. ALERT YOUR HIGH SCHOOL COUNSELOR ABOUT THE DEFERRAL

Let your high school counselor know of your deferral and express your disappointment at not being accepted. Reassure him or her of your continued enthusiasm for the school and ask the counselor to go to bat for you by calling the admissions office to find out a) why you were not admitted, and b) what you can do to become a stronger candidate for the regular admissions cycle.

If the counselor is not willing to call the admissions office, then call the office yourself.

5. REAFFIRM YOUR FIRST CHOICE INTEREST IN THE COLLEGE

After you receive first semester grades at the end of January or early February, **send an upbeat letter to the Dean of Admissions** and the admissions representative assigned to your school, reaffirming your first choice interest in the college and detailing any new or compelling information since you turned in the original application. New information might include the following:

> **adMISSION POSSIBLE TIP!**
>
> Students who are deferred in an Early Decision program are no longer contractually bound to enroll in that college, even if they are accepted later in the regular application cycle.

* **Identify why you and the college are a perfect match,** including what you are looking for in a college, and specific examples of courses, professors, activities, and programs you would get involved with.
* Specifically **how you would contribute** to the college and community.
* **Note your first semester grades** (and make sure that your school sends the college a new transcript) and any new, improved test scores.
* **Update the admissions office** about any **new awards, honors, successes, or accomplishments** in your academic, activity, work, and/or volunteer involvements. This can be described in the letter and/or shown in an updated résumé.
* Send the admissions office a copy of **any special work or project** you have done, including a paper, research project, art portfolio, CD of a musical performance, etc.
* If you already know, include your **summer plans,** especially if they are impressive.

A sample letter to the admissions office can be found in the Checklists section of www.admissionpossible.com.

6. HAVE GLOWING LETTERS SENT TO THE ADMISSIONS OFFICE

Have your high school counselor, high school principal (if you know him or her), a teacher (that did not write your first letter), and/or another person outside of school who knows and likes you a lot **send additional letters of recommendation** that offer new insights and information about you, your personal qualities, and how you would contribute to the college. Make sure they sing your praises.

Don't overdo it, though; a couple of letters will do.

7. CONTACT A PROFESSOR, ADMINISTRATOR, OR DISTINGUISHED ALUM FROM THE COLLEGE

If you have **excellent college contacts,** now is the time to ask them to call or write the college on your behalf.

8. MAKE A SPECIAL VISIT TO THE COLLEGE TO PLEAD YOUR CASE

If your family can afford it, **see about making a special trip to the admissions office** to talk with them about your application. Before you drive/fly/take a train to the college, call the admissions office to see if they would be open to and welcome such a visit.

9. CONTINUE COMPLETING APPLICATIONS FOR REGULAR ADMISSIONS COLLEGES

In the early application phase, some applicants are admitted, some are not. Admitted applicants usually have sterling applications, including the best grades, the best SAT scores, very notable activities or interests, wonderful letters of recommendation, and unique, well-written essays.

As with most things in life, in early admissions there are never any guarantees. But each year a good number of applicants are accepted, some say as many as 20–40 percent of the next freshman class. If you are not accepted during the early application phase, continue applying regular admission to other colleges.

ENDNOTE

Early applications are not for every student, but they can be a very useful strategy for excellent students who are certain about where they want to go to college and/or for certain "hooked" students.

» FRESHMAN AND SOPHOMORE YEAR AND PARENTS

Freshman and sophomore years are wonderful times to research and visit colleges to begin finding out what you like and don't like about them.

» JUNIOR YEAR

FALL SEMESTER

- Start researching colleges online and in guidebooks.
- Get the best grades you can.

SPRING SEMESTER

- Complete all of your testing—SAT and/or ACT, as well as Subject Tests—by June of your junior year.
- Put together a list of colleges in which you are interested.
- Visit colleges during spring break.
- Get the best grades you can. Remember, colleges only see your grades through junior year if you apply early.
- Before you leave school, ask two teachers if they will complete the Teacher Evaluation forms for your applications.

» SENIOR YEAR

FALL SEMESTER

Early Action and Early Decision deadlines are usually the first of November. All application materials must be mailed by the specified due date. Students usually receive notification about admissions decisions **by the middle of December.**

Early Action and Decision II deadlines vary, but are usually sometime between the **end of December and middle of January.** Students usually receive notification about **six weeks after the EDII deadline.**

AUGUST

If your testing is not complete, register for the September or October ACT tests and/or the October SAT or Subject Tests.

adMISSION POSSIBLE TIP!

If at the beginning of your senior year you haven't researched colleges and come up with a good college list (and taken the required SAT or ACT and Subject Tests), the early admission programs are probably not a good choice for you.

adMISSION POSSIBLE TIP!

The last SAT, ACT, or Subject Test dates that accommodate Early Action and Early Decision applications are those offered in October.

SEPTEMBER/OCTOBER

* **Begin filling out the early application(s), including writing one-of-a-kind essays.**
* **Be sure to photocopy or print a copy of all application materials before you send them.**
* **Take any SAT or ACT or Subject Tests that you have not taken before or those on which you want to get higher test scores.**
* **Provide your counselor and two teachers with letter of application packages.** For what to include, see www.admissionpossible.com.
* **By the required due date, also send:**
  - **the completed application and fee**
  - **a copy of your high school transcript** (and other transcripts if you have taken classes outside your school)
  - **test scores from the College Board and/or ACT**
* **See about signing up for an admissions interview.**

NOVEMBER

* **Call the college admissions office to make sure that all of your application materials have been received.**
* **Continue filling out regular decision applications** should you not be accepted by your early application school.
* **Complete the College Board PROFILE financial aid form.**

JANUARY

* **Complete and send the FAFSA financial aid form.**

SPRING SEMESTER

* Students choosing the **Early Action, Early Action Single Choice,** or **Rolling Admissions** option have until **May 1** to accept or decline admission offers.

CHAPTER 11

COMPLETING UNDERGRADUATE APPLICATIONS

How to Make Your Best Case to Colleges

DEFINITION of COLLEGE APPLICATION: *Whether a student applies Early Action, Restricted Early Action, Early Decision I or II, Rolling Admission, or Regular Decision, each of these plans requires completing a college application form.*

There are two major types of applications:

The Common Application

In 1975, fifteen colleges who wanted to provide a standardized application for undergraduate applicants created the Common Application. Today, over 450 private and public colleges and universities make use of "The Common App."

A College's Own Application

Many public universities (such as the University of California) and some private colleges (such as Georgetown University) have their own applications that students must use.

adMISSION POSSIBLE TIP

One of the most important goals in completing each application is to let a college know that you have carefully thought through your college list and that their college is a very serious choice. This should be the message to every college to which you apply, even those you think of as back-up schools. You never know when a back-up school will become a top choice.

FAQ #1: I have heard there is a new application that's supposed to be like the Common Application. Should I use it?

ANSWER: The Universal College Application (UCA) is a relatively new (as of 2007) application available to students, both online or as hard copy. About fifty colleges in the United States accept the UCA, which like the Common Application offers college-specific supplements. Your decision to use it depends on whether the colleges to which you are applying use this application. You might also want to consider whether it's worth adding a third type of application form to your application lineup.

While the different applications vary some, they usually include one or a number of the following forms:

USUAL COLLEGE APPLICATION FORMS

* Preliminary form (also called Pre-Application or Part I Application by some schools)
* First-Year Application form (also called the Student form, Main form, or Part 2 Undergraduate Application)
* College-Specific Supplement forms
* Secondary School Report form (also called School and Transcript form)
* Teacher Evaluation form (also called Instructor's Recommendation or Teacher Report form)
* Mid-Year Grade Report form
* Final Report form

SPECIAL APPLICATION FORMS

* Arts Supplement form
* Athletic Supplement form
* Early Decision Agreement form
* International School Supplement to the Secondary School Report form
* Home School Supplement to the Secondary School Report form
* Peer Recommendation form (also called Peer Evaluation form)
* Financial Aid form

Heads-up: undergraduate students wanting to transfer from one college to another complete special Transfer Application forms.

{ **THE BOTTOM LINE** } While each phase of the college admissions process is important, nothing is more important than actually completing the application itself. This is when a student finally makes his or her admissions case. When all is said and done, the best case is letting colleges know exactly who you are as a student and person in as articulate and complete a way as you can. Done correctly, that is what will make you stand out from other applicants.

KEEPING TRACK OF YOUR APPLICATIONS

Students (and their parents) often ask for ways of keeping track of their applications, including what needs to be done by when and a system for making sure that all pieces of an application are completed. adMISSION POSSIBLE has created four grids/checklists to do that, including 1) Application Due Dates Master List, 2) Application Essays Master Grid, 3) Individual Application Checklist (for one application), and 4) Master Admissions Applications Checkoff Grid (for your applications).

These tools can be found in the Checklists section of www.admissionpossible.com.

ORGANIZING A SYSTEM FOR HANDLING ADMISSIONS MATERIALS FROM 9TH THROUGH 12TH GRADES

It is very useful if you can establish a college admissions "center" someplace in your home. This can be anything from a desk in your bedroom to a bookshelf or card table somewhere else. Once you start filling out the applications, you can move all your materials to this workspace.

★ **Admissions "Stuff" Sent to You by Colleges**

Basically there are two ways of dealing with all the "stuff" sent to you by colleges: **save what you need and want and recycle everything else. Perhaps the best approach is to do a little of both.**

★ **College Visit Files**

For students who plan to visit colleges, **it is useful to have a folder set aside for information you gather about a college and the city and region where you will be,** including newspaper or magazine articles, notes from friends who tell you what to see and do, you name it.

★ **Information from/for Your High School Counselor**

There is a huge disparity from one high school to another regarding what they provide students about colleges and admissions. Some high schools start giving students information about college admissions when they are ninth or tenth graders; others barely give out information when students are seniors. Some high schools have extensive questionnaires that they ask juniors and seniors to complete for their high school counselor; others do nothing. Because you want to take seriously whatever your counselor gives you—and especially not lose it—**create a special place (manila envelope, or open-ended folder, binder, etc.) for anything your counselor or the high school counseling office gives you.**

★ **Books and Other Materials**

It is the rare student or parent who doesn't buy (or borrow) at least one book about college admissions.

Many families end up with quite a few. **Designate one space in your home as the college admissions place for whatever books you get, so that whenever someone wants to consult them, you'll know where they are.**

INSIDER ADVICE, COMMON SENSE, AND WHAT MATTERS REGARDING APPLICATIONS

As you complete your applications, here are a few things to keep in mind:

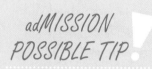

adMISSION POSSIBLE TIP!

No matter who you are or what you have done, admissions officers only know and make decisions about you by what you and others say in your application. If you leave out something, they will never know.

A. KEEP YOUR AUDIENCE, THE ADMISSIONS OFFICERS, IN MIND

1. College admissions officers read hundreds, if not thousands, of applications, many of which say the same things year after year. After awhile, this can become a mind-numbing job. **What you want to do is offer something that is a little different and better than the ordinary application.**

2. There is no such thing as a perfect applicant or a perfect application. However, every person has the potential to put together an application that captures the attention of, entertains, or delights admissions people.

* In general, **admissions people look for** applicants who in their academic and extracurricular pursuits demonstrate such characteristics as **intellectual curiosity, honesty, persistence, ability to deal with challenges, leadership, energy, maturity, resourcefulness, creativity, and especially a good sense of humor.**

* They **also want people who show unusual talents or involvement** in anything ranging from the arts to athletics, community service to student government, writing to computer programming, and also esoteric pursuits such as gourmet cooking, sky-diving, orchid-growing, car restoration, trapeze flying, you name it.

* **Colleges want to know who you are and especially how you and their college are a good fit.**

3. **Admissions people also look for a well-rounded class** that includes individuals from a broad range of personal, geographic, socioeconomic, ethnic, and religious backgrounds, each one of whom will take advantage of what a campus offers, as well as contribute to the campus.

B. PUT YOUR BEST FACE FORWARD ON APPLICATIONS

To maximize your chances of being accepted at colleges, here are some actions you can take with each application:

1. **You need to make the most of each application,** remembering that for each college to which you apply, you have one application, one shot for gaining admission.

2. Many students approach college applications as a distasteful job they want to get over with as fast as they can, often racing from one question to another almost mindlessly filling in the blanks. **To put your best face forward, think about what you write, and the messages the words will elicit as someone reads them.** Even the simplest of informational questions can be answered with care and style.

Before filling out an application, ask yourself these questions:

★ What do I want the admissions people "to get" about me?

★ How can I distinguish myself? Where do I "shine"?

★ Who am I as a person? What is important to me?

★ What makes me interesting, unique, or different from other people?

3. You can **find clues to answering these questions** by looking at your Activities Résumé, at how and with whom you spend time, by talking with your counselor, friends, and family, and especially by going over the personal stories and anecdotes that you collected as a result of reading chapter 9, "Collecting Personal Stories and Anecdotes."

4. Some students worry about putting too much in their applications for fear that colleges will think them arrogant. **However, there is a big difference between identifying and describing what you do or have done, and bragging about it.** In an honest and upbeat way, tell the reader about your academic background, document your talents, explain how you spend your time when you are not in class, give evidence of how well you express yourself, and do this in your own voice. After you have done that, then let others—your counselor, teachers, and people who know you well—sing your praises and do the boasting for you.

5. In order to communicate the whole of who you are, **make sure that you don't use the same experience, activity, or example in more than one essay response.** Not every essay should be about soccer, even if you are a star player. Change and balance your responses. Colleges want to know about the various aspects of your life.

C. MAKE A DIFFERENCE WITH NEATNESS AND ACCURACY

1. **The appearance of an application is almost as important as what it says.** Whatever method you use to fill out applications you use, it is extremely important that you do it right. "Right" means perfect or near perfect in terms of neatness, and absolutely flawless when it comes to spelling, grammar, punctuation, and lack of typos. Your goal in filling out the application neatly is to make it EASY for the admissions officer to read.

2. **A sloppy or incomplete application gives the readers one or more of these messages** that you DON'T want to convey:

   a) You're immature.

   b) You don't respect the reader.

   c) You are not taking the college admissions process seriously.

   d) Their college is a back-up school.

3. **Having a good proofreader go over your application** is one way of making sure that there are no silly mistakes, omissions, or errors. This is where a trusted parent, counselor, teacher, older sibling, or friend comes in. Ask for help. This may make the difference between being taken seriously as an applicant, or not — the latter being the quickest route to getting a rejection letter, something that you don't want.

D. FOLLOW THE APPLICATION DIRECTIONS

1. Before you type information onto online applications, the Common Application, or otherwise, **be sure to first read the application instructions.** It usually helps if you download and print directions, noting (better yet, highlighting or flagging) specific instructions. Know that Common Application colleges will often have additional directions in their respective Supplement sections.

2. **Admissions people take note of when you don't pay attention to their directions,** and, frankly, they don't like it at all. So if the directions say to write a 250-word essay, you'd better stick close to that number of words. If instructions specifically tell you to use the provided Activity List grid and not to submit a résumé, do as they say. Fill in the grid or space they provide; don't say, "See attached list" in the middle of it.

   Following directions is a way of saying to the admissions reader that you are a responsible, attentive, and competent person, messages you want them to get.

> **FAQ #2: I don't have access to a computer. Can I handwrite answers on a paper application?**
>
> **ANSWER:** Admissions offices would like you to use online applications, but if circumstances prevent you from doing that, they will accept a handwritten application. Of course, it makes sense for you to explain in an accompanying letter why you are sending them a hard copy application. Public libraries often make computers available to students.

E. IF SOMETHING IS OPTIONAL, DO IT! NEVER LEAVE ANYTHING BLANK, UNLESS...

1. Since the content of your application is the only data admissions officers have to make their judgments, **it is imperative that you take advantage of every single line, space, and question in order to make your case.** The reasons for doing this are pretty simple: you don't want to give the appearance of being lazy or uninterested.

2. **If you don't know the answer to a question, find out; don't leave it blank.** If you come upon a question that asks, "Is there anything else you want us to know?" answer it. This latter question is a perfect opportunity to tell the admissions people about a challenge you have faced, an unusual hobby you have undertaken, the reason your grades may have gone down one semester, or something unique or unusual about yourself.

3. **Whatever the question, fill it in, unless it is not relevant to you** (e.g., immigration status, foreign language spoken at home, relatives who have attended the college), then simply type in N/A, the standard abbreviation for "Not Applicable."

F. DESCRIBE AND EXPLAIN EVERYTHING

1. **If there is room available, describe the various awards or activities that you identify on applications.** Use action verbs to explain what the position is, e.g., "One of five major student body officers who meet weekly to plan and carry out school governance and activities."

2. Because most applications have limited space, **sometimes it is necessary to use common abbreviations** (e.g., ASB for Associated Student Body, VP for vice president, 12 for senior year).

3. For some students, **certain issues warrant detailed explanations.** For example, it is not enough to identify that you have **a learning or some other disability.** In an essay or separate letter, you need to provide information that helps the admissions reader understand what you have, how it has affected you, and what you have done or are doing to deal with it.

4. It is especially important to explain **anything negative that might show up in any part of the application.** For example, if you think that your test scores do not reflect how smart you are, or how well you will do in college, then provide a well-thought-out explanation. If you received a poor grade one semester against the backdrop of otherwise excellent grades, don't leave the issue there for admissions people to guess or interpret; explain what happened.

> **adMISSION POSSIBLE TIP!**
>
> Be sure that explanations about challenges you have faced don't come across as whiney or "poor me," but rather as illuminating, descriptive accounts, including what you have learned or gained from the experience.

G. EMERGENCIES: LATE APPLICATIONS AND EXTENSIONS

It goes without saying: **Unless you experience an emergency, your application should never be late.**

John Lennon once said, "Life is what happens to you while you're busy making other plans." Unfortunately, this is true for students working on college applications. **Of all the times for an emergency to happen, the first semester of a student's senior year is obviously one of the worst.**

If you should become very ill, or have some kind of accident when applications are due, here is some advice for either you or your parents:

* As early on in the admissions process as you can, call the admissions office and ask to speak with the representative for your school or the Dean of Admissions.

* Explain the circumstances of your calling—illness, accident, whatever—and ask for an extension to the application deadline. Try to give the admissions person some idea of how long you may need (two weeks, a month).

★ Follow up the phone call with a letter summarizing your conversation, including the name of the person with whom you spoke, and what that person told you to do about requesting an extension. Document any communication with the admissions office—whether by phone or email.

As soon as is reasonably possible, complete the application.

FAQ #3: My parents keep telling me that I have to get my applications in early. Will that make any difference?

ANSWER: First of all, the answer to this question has nothing to do with applying Early Action or Early Decision. If you want to know the pluses and minuses of applying through one of those programs, see chapter 10, "To Do or Not to Do the Earlies."

Sending in an application early is almost always a good move, provided that your application is as well done as it can be. To begin with, the earlier you start completing applications, the easier your life will be. While applying early doesn't necessarily change your chances for acceptance, admissions officers might interpret an early application as a reflection of your serious interest in their college. That in itself is not a bad thing.

Just so you know, the earlier you submit a Rolling Admission application, the better your chances for acceptance are.

H. WHEN IN DOUBT, ASK

As students fill out applications, often they have questions about specific parts. Many choose to answer a question, right or wrong, and be done with it. That's not a good choice because frequently their best guess is an incorrect one.

1. If you have questions about anything on an application, first look at the application booklet for the answer. If that doesn't work, ask your high school or independent counselor for help.
2. If you are unsatisfied with the answer you get, then don't hesitate to email or call the college (or application program) whose application is confusing you. Except for the large, mega-universities, most college admissions people are very responsive to students who ask for help.

I. MAKE COPIES OF YOUR APPLICATIONS BEFORE YOU SEND THEM OFF

As noted previously, colleges do not act on applications unless they are totally complete. It is your responsibility to make sure that every single application piece is not only sent, but also received by a college.

1. One of the most important tasks in the entire admissions process is to photocopy a finished application in its entirety before you send it off. If you do not have a copy of your finished application, you have no proof that you have completed it.

2. More importantly, if the application is lost—somewhere in Internet space or even at the admissions office—with no copy, you have no other recourse except to do it all over again. What a drag that is!

J. AVOIDING DISASTERS AS YOU USE ONLINE APPLICATIONS

Online applications have made applicant lives a lot easier. Imagine what it was like just a few years back to sit in front of a typewriter, parceling out each letter and using whiteout to cover up mistakes on application form after form. Thank God those days are gone! But online applications are not free of missteps and an occasional disaster. Here are some things you can do to avoid them:

1. USERNAMES AND PASSWORDS

In a safe and known place, be sure to keep a record of your Usernames and passwords for each college application. (If you can, use the same names and passwords for all applications.) Keep login information in a logical place on your computer and also on a piece of paper near your computer or on your cell phone so that you can easily find it. Also, tell one of your parents the names and passwords, in case you are away from your home computer, need the login info, and can't remember it.

2. "SAVE" EVERYTHING, AND OFTEN, AS YOU WORK ONLINE

As you work with online applications, always "Save" whatever you do every fifteen to thirty minutes to avoid losing what you have just typed. Some online applications automatically shut down after awhile, which means that everything you have done simply disappears.

3. WRITING SHORT AND LONG ESSAY DRAFTS

Write both short and long essay drafts away from the actual online application. Once you have a final, edited draft, then copy and paste or upload it into the online application space.

---

adMISSION POSSIBLE TIP!

If you now use aol or hotmail email systems, it would be useful to change to yahoo, gmail, cable, or other services so that you can make full use of online college applications. Also, download the highest level of Internet Explorer or Netscape, the browsers that college applications require.

Little Known Fact

There are wildly differing practices among college admissions officers with regard to searching YouTube, Twitter, and Facebook for information about applicants to their respective colleges. Students should know that what they post on these websites is public information that anyone can access. Admissions counselors recommend that if a student is going to post information about him or herself, it should pass the Grandma test. If you wouldn't want her or an admissions officer or scholarship committee to see what you have posted, don't post it.

4. EMAIL AND IM ADDRESSES

Admissions offices often communicate with students (and students with them) by email or instant messaging. One frequent complaint is that students' email and IM addresses are incorrect or change. **On your applications, make sure that you provide a correct email/IM and then stick with it throughout the admissions process.** If for some reason you have to change your addresses, be sure to let the admissions people know.

A word of advice: Email or text communications with admissions offices should involve proper English—not Internet slang such as "ur" (you are), "B4" (before), "TIA" (thanks in advance). Communications should also use formal salutations (Dear Mr. X: or Ms. Y:), and be written as a formal letter.

Also, take a careful look at your email address to make sure that it doesn't give the wrong impression of you, as in "slackerguy" or "boycrazy#1." Also, stay away from anything that is sexual, profane, or illegal, e.g., "sexylady," "f___u29," "coke-lover." While your email address might not make or break your admission, why risk raising someone's eyebrows?

SUMMARY OF COLLEGE APPLICATION STEPS

Here are the steps to complete an individual undergraduate admissions application:

1. **Determine which school you want to apply to** and whether it uses its own application, the Common Application, or the UCA.
2. Through the college's admission website or the Common Application requirements grid, **find out what and when forms must be completed.** Determine if the school has a Preliminary form that must be completed and by what date.
3. **Complete all forms** for which you are responsible.
4. **Download and fill out your section for other required forms and distribute them to your recommenders.** (See chapter 13, "Letters of Recommendation," for what to provide counselors, teachers, and other recommenders.
5. **Identify essay questions.**
6. **Decide on a focus** for your application and topics for the essay questions.
7. **Write, edit, and upload essays** onto the online application.
8. **Gather any supplemental materials** (e.g., Activities Résumé, art portfolio, etc.).
9. **Photocopy and then send in all application materials** by the due date.
10. **Contact the College Board to send your transcript** of SAT and/or Subject Test scores to the college, and/or **contact ACT to have your ACT transcript sent to the college.**
11. **Have your high school and other academic transcripts sent** to the college.
12. Make arrangements for an **admissions interview** (if possible).
13. Two weeks after all application materials have been sent, **check with the college to make sure all your materials have been received.**
14. Make sure your **Mid-year Report** is sent to the college after first semester grades come out.

SECTION BY SECTION ADVICE ABOUT FILLING OUT APPLICATIONS

While the Common Application, UCA, and different colleges offer different applications, there are many elements that are the same. The following are suggestions for how to effectively complete the different application sections.

1. FIRST-YEAR APPLICATION

To avoid making mistakes or leaving out critical information, first follow these tips:

* Download the application from the college or application website.
* Carefully read through the application, highlighting or flagging any specific directions.
* Identify due dates, including financial aid, and put them on your calendar.
* Write down the short and long essay questions on your essay grid. (See the Checklists section of www .admissionpossible.com).
* Before you input data onto an online application, handwrite your draft answers on a printed application, proofread the answers, and then type the information onto the online application.
* After that, you can use a printed copy of the first application as a guide for completing all other applications.

2. PRELIMINARY FORM OR PART I

Some colleges and universities require applicants to complete a one- or two-page Preliminary Information form that asks for basic information. After completing this Part I form, the remainder of the application then becomes available. Just so you know, this form usually has a due date that is earlier than the regular admission date.

3. STUDENT (APPLICANT, PERSONAL) INFORMATION

Colleges want a lot of personal information about you, including your name, address, birth date and city of birth, etc. Here are some things to watch out for:

Social Security Number

Not long ago, colleges were insistent about having an applicant's Social Security number because this number was a way to keep track of a student during the application process, as well as during the time he or she was an undergraduate at the school. Some colleges and application groups now leave this as an optional piece of information.

Identification with an Ethnic Group

Even though by law you do not have to answer questions regarding your race or ethnic origins, if your family background is African American, Native American, or Hispanic, **it is clearly to your advantage to note this on the application.** If your family is of a mixed background, then identify the different categories or explain what it is in the "Other" section.

Also note any language other than English that is spoken in your home.

4. FAMILY INFORMATION

Students are often surprised by the information that applications ask regarding their parents and siblings. Consequently, at the last minute many applicants end up frantically tracking down information that only their parents can provide. So if you're smart, gather this information way before you need it:

* Your mother's and father's professions, positions, and names of employers (and sometimes even their previous occupations)
* The undergraduate and graduate colleges that both your mother and father attended, degrees attained, and years of graduation
* Your parents' gross annual income for the year you apply, as well as the previous year, and also the number of dependent students in the family (for some colleges)
* The names and ages of your siblings, as well as the colleges they attend (or have attended), the degrees earned, and their dates of attendance at the colleges (for some applications)

5. HIGH SCHOOL ACADEMIC INFORMATION

All undergraduate applications ask about your educational background. While the exact information they require varies, here is what you should be prepared to provide:

High Schools, Summer Schools, and Other Academic Programs You Have Attended

* You need to have ready the name of the current high school you attend (and any others you have attended), its address, and the CEEB/ACT codes for each. You can get this information at these two sites:

SAT: www.sat.collegeboard.com/registerlsat-code-search

ACT: www.actstudent.org/register/lookuphs.html

* You also need to provide your high school counselor's name, title, email address, phone, and fax.

Participation in Educational Preparation Programs

Some applications ask for the name of any college counseling you have received from a community-based program (e.g., AVID, Questbridge, Upward Bound, etc.).

The Titles and Semester Grades of Courses 9th–12th Grades (and sometimes even 7th and 8th grades coursework in math and foreign languages)

Most applications ask for a listing of an applicant's senior year courses; some ask for a listing of all courses, ninth through twelfth grades. The best source of this information is your high school transcript. Be sure to request a copy as soon as school starts in the fall (better yet, get it before).

Some colleges ask for your unweighted Grade Point Average (GPA), others allow a weighted GPA, and many applications don't ask for your GPA (they take what they want from your high school transcript).

6. COLLEGE ACADEMIC INFORMATION

This part of the application is about your plans for a major and for a future career.

Major

Many students don't think twice about what they put down as a major. Often they think this information is of no admissions consequence. **However, what you list as a major can have implications for your admission and even later as a college student.**

A few universities, such as those in the UC system, see identified majors as a major commitment. Therefore, **what you list as your major on an application is what you are when you arrive in the fall. Especially at large public universities, it can be a hassle to change majors, but you can do it.**

Colleges such as Stanford University **say that they don't pay much attention to majors,** that accepting the best possible students in each freshman class leads to the university having students in all of the possible majors. For them, somehow it all works out.

Some admissions offices pay a lot of attention to what students identify as a major, especially since **various majors are more popular than others.** These days, a few of the most popular include computer science, engineering, premed (pre-vet, pre-dental), business, communications, and film. More importantly, for admissions offices, the acceptance rate for students interested in popular majors might be 20–50 percent lower than for students identifying other less-trendy ones. In other words, the more popular a major you choose, the harder it might be to get accepted at a school.

Likewise, the acceptance rate for less popular majors might be 50 percent higher than popular ones. **Thus, the less popular a major you choose, the easier it might be to get accepted.**

Little Known **Fact**

Some admissions offices pay attention to the gender of the applicants for certain majors. For example, they like to find women wanting to major in math, the hard sciences, or other more traditionally male fields. They also like to see men identifying majors in female associated fields such as education, child development, or nursing. Students indicating gender contrary majors might get a slight edge in admissions.

---

adMISSION POSSIBLE TIP

Many college students end up changing majors at least once during their college career. A good number change their major two or more times.

Of course, one should not identify a major in which you are not interested just for the sake of possibly increasing your admissions chances. It's always a bad idea to misrepresent yourself.

Here then are some considerations for when you identify a major on an application:

* For each college you plan to apply to, **find out how competitive your major is.** You can usually determine more or less popular majors from the admissions office and/or academic departments.

    Information about majors has implications that go beyond admissions. Oversubscribed majors may have larger than usual class sizes, taught by TAs rather than professors, and be difficult to get into. Because of the large class size, faculty may be less accessible.

* **If you want to major in a popular field at a college, you might first look for some closely akin major that is less popular.** Listing Undecided on an application form is also a viable choice.

* To help colleges see you as a focused person, **it is OK to designate a major even if you are not totally sure about it.** For example, if your academic and extracurricular background in high school involved a lot of science, then choosing a science major will make sense. What colleges are looking for are students with real intellectual interests.

Career Plans

Most high school students have no idea about what their career interests are. Does any seventeen-year-old really know what to do with his or her life? But there are a number of ways to handle this application question: **a)** Indicate "Undecided," but say that you are looking forward to attending college as a way of exploring your options and coming up with an answer; **b)** Offer two or three alternatives that you have been thinking about, e.g., a career that matches your academic strengths and/or extracurricular activities.

7. TEST INFORMATION (SAT, ACT, SUBJECT TESTS, ADVANCED PLACEMENT {AP}, AND INTERNATIONAL BACCALAUREATE {IB})

What colleges want in standardized test information varies. Individual college admissions websites provide information about what their respective requirements are.

The Common Application website also provides information about test requirements for its four hundred colleges on its requirements grid.

SAT and ACT

* More than eight hundred four-year colleges and universities do not require their applicants to submit SAT I or ACT scores.

    You can find out what these schools are on the FairTest.org website.

* Of the colleges that do require test scores, all accept equally the SAT and the ACT.

* Some colleges ask for your best individual SAT scores: Critical Reading, Math, and Writing, no matter when you took the tests; others want you to submit the best scores from one test date.

Subject Tests

The most Subject Tests any college or university requires is two.

Colleges will not accept photocopies of College Board or ACT test reports. Many colleges will not even accept the test scores noted on high school transcripts. Therefore, you must contact the College Board directly and ask them to send a copy of your test report that includes SAT I and Subject Tests to every college to which you are applying. Likewise, you must also ask the ACT organization to send a copy of your test report to every college to which you are applying.

AP and IB Tests

Some colleges and the Common Application ask for a listing of your AP and IB courses, test dates, subjects, and scores.

FAQ #4: Do I have to have a test score report for my AP and/or IB scores sent to the colleges?

ANSWER: AP and/or IB test score transcripts are not usually a required part of regular admissions. However, for college credit and course placement reasons, they should be sent to your college of choice after you have been accepted.

---

8. APPLICATION GRIDS

Most college applications ask students to fill in grids or spaces about such things as Honors, Activities, and Work Experiences. Most students think that essays are the only arena in which they can demonstrate their resourcefulness and creativity. As long as you follow application directions, these grids offer another opportunity to show admissions people a lot about who you are.

Academic Distinctions, Other Honors, and Awards

In a grid that offers as little as five lines, sometimes in an open-ended space, all applications ask about the honors and awards students have received. A number of application directions specify that they only want academic awards, such as National Merit, National Honor Society, Cum Laude Society, etc.

What do you do? First, **from your Activities Résumé identify everything that might be appropriate for the Awards and Honors space.** Then organize what you write by the directions offered in the application. Sometimes, directions will say to start with the ninth grade and move forward through the rest of the grades. If no directions are given, begin with the most important honors first, and then list the rest. Try to give as much descriptive information as there is space for.

Honors Grid

Here is an example of how one very competitive student filled out a typical pull-down grid:

HONOR	GRADE LEVEL				RECOGNITION	
	9	10	11	12	School, State/Reg	National
NATIONAL MERIT SEMI-FINALIST			x			x
AP SCHOLAR WITH DISTINCTION			x			x
MATH DEPARTMENT AWARD, only student in upper school	x	x	x		x	
MODEL U.N. CONFERENCE, Outstanding Delegate	x				x	
JUNIOR THEATER, best student actor				x	x	

As you can see, one way of making an Honors grid more readable is to capitalize the names of the different items, followed by descriptions in lowercase.

Extracurricular Activities and Work Grid

The activities grid is a very important part of any admissions application. Not only can you document what you have done, but you can also distinguish yourself from the rest of the crowd.

Sometimes the directions for an activities grid call for all extracurricular involvements, including community service and work. These grids usually allow for five to twelve entries. Activities grids might involve "pull-down" lists of activities or simply offer an empty space to fill.

Most activity grids ask for the following information:

★ Activity
★ Grade level(s) during which you participated
★ Approximate hours per week and weeks per year spent on activity
★ Positions, honors, or athletic letters held or won

Usually there is a strict limit to the number of words or characters you can use to describe what you have done.

adMISSION POSSIBLE TIP!

Even though an application allows you to submit an Activities Résumé, be sure to fill out the application activities grid. Do not type in "see attached résumé" unless you want to ruffle the feathers of the admissions folks.

Activities and Work Grid

Here is a process for deciding what to put into an activities grid:

1. Go to your Activities Résumé and identify your most important activities.
2. Choose those experiences in which you have
   ★ Founded, initiated, or demonstrated remarkable leadership
   ★ Held offices or assumed major responsibilities
   ★ Shown a long-term talent or interest, perhaps going back many years before high school

Typical entries into an activities grid might look like this:

ACTIVITY	DESCRIPTION OF ACTIVITY	GRADE LEVEL	POSITIONS HELD, HONORS WON	HOURS PER WEEK	WEEKS PER YEAR
Community Service Bd	Bd plans and offers activities on and off campus	11, 12	Secretary; Presidential Certificate	6	40
Varsity Tennis	Practice and play high school and competitively	9, 10, 11, 12	Most inspirational player	20	46
Independent Artist	Take private lessons, draw, and paint	9, 10, 11, 12	Blue Ribbon, County Fair	5	52
Art	Teach disadvantaged students	9, 12	Assistant to art teacher	2	40

Volunteer and Community Service Sections

Colleges want people on their campuses who not only take advantage of all the resources they offer, but who also are willing to give back. The best prediction of whether a student will be a giver in the future is to look at how he or she has given in the past. Therefore, colleges pay attention to students who identify community service on their activity lists.

Admissions people particularly like when students do their community service voluntarily, rather than as a high school requirement. More, rather than fewer, hours is useful, as well as commitment to an activity over a longer rather than a shorter period of time. It is also helpful for students to convey that their experiences have helped them to grow as a person or learn something new.

It will not be lost on admissions staffs if middle class and privileged students demonstrate their concern for others by participating in community service projects.

Work Experience, Employment

No matter how menial or little the pay, colleges appreciate seeing that a student has spent some of his or her after-school, weekend, or summer time working. In the activities grid, be sure to include any kind of work, including baby-sitting, working for your parents or other relatives, and, of course, employment outside the family.

9. MISCELLANEOUS QUESTIONS

Students must inform colleges of any major disciplinary action, dismissal, suspension, criminal conviction, or juvenile probation they have had while in high school. Do not be tempted to overlook this question or lie about it. Most Secondary School report forms ask high school counselors the same question; so even if you wanted to hide the situation, you can't. The best way of handling this question is to give a simple, honest description of the circumstances of what happened, as well as what you might have learned from it. It doesn't hurt to say that you regret having done it, and that it will never happen again.

Where else are you applying?

At first sight this may appear to be an innocent inquiry, but be careful. **How you answer this question could affect your admission. Colleges not only want to keep tabs on who their competition is, but also might use your answer to interpret your interest in their school.** In no way should a college interpret from your answer that theirs is a back-up school.

One way of handling this question is to say something such as, "While your college has always been a top choice, to make sure that I have other viable options, I am also applying to A, B, C, and D." Then list colleges comparable to that college.

Question regarding taking time out after high school graduation

A growing number of high school students take a year off between high school and college, a practice called gap year. If you have taken a gap year, this question is a wonderful opportunity to tell admissions people what you did, why you decided to do it, what you learned from the experience, as well as how the year changed or helped you.

10. SHORT AND LONG ESSAYS

The subject of short and long essays is important enough to deserve a chapter of its own. (See chapter 12, "Writing Admissions Essays.")

11. SUPPLEMENTAL MATERIALS

Some admissions offices welcome supplemental materials that testify to a student's talent. Other colleges don't. Possible submitted materials include drama, music, or dance CDs or DVDs, artwork including photography, scientific research projects, or writing and poetry samples.

Before you go to the trouble of pulling together supplemental materials, first make sure that a college will accept them; second, follow application directions for how to submit them; and third, think twice before submitting anything that is less than stellar and special.

Be careful about sending along random musings or journal entries, loose drawings, even an ordinary paper for which you may have received an A. If you send anything, **make sure that it is the best representative of what you are able to produce.** Particularly if supplemental materials are in the arts and scientific arenas, admissions people, themselves, probably won't look at them. They will send submissions on to college departments who have the expertise to evaluate them.

> **FAQ #5: My friends tell me that one way of getting an admissions office to pay attention to me is to send them cookies or something a little weird or very creative. What do you think?**
>
> **ANSWER:** What doesn't work in admissions is gimmicks such as fancy cakes and tins of cookies decorated with the name of an applicant. These attention grabbers often have quite the opposite effect. Don't do it.

12. RECOMMENDATION FORMS

Except for the large public universities, most college applications include a Secondary School Report form, a Teacher Evaluation form, and sometimes an Optional and/or Peer Reference form.(See chapter 13, "Letters of Recommendation," for a thorough explanation of what to do about these forms.)

When students give their counselor, teachers, and others the Secondary School Report, Teacher Evaluation, and Optional Reference forms, we urge them to waive their right to see the recommendations. If the right is not waived, college admissions offices might not treat the recommendation with the same weight as when it is waived.

13. HIGH SCHOOL AND COLLEGE TRANSCRIPTS

Students must provide an official copy of their high school transcript for each school they have attended, as well as any coursework completed at another high school, college, or university.

Counselors at many private high schools include a copy of a student's transcript with their School Report form. Because of the incredible number of students public high school counselors must cover, they usually don't include student transcripts with their forms. This means that you must go to the administration office to request that a transcript be sent to each college to which you are applying.

14. SCHOLARSHIP APPLICATION FORM

If a student wants to apply for financial aid, each college provides its own forms for doing that. In addition, students are asked to complete a Free Application for Federal Student Aid (FAFSA) form (for public colleges) and a College Board Profile form (for private colleges). Deadlines for financial aid forms are often different from application deadlines. Be sure to pay attention to and adhere to these dates.

adMISSION POSSIBLE TIP

Resist the temptation to throw out all of your college admissions files after you have completed the applications. You never know when you might need to resend a lost application or a piece of it, or just refer to something in the file.

15. MID-YEAR GRADE REPORT FORM

A Mid-Year Grade Report form is an update of a student's academic progress sent at the end of first semester senior year. Students must provide their school counselor with this form, the top section filled out, as well as a stamped, addressed envelope.

16. FINAL REPORT

Completed by your secondary school counselor or other school official, the top section must be filled out by you and then the form sent/emailed by the counselor when final grades are available.

FOLLOW UP ON YOUR APPLICATIONS

There are two ways of following up on an application. The first is to call the admissions office at each school to which you apply to make sure that they have received all of your application forms and materials. Some colleges leave messages for students online or get in touch with them by postcard or email when everything has been received; if that happens, you are in good shape. Be sure to keep a copy of that notice.

The second follow-up step for applicants is to send admissions offices any new information that emerges after an application is sent. Colleges want to be alerted about new honors, achievements, developments, and especially a student's first semester grades. Sometimes this information can make the difference between getting into the college or not.

ENDNOTE

As you finish each application and send it in, congratulate yourself and enjoy the good feeling. When they are all in, then it's time to really celebrate.

Timeline for Completing College Applications

» FRESHMAN AND SOPHOMORE YEARS

Freshmen and sophomores might find some sort of cardboard or plastic file box in which to place application materials that they collect.

» JUNIOR YEAR

Junior year is a good time to develop individual college file folders so that you have a place for admission rep business cards, personal notes, or college-specific materials you collect at college fairs, from newspaper, magazine, or Internet articles, or while visiting colleges.

FALL SEMESTER

Juniors can get an edge on their peers by acting on these suggestions in the fall:

* Because the **best test tutors are often booked way in advance**, this is a good time to begin the process of finding the best one for you.
* **Take the October PSAT.**
* **Take a practice SAT and ACT** (often offered free by the likes of Princeton Review) to see which test better suits you.
* **November is the only time students can take a Language with Listening Subject Test** (e.g., Spanish or French with Listening).
* **Junior year is the most critical year for getting good grades.** Get a jump-start first semester.
* **Junior year is also the time to develop leadership positions** in whatever you do, or lay the groundwork for such positions in your senior year.
* **Begin thinking about your college list and making contact with the college reps** assigned to your high school from every college.
* **As your family takes trips and vacations, drive through college campuses** that are on your way to your final destination.
* **Give some extra attention to your special teachers** who might be writing recommendations.

SPRING SEMESTER

* **Decide when you are going to take the different admissions tests.** If you haven't already, sign up for test tutoring. Have all of the tests completed by June.
* **Make plans for what you will do in the summer.**
* **Put together a first draft Activities Résumé.**
* **Begin getting serious about a college list;** research colleges through guide books and the Internet.

* **Use Spring Break to visit some colleges.**
* **Attend the National Association of College Admissions Counseling** (NACAC) **college fair** in your area.
* **Before school ends, ask two favorite teachers to write application recommendations.**
* **Carefully choose your senior classes**, taking into consideration the rigor of your program and balance in your life.

SUMMER BEFORE SENIOR YEAR (BEFORE SCHOOL STARTS)

* **Ideally, this is the time when your application organization should begin in earnest.**
* **Develop a file for each college** to which you plan to apply.
* **Narrow down your college list** to ten to fifteen of those you like best.
* **Finalize your Activities Résumé.**
* With your résumé in hand, **identify activities, talents, or interests about which you can write essays.**
* **Make plans to visit colleges** during the summer and/or fall.
* **Sign up for any SAT I, Subject Test, or ACT tests** that you need to take in the fall.
* **Decide if you are going to apply through an early admissions plan** to a college(s).
* **Determine which colleges accept the Common Application** (or UCA) and which have their own application.
* **Complete at least one application**, including the essays, before the beginning of school. This is particularly important for students who play fall sports or are engaged in time-intensive fall activities.

» SENIOR YEAR

SEPTEMBER

* **Get a calendar.** Taking into consideration scheduled academic, sports, and activities, block out time each week through December to work on applications, noting which applications you want to complete by when.
* **Begin working on any Early Applications** and/or "Most Important" applications.
* **Download the applications for your final college list.**
* **Identify the due dates** of all the applications you plan to complete (noting when Preliminary App, Early App, and Regular App deadlines are).
* **Identify the essay questions** for all of your applications. Decide on a focus for your applications and what topics you will use to write the essays.
* **Brainstorm ideas for essays;** write first drafts; have someone edit the essays; finish final drafts.
* **Prepare Recommendation packages** for your counselor, teachers, and others. (See chapter 13, "Letters of Recommendation," for what to include.)

* **Meet with your high school counselor, teachers, and other recommenders** and give them their respective Letter of Recommendation packages.
* **Find out which college reps are coming to your high school** or town and make arrangements to meet them.
* **Give some extra attention to your high school counselor** (who will complete the college Secondary School Reports for you next fall) and special teachers who might be writing recommendations.

OCTOBER

* **Most early application deadlines are at the end of October.** Complete your early, rolling, or first choice school applications.
* **Make sure your high school counselor, teachers, and other recommenders are prepared to send off recommendation packages** for the early apps.
* **Contact College Board and/or ACT to have admission test transcripts sent** to early app colleges.
* **Send your high school transcript** to early app colleges.
* **Finalize arrangements for admissions interviews.**

NOVEMBER

* **Continue completing other top-choice applications**, including making sure that letters of recommendation, test scores, and transcripts are sent.
* **Check in with Early App colleges** to see that they have received all of your application materials.
* **Continue working on and completing three or four applications** based on their respective due dates.
* **Complete the College Board PROFILE** financial aid form.

DECEMBER

* **Complete any applications that have January due dates.**
* **Complete and send the FAFSA financial aid form.**
* **Make sure that the high school counselor, teachers, and other recommenders have or are sending in their respective forms or letters.**

JANUARY/FEBRUARY

* **Complete all remaining applications.**
* **Confirm with any colleges to which you have applied that they have received your application** and other requirements.
* **Give your high school counselor all of your college's Mid-Year Reports** to complete and send.
* **If you have been deferred by a college, meet any requirements noted on their letters to you.** Update your file with new information. (See chapter 15, "The End of the Admissions Road," for what to say and do about deferrals.)

MARCH/APRIL

- ★ A few colleges begin notifying students about their admission decisions as early as late February, and some send notices in March. The Ivies and other very competitive schools notify their applicants around April 1 or shortly thereafter.

- ★ **Comply with any requests from colleges for additional information.**

- ★ April is the month during which many colleges offer accepted students on-campus and local **Pre-Admit programs and receptions.** If you can, **take advantage of these college-sponsored events**, as well as visit campuses on your own.

- ★ **From the acceptance options** available to you, **decide which college you want to attend.**

- ★ **Follow-up with any college to which you have been wait-listed** with whatever materials they ask of you. (See chapter 15, "The End of the Admissions Road," for what to say and do about wait lists.)

- ★ **Let your college counselor, teachers, and other recommenders know about your college admissions results.** Be sure to thank them for their help.

MAY

- ★ **By May 1, you must notify the school you have decided to attend** of your decision to enroll. Send in the admission deposit.

- ★ **Also return any housing and scholarship forms.**

- ★ Early May is also the time for you to **inform all other colleges that you will not attend their schools.**

- ★ **Take your final AP tests.**

JUNE

- ★ **Make sure that your final high school transcript is sent** to your college choice.

- ★ If you want to get college credit for high school AP courses, have College Board **send an AP transcript to the college.**

- ★ **Let your parents know when tuition and room and board bills are due** at your college.

[CHAPTER 12]

WRITING ADMISSIONS ESSAYS
How to Be More than Your GPA and Test Scores

DEFINITION of ADMISSION ESSAYS: *Most colleges have essays as a part of their respective application forms; a few don't. As students fill out their applications, they are likely to find one or more of the following:* **1) very short answer questions** *ranging from a few words to one to four lines;* **2) short answer essays** *asking for up to 250 words or 1/4–1/3 single-spaced page;* **3) long answer essays** *that require between 250 and 500 words, or 1, 2, or 3 pages;* **4) previously written class papers** *with teacher comments. The Common Application and other applications often specify character, as well as word counts.*

The number and types of essay questions on applications vary. Many colleges use the Common Application (with its predictable choice of one short-answer question, and a choice of a long essay question and an additional information question), but most Common Application colleges also have supplemental forms of their own that contain additional requests for information and sometimes essay questions. Quite a few colleges offer a menu of questions and ask applicants to choose one or two to answer.

 **THE BOTTOM LINE** While student grades and test scores are critical factors in making admission decisions, essays may be an even more important factor, especially for private liberal arts colleges and the more selective universities. Like nothing else, essays give readers a sense of how well you express yourself, and particularly how unique and different you are from the rest of the applicants. Essays have the potential to help you stand out from the crowd.

Even if you have great test scores and grades, a poorly written essay can diminish your chances for acceptance. On the other hand, if your grades and test scores are mediocre, but your essays are great, sometimes this can turn the tide toward acceptance. At their best, essays offer a peek into a student's soul.

SAMPLE ESSAY QUESTIONS

Here are some examples of essay questions from a variety of schools. Because they change on a regular basis, for the most up-to-date questions, go to individual college websites or The Common Application.

adMISSION POSSIBLE TIP!

The purpose of a college essay is for college admissions people to find out more about who you are as a student and a person.

adMISSION POSSIBLE TIP!

Sometimes essay questions are almost hidden in the application directions, so students must be on the lookout for and answer anything and everything that is asked.

VERY SHORT ESSAYS

⭐ **What historical moment or event do you wish you could have witnessed?** (300 characters, Stanford University, CA)

⭐ **How did you learn about SMU?** (250 characters, Southern Methodist University, TX)

⭐ **Please mention any international experiences, special study programs, or significant service projects in which you have participated.** (200 characters, Earlham College, IN)

⭐ **Nothing bores me more than…**(100 characters, Wake Forest University, NC)

⭐ **What do you consider to be the most significant factor in your decision to apply to MSU?** (4 lines, Montana State University, MT)

SHORT-ANSWER ESSAYS

⭐ **Please tell us how you have spent the last two summers, including any jobs you may have had.** (2,500 characters, Princeton University, NJ)

⭐ **How does the University of Chicago, as you know it now, satisfy your desire for a particular kind of learning, community, and future?** (Not specified, University of Chicago, IL)

⭐ **Describe an experience when you worked in partnership with others to achieve something you could not have done alone.** (1,500 characters, Kenyon College, OR)

⭐ **When Smith College was founded in 1871, there were few educational opportunities for women. Is a women's college still relevant in 2009?** (1,000 characters or 150 words, Smith College, MA)

⭐ **What work of art, music, science, mathematics, or literature has surprised, unsettled, or challenged you, and in what way?** (1/2 page or 250 words, University of Virginia, VA)

LONG-ANSWER ESSAYS

⭐ **You have just completed your 300-page autobiography. Please submit page 217.** (No specification, University of Pennsylvania, PA)

⭐ **In a clear, well-organized essay, tell us about something that you have done on your own in the last two years that makes you feel good about yourself.** (500-word maximum, University of Oregon, OR)

⭐ **Please provide us with information about your academic preparation and why you feel you're ready for college-level studies at Evergreen. In addition, you should describe your educational and career**

goals and how you believe attending The Evergreen State College will help you reach them. (2 pages, Evergreen State College, WA)

⋆ **Describe the world you come from—for example, your family, community, school—and tell us how your world has shaped your dreams and aspirations.** (Maximum 1,000 words, University of California, CA)

⋆ **Given your interests, values, and goals, explain why Oberlin College will help you (as a student and a person) during your undergraduate years.** (3,000 characters, Oberlin College, OR)

FAQ #1: The directions for one of my essays say that it is to be 500 words. What I have written is 700. Will that be a problem?

ANSWER: This might be a problem for some colleges. Admissions officers want you to follow application directions and are pretty strict about that. Essays that are far short of the word limit or way over might elicit a negative response from an admissions reader. Why risk it?

If the word count of your essay is just a few words over the prescribed number, that shouldn't be a problem. One way of checking is to cut and paste your essay into the space provided on the online application to see if it fits. If it does, no problem. If it doesn't, then begin cutting.

THE TABOO SUBJECTS FOR ESSAYS

While admissions officers are thrilled to come upon an essay that is eccentric or "new," there are some essay topics that are risky. You should not write about anything that is silly, stupid, gross, or false. Also, avoid subjects that might make people uncomfortable, or raise red flags about your future behavior. Therefore, it is best not to write about:

⋆ **Sex**

⋆ **Your use of alcohol or drugs**

⋆ **Personal struggles with bulimia and/or anorexia, a mental illness, or attempted suicide**

⋆ **Your family's dysfunction,** especially if you whine and moan about it

⋆ **Girl- or boyfriend problems**

⋆ **Any secret revelations of stealing or shop-lifting** (Of course, you must truthfully answer any application questions about being convicted of a crime or an experience with juvenile court.)

⋆ **Negative attitudes about anything,** especially individuals or groups

There are also a few essay subjects about which admissions people feel burnt out. They include

* **Predictable favorite books such as *Catcher in the Rye, Huckleberry Finn*, and *The Great Gatsby***
* **Travelogues** (I visited here and there and there.)
* **The catch, hit, or basket that "won the game"**
* **A superficial take on wanting to save the world**

adMISSION POSSIBLE TIP!

Gifted writers can make just about anything appropriate, compelling, and fresh, taboo or overdone subject or not.

AUTHOR'S TIPS ON WRITING

Whether one is a high school student or a Pulitzer Prize-winner, most writers seem to share this sentiment: writing is not easy. As a published author of a number of books, writing is something that I both love and at times hate.

Over the years, other writers have generously shared their "tricks of the trade" with me, the effect of which has been to make my writing experiences easier and more pleasurable. Some of this advice is very applicable to the process of writing admissions essays. Following are some of those tips.

WRITE AS IF YOU ARE TALKING TO THE READER

Perhaps the best advice I ever received came from a publishing executive at a writers' conference. I will never forget the moment when she said, **"The most effective authors write as if they are talking with someone. To write well, be yourself; be natural; write like you're talking on paper."** As soon as I heard this advice, I changed how I wrote. After that, words just seemed to flow.

You can and should do the same with college application essays. After all, if the purpose of a an admissions essay is for the reader to get to know you, then a step in that direction is to write as if you are talking to the admissions person who will read it.

WRITE IN THE FIRST PERSON

Many writers have told me that in order to write well, they had to unlearn much of what they learned in high school English classes. Among the most important unlearnings was giving themselves permission to use the pronoun, I. Teachers often tell students to write only in the third person, using the pronouns he, she, and they. **Because college admissions people want to hear about you in your own, unique voice, you need to find that voice; and one of the best ways of accomplishing this is by using the first person, I.**

SHOW; DON'T TELL

Over and over, skillful writers tell me that the key to good writing is "showing, not telling." **Rather than writing that you are passionate about something, describe it in detail, tell a story, show the reader why you love it so.** Rather than saying that you love animals, write something such as, "Whether a tiny, slithery salamander or a magnificent, giant elephant, I am simply a nut about animals. I have spent most of my life raising, caring for, and rescuing them."

Natalie Goldberg says, "…a writer's job is to make the ordinary come alive."

DON'T START WITH AN OUTLINE; BEGIN WITH A BRAINSTORM

Author and writing teacher Natalie Goldberg urges students to **"…think the thoughts that come, and to write them down and make sense of them in any way they wish."** This is in direct contrast to what many writing manual authors advise. How often have you heard (or read) that you should start with a primary idea, followed by subordinate ideas, etc.

What many accomplished writers say is that when they do the primary subordinate idea thing, they feel choked, stifled, and anxious. By contrast, **successful writers often get started by brainstorming ideas, writing down anything that comes into their heads.** Goldberg also urges writers to "…stop battling youself…shut up, sit down, and write." It really doesn't matter what you write; just get a lot of stuff down on paper or on the computer.

Examples of Successful Essay Titles

» **Nothing Stops Me**
Written by a near-deaf student about how there is little he can't do.

» **Autobus Numero 48**
About an exchange student's experience in Spain.

» **"Michael, being young is serious, but not necessarily fatal"**
About a student who turned around his academic record midway through high school.

» **The Devil Makes Me Do It**
Why a student is involved in all the activities he is.

» **What's a Jock Doing in Academic League?**
Why a football player quit his team and joined an academic group.

» **The Freeway Epiphany**
A brief three-act play that explains how a girl went from being a bad to very good student.

» **My Life Is Like a Coloring Book**
What it is like to be a Mexican Jewish student living in California.

» **Musings from a Personal Computer**
A note from a student's PC about him.

» **A Culinary Odyssey**
What a prizewinning cook would learn from a trip around the world studying different cultures through their food.

(continued)

(continued)

» **When Elephants Fight It Is the Grass that Suffers**
A description of a student's volunteer experience in the racially tense world of Crown Heights, New York.

» **The Wisdom of Grandma Esther**
What a student learned from his grandmother who was married seven times to six different husbands.

» **How, When, and Why I Became a Kid Entrepreneur**
The adventures of a student who opened up a neighborhood take-out food stand in his sister's playhouse.

» **A Klutz Except on a Trapeze**
How a student learned that she could be graceful and accomplished as a trapeze artist, after failing all other athletic endeavors.

» **It's All in the Stroke**
A champion crew member's thoughts about what it's like to be a rower.

» **How Can You Be Intellectually Intense without Being a Nerd**
A bright student's musings about how to not appear to be a nerd, even though he engages in many nerd-like activities.

» **Why Does a Nationally Ranked Swimmer Suddenly Stop Swimming?**
Why a swimmer decided to become a volleyball player.

» **The Day I Became a Mexican**
One student's experience of embracing his cultural heritage after a trip to Mexico City.

BE SPECIFIC AND DESCRIPTIVE

Another piece of good writing advice is to be specific and descriptive. "Don't just write about a fruit," I was told. "Write about a luscious, white nectarine that is so sweet and juicy you want to cry."

While most essay questions are pretty broad and vague, **colleges want just the opposite: answers that are specific, and with plenty of details. Application essays that really work are focused on one minor incident, one interaction, or a small slice of life.**

AVOID GENERALITIES, CLICHÉS, BROMIDES, AND PHILOSOPHICAL/ PSYCHOLOGICAL BABBLE

In other words, stray away from these:

• **Generalities**—Don't say, "I'm very hardworking"; describe a situation in which you are hardworking, and why and how that affects you or other people.

• **Clichés**—Don't say, "…and from the AFS experience I learned how to appreciate other cultures." Explain what you experienced, why it touched you, what you learned from the experience, or how it changed you.

• **Bromides**—Don't say, "I began to see that if people would just talk to each other, we could have world peace." Rather, describe a specific problem, discuss how it developed, identify what could have been done differently, and note what you might do differently should it happen again.

EIGHT STEPS TO WRITING A GREAT ADMISSIONS ESSAY

Is there anything more intimidating than sitting before an empty computer screen or blank piece of paper and thinking, "I now have to write something that will determine my future college choice, if not the direction of my life"? I don't think so.

As a writer myself, if I begin thinking about having to write an entire book, writer's block immediately sets in. Over the years, I have learned that **the best way to approach a major writing task is to block out the time to do it, and simply take on the writing one step at a time.**

The following are steps you can follow that will not only help you get started, but move you forward on a predictable writing path, hopefully ending up with an essay about which you feel very proud.

To help you do this, we're going to follow Peter Jensen (not his real name), an outstanding student who was also a chess champion, as he wrote his college essay. From now on, anything in orange font will be about Peter or use his words.

1. SET ASIDE A BLOCK OF TIME IN A PLACE THAT IS FREE FROM DISTRACTIONS

There are a lot of things you can do in fits and spurts—clean your room, shoot a few baskets, talk to friends on a cell phone—but writing is not one of them. In order to concentrate on what you're doing, **you need to set aside at least an hour for each writing session. Designate one, quiet place** such as a desk in your room, a dining rooms or kitchen table as your writing station. Some students like going to a quiet coffeehouse or nearby public library. **Bring together all of your supplies and resources**, including the college application you're going to work on, a laptop computer or writing pad, pens or pencils, your Activities Résumé, notes with personal stories or anecdotes, and water to drink.

Announce to whomever is nearby (family, friends, etc.) that you are going to be writing now, and don't want to be disturbed. If you're smart, you'll turn off your cell phone and email functions on your computer. All writers know how easy it is to become distracted by anyone or anything in the middle of writing. You have to be very proactive in order to prevent that from happening.

(continued)

» **The Nincompoop and Me**
How a student identified with Voltaire's *Candide*.

» **I Come from a Long Line of Soft-Spoken Feminists**
A letter written to a girl's grandmother about all she had learned from her.

» **Polele or Poulet?**
A student's humorous experiences when she spent a year with a gastronomically challenged French family.

» **Short People Got No Reason to Live**
How a very short student made it onto a varsity volleyball team.

» **Curiosity Killed the Cat and Nearly Got Me**
How a student got himself rescued in Israel by a general when he ventured into a mine field.

» **The TAL Soccer Academy: A Soccer Camp for Disadvantaged Kids**
How an accomplished soccer player set up a summer soccer camp for students who ordinarily don't have access to such a thing.

» **Awakening**
How a student from Mexico City was affected by her grandmother's awakening to personal possibilities.

» **A Profile in Courage**
A student's tribute to his mother, who suffered an irreparable neurological accident a few years before he was born.

» **Sweet as Sugar, Tough as Nails**
Musings from a female athlete.

Peter set aside two hours every Sunday afternoon, from 1 to 3. As he went to the big desk in his room, he announced to the family that he was not to be disturbed.

2. IDENTIFY THE QUESTION YOU ARE GOING TO ANSWER

After you have gotten yourself ready to write, **the first thing you need to do is identify the essay question on which you want to work.** If you haven't yet written an essay or are just starting on a new application, sometimes it's good to start with a short, rather than a long or major essay question.

Peter began his writing session by looking at his essay grid to see which question he was going to work on. He chose the following:

Of all the activities, interests, and experiences you have identified, which is the most meaningful to you? (1/4 page)

3. BRAINSTORM IDEAS FOR A TOPIC TO ANSWER THE QUESTION, LOOKING FOR A THEME OR TOPIC THAT FITS

There are a number of places where you can look for ideas about a theme or topic for essay questions: Think about your long-term activities or what you love to do; take a look at your Activities Résumé or the notes you generated when you brainstormed about personal stories or anecdotes, if you have done that. If you feel stuck, bring in a parent or someone else you trust to help you brainstorm ideas.

Peter looked over his résumé and saw that there were a lot of potential essay topics that could relate to "a most meaningful activity, interest, or experience." Among other things, he

- ★ **Had a number of activities that involved his math talents**
- ★ **Was president of his school Chess Club, as well as a nationally ranked chess champion**
- ★ **Was a member of his school's Academic League team**
- ★ **Had been taking karate lessons since he was seven years old**
- ★ **Was a member of his high school varsity basketball team**

4. CHOOSE A TOPIC

Choose a topic that specifically answers the essay question.

Peter had determined that his main essay was going to be on chess, so he quickly ruled out that topic for the shorter meaningful activity question.

Math was a real interest, but Peter figured he could write about it in questions that asked about academic or intellectual concerns.

As Peter thought about different messages about himself that topics might provide, Academic League was too similar to chess and math, but karate and basketball were completely different. Basketball was his real passion, so he decided on it as the topic for the meaningful activity essay.

In using the criteria established above, Peter found that

- ★ **Basketball was a topic that fit the essay question**
- ★ **It was a subject about which Peter was a total nut**
- ★ **He had some interesting things to say about it**

⭐ Because of his unusual "take" on basketball, admissions readers would learn something very important about him

⭐ He liked the idea of writing about basketball because he thought it was going to be so much fun. Peter couldn't wait to start writing his essay.

5. GATHER YOUR IDEAS AND MATERIALS FOR THE CHOSEN TOPIC

Once you have your topic, the next step is to gather all the information you have about it, including personal stories and anecdotes. This is also a good time to brainstorm ideas for the topic on your own or with someone you trust. As you come up with all kinds of thoughts, stories, and ideas, jot them down on a piece of paper or on a computer. It's very important that you keep written notes of brainstorming sessions because after a few minutes—let alone days—it will be nearly impossible to remember what you have thought or said. You don't want to lose the good "stuff"!

Here are the notes Peter took from a brainstorming session about basketball:

BASKETBALL BRAINSTORM NOTES

- *I'm better at playing basketball than the average person on the street who doesn't play basketball.*
- *But I'm probably the worst player on the best team in my division.*
- *I absolutely love basketball for a number of reasons:*
  - *Unlike football, soccer, or even tennis, I can be a part of a team, but I can also practice on my own or pick up a game just about anywhere.*
  - *Like chess, basketball is a very strategic game. Coaches are always saying that basketball is like chess. There are strategies for offense, defense, winning. Like chess, you play to the weaknesses of other players. You have to have a plan.*
  - *I love running around. Basketball uses up my physical energy.*
  - *I started playing basketball in fourth grade.*
  - *Even though I'm not very good, I get to play enough. Get to play when our team is killing the other team. Can't hang onto the rim; don't do dunks.*
  - *Main reason I'm on the team is because I work so hard. Never slack off, always there; arrive early; bust my butt. Seems like even though I lack the skills, I'm kind of a team leader (team cheerleader).*
  - *Like that I'm with a different group of guys I don't usually hang with: jocks. Diverse: white boys and "bros." Never talk about school. Talk about girls, the game, cars, other sports, music. It's fun.*
- *How basketball has changed me:*
  - *Introduced to different kinds of music from other guys. Now listen to rap music.*
  - *The guys are from a different social group.*
  - *Have gotten confidence; even an athletic letter.*

> - *Have gotten more respect from other students.*
> - *You really get to understand the game; you can talk the talk.*
> - *It's so much fun.*
> - *Wouldn't give it up for anything.*
> - *Thrill of being at the Sports Arena for a championship game, to be a part of a championship team.*
> - *Love the process: everything from the coach coming out with his clipboard to talking strategy to practicing.*
> - *What makes a good player: Talent + smarts + practice + heart.*
> - *You really have to love it in order to put up with all the practices. Gets hard around the latter part of the season. Sometimes have even thought, "Can't we just lose so that I can go home and study?"*

There were all kinds of messages in the above notes that Peter wanted admissions people to get about him: there is a lot more to Peter than his brain: he is humble, has a great sense of humor, is a hard worker, and works well on a team. Who wouldn't want admissions officers to know about these things?

6. ORGANIZE ALL YOUR THOUGHTS AND WRITE A FIRST DRAFT

The next step is for you to take your notes, organize them into some kind of order, and write a first draft. For the moment, don't worry about how long it is. Also forget about making the first draft perfect. All you want to do is to get the words down. After all, you and others will edit the essay once, twice, or three times after this first attempt.

SHORT ESSAY ROUGH DRAFT

Here is Peter's first draft:

Sports have always been a very meaningful part of my life. As a child I was always playing one sport or another.

I've been on soccer teams and baseball teams, and I even helped coach my little brother's tee ball team. For the past ten years, I've been actively involved in the martial arts, taking lessons, competing in regional tournaments, and helping out little kids at fun summer events like "Ninja Camp." But even with all that I must say that being on the varsity basketball team has by far been the most meaningful experience of my high school days. Why? Because I'm so passionate about it. I love so many things about basketball: the camaraderie of the team, the fierce competition, the nervous tension I feel before a big game, and even the way Coach throws his clipboard at the ground when he's mad. This is not to say that I'm any good at the game; in fact, I'm really bad compared to the other Varsity players. I'm a scrawny white kid of 5'10" who can't dribble, doesn't shoot that well, and I am the only player on my team who can't touch the rim. Despite my lack of talent, I can't help myself—I love the game. I have a spot on the team solely because I work harder than anyone else on the court to execute our game plan—not because I score a lot of points. Coach and the team know they can count on me to be in the right place, doing the right thing, and giving my all. Because of this, over the seasons, I've become somewhat of a team leader, helping the team with my attitude and my understanding of the game, rather than coming up with fancy moves and nasty dunks. In order to be as useful as possible to the team, I've had to learn how to play every single position on the court, and play it well enough for us to win. I've been laughed at many times when I've had to play center and guard someone two heads taller than I am and 50 pounds heavier. But after four quarters of fighting, scrapping, and clawing, my opponents stop laughing. I may not be good but I'm not afraid of anybody. Not only has basketball given me a chance to run around and compete, it has also introduced me to a completely different social group, which has educated me as to the meanings of words such as "flossin" and "blingin," exposed me to rap music (which is now my favorite), and I'm even a teammate's "dawg." I'm absolutely crazy about the game and, honestly, would not give it up for anything.

7. EDIT, EDIT, AND EDIT YOUR DRAFT

People who write for money or because they love it have come to a major understanding about writing: It is not just a one-time event. It is writing and editing; then re-editing, and then editing some more.

First editing involves making sure that you have answered the essay question, and that there is organization to the essay. Make sure you have an introduction, a theme, a development of that theme, and some kind of wrap-up or conclusion.

Admissions officers also like to **know what you have learned or gained from an activity or situation.**

Then read the essay to see if it makes sense. Examine the sentences and paragraphs to make sure that they are well-written. Look for transitions from one paragraph to another, and how one thought leads to another. Check to see if the draft is focused and specific, yet contains enough detail so that the writing is alive. One good technique is to read the essay aloud to make sure that the words and sentences run off your tongue naturally, like a conversation.

Next look for any spelling, punctuation, or grammatical errors, as well as improper use of words. Cut out any extraneous words or sentences.

Don't be "married" to a particular phrase or sentence, no matter how great. If it does not really fit into the whole story (or advance it) but is there to show off the writer's technique, wit, or whatever— leave it out!

Finally, **make sure that the essay fits the space provided or the number of words specified on the application.** A few words under or over won't make that much difference, but colleges are very picky about applicants following their directions, whatever they are.

adMISSION POSSIBLE TIP!

Some students are tempted to use an old paper written for a high school class as an admissions essay. Be careful about doing that. Traditional high school papers are not usually what college admissions people want (unless, of course, they ask for a sample high school paper). Unless a previously written paper is very personal—shows something about who you are, directly answers the essay question, and takes account of the above-mentioned writing tips, don't use it.

adMISSION POSSIBLE TIP !

A good rule of thumb is to edit an essay, put it aside for a period of time or have someone else edit it, and then edit it again.

Ask someone you trust, such as an English teacher or your college counselor, to go over your essay for comment and feedback.

Peter edited his essay, and then asked his college counselor to do the same. The following page is what he ended up with (edits: deletions are crossed out and new words are in orange font).

SHORT ESSAY WITH EDITING MARKS

Being on a varsity basketball team has by far been the most meaningful experience of my high school career. Why? Because ~~for the simple reason that~~ I'm so passionate about it. I love ~~many things about basketball:~~ the camaraderie of the team, the fierce competition, the nervous tension I feel before a big game, even the way Coach throws his clipboard at the ground when he's mad. This is not to say that I'm any good at the game; in fact, I'm really bad. ~~atrocious.~~ I'm a scrawny white boy of 5'10" who can't dribble, doesn't shoot that well, and the only player on my team who ~~that~~ can't touch the rim. Despite my lack of talent, I can't help myself—I love ~~ing~~ the game. I have a spot on the varsity team solely because I work harder than anyone else on the court, not because I score a lot of points (or any points!). Over the years, much to my and the coach's surprise, I've become somewhat of a team leader, ~~able to~~ helping the team with my understanding of and creating strategies for the game, rather than doing all the ~~with a display of~~ fancy moves and nasty dunks. ~~Basketball has given me so much!~~ Not only has basketball given me a chance ~~do I get~~ to run around and compete, but it ~~the game~~ has also introduced me to a completely different social group who has taught me the ~~My basketball friends have educated me as to the~~ meaning of such words as "flossin'" and blingin'," as well as exposed me to rap music (which is now my favorite). I'm absolutely crazy about ~~this~~ the game and ~~honestly,~~ would not give it up for anything.

adMISSION POSSIBLE TIP !

All good writers make use of other people to give them feedback, edit and proofread their writing, and provide them with advice. While it is totally inappropriate to ask someone to write an essay for you, most colleges have no problem with your asking others for writing advice, as well as feedback and edits on your essays.

8. GIVE YOUR ESSAY ONE FINAL PROOFREAD; THEN UPLOAD IT INTO THE SPACE THE ONLINE APPLICATION PROVIDES

Before you upload your essay, it's a good idea to give it one final edit or proofread. It is so easy to miss an error or two. How silly it would be to let something small diminish all your hard work. Be especially careful to note computer spell-check errors, e.g., the word hair coming out as hare.

Here is a copy of Peter's final essay:

FINAL SHORT ESSAY

Being on the varsity basketball team has been the most meaningful experience of my high school career. Why? Because I love the camaraderie of the team, the fierce competition, the nervous tension I feel before a big game; even the way Coach throws his clipboard at the ground when he's mad. This is not to say that I'm any good at the game; in fact, I'm really bad. I'm a scrawny white boy of 5'10" who can't dribble, doesn't shoot that well, and the only player on my team who can't touch the rim. Despite my lack of talent, I can't help myself—I just love the game. I have a spot on the Varsity team solely because I work harder than anyone else on the court, not because I score a lot of points (or for that matter, any points!). Over the years, much to my surprise and the coach's dismay, I've become somewhat of a leader, helping the team with my understanding of and creating strategies for the game, rather than doing all the fancy moves and nasty dunks. Not only has basketball given me a chance to run around and compete, it has introduced me to a completely different social group, people who have taught me the meaning of words such as "flossin'" and "blingin'" and exposed me to rap, now my favorite kind of music. I'm absolutely crazy about basketball and would not give it up for anything.

HOW TO RECYCLE AN ESSAY

Many students approach their applications with the notion that every application will require a totally new answer for each essay question. Fortunately, this isn't true. **In many cases, students can recycle the answer to a question a number of times. One of the benefits of putting together an essay grid is that you can literally see where certain essay topics or essays can be used over and over again.**

Of course, if you use the Common Application, you will be submitting the same short, long, and additional information answers to every school that accepts the Common App. If you use a college's own application, you need to pay a lot more attention to individual questions.

In some cases, one essay answer to a question can be used almost word for word for another because two different college application questions are so similar to one another. For example, one question might ask, "Of all the activities, interests, and experiences you have identified, which is the most meaningful to you?" (1/4 page), while another says, "Tell us about a favorite way you spend your time?" (1/4 page).

The following is Peter's short essay recycled and expanded to be a longer essay.

SHORT ESSAY RECYCLED TO A LONG ESSAY

All new words are in a orange font.

BASKETBALL: LEARNING ABOUT "FLOSSIN'," "BLINGIN'," AND "DAWG"

Sports have always been an important part of my life. As a child, if I wasn't playing soccer, I was playing baseball or something else. I was even an assistant coach for my little brother's tee ball team for a while. For the past ten years, I have been actively involved in martial arts, the Eastern version of sports. I have taken lessons, competed in regional tournaments, and taught little kids karate at fun summer programs such as the "Ninja Camp."

Having said all that, I must admit that being on the varsity basketball team has been by far the most rewarding experience of my high school days. Just how and why I am involved may say more about me than anything else. I love so many things about basketball: the camaraderie of the team, the fierce competition, the nervous tension I feel before a big game, and even the way Coach throws his clipboard at the ground when he's mad. This is not to say that I'm any good at the game; in fact, I'm really bad compared to the other Varsity players. I am a scrawny "white boy" of 5'10" who can't dribble, doesn't shoot that well, and the only player on my team who can't touch the rim.

Despite my lack of talent, I can't help myself—I have a real passion for this game. I have a spot on the team not because I score a lot of points, but because I work harder than anyone else on the court. Coach and the team know they can always count on me to be in the right place, doing the right thing, and giving my all. Because of this, over the seasons, I have become somewhat of a team leader, helping the team with my attitude and my understanding of the game, rather than coming up with fancy moves and nasty dunks. In order to be as useful as possible to the team, I have learned to play every single position on the court, and play it well enough for us to win. I cannot tell you how many times I have been laughed at by the opposition when I have been called upon to play center and guard to someone two heads taller and 50 pounds heavier than I am. But after four quarters of fighting, scrapping, and clawing, my opponents actually stopped laughing. I may not be good, but I'm good enough and not afraid of anybody.

Not only has basketball given me a chance to run around and compete, it has also introduced me to a completely different social group. I have become educated as to the meaning of such words as "flossin'" and "blingin'," exposed to rap music (which is now my favorite), and even become a teammate's "dawg." This is all to say that I'm nuts about basketball and wouldn't give it up for anything.

ESSAY DOS AND DONT'S

DO	DON'T
1. Write short, concise essays that inform, reveal, and/or amuse.	1. Try to say too much, ramble on; think that more is better: it's not.
2. Appear to be humble, even somewhat self-effacing. Show how you have taken advantage of the resources made available to you.	2. Appear to be self-centered, boastful, a person who likes to toot his or her own horn.
3. Give the impression that you take very seriously the college application process, and especially the essay questions; you value education and learning and will exceed the college's expectations.	3. Give the impression that you dislike or are tired of the application process, especially the essay questions; that you want to go to college only to have a good time.
4. Be yourself.	4. Write as if you're trying to impress the essay reader by using affected words or dealing with ostentatious subjects.
5. Give the message that you are mature, positive, sensitive, upbeat, modest, reflective, thoughtful, intelligent, contemplative, secure, confident, persistent, tenacious, courageous, curious.	5. Give the message that you are arrogant, disrespectful, sarcastic, melodramatic, overly emotional, money-grubbing, superficial, insecure, a slacker, prissy, judgmental, or negative.
6. Show evidence of having done research about a particular college; having real knowledge about a campus, its programs and activities, as well as its students.	6. Give the impression that you know little about a college by writing trite things, e.g., it has a beautiful campus, has a great football team, is prestigious.
7. Write about anything that is counter-intuitive about yourself: a football player who has an academic passion, a girl who is interested in math or physics, a guy who is interested in education.	7. Make something up about yourself to impress the application reader.
8. Use a variety of words or phrases to describe a certain idea.	8. Use the same words over and over (certainly more than twice).
9. Explain anything that needs explaining: an illness, a tragedy, a bad quarter, etc.	9. Make excuses for anything such as bad grades, an infringement of rules.
10. Go for a smile or a giggle. Use your sense of humor.	10. Try to be funny but end up sounding immature or inappropriate.

College essays are one of the most important ways that students can reveal their hearts and minds, something that admissions officers want to see. Students who take the time to write an original, thoughtful essay that reveals something about themselves really enhance their admissions possibilities.

FAQ #2: Some of my friends are buying application essays from websites that guarantee to bring them application success. What do you think?

ANSWER: For personal, moral, and ethical reasons, don't do it. Application essays are supposed to be by and about you (not by a website, your parents, an older sibling, or a paid gun). And if you should go that road and be found out, your reputation with colleges (and possibly future employers) will be compromised forever.

ENDNOTE

Application essays are the most powerful tool for letting colleges know who you are as a person and student. They offer you a unique opportunity to show your good writing skills, how well you think, and even your sense of humor.

Timeline for Writing Admissions Essays

» SUMMER BEFORE SENIOR YEAR

JULY

The new Common Application is available for students every August. For students who will be very active in a sport and/or activities during fall semester, July is a good time to begin brainstorming ideas for the short, long, and additional information essays.

AUGUST

Go to the website's admissions section of each college to which you plan to apply to see if their application is available online. If you find that one or more are, then download and print a copy of the application, making note of what the application essays are.

★ **Continue brainstorming ideas for the application essay questions.**

» SENIOR YEAR

SEPTEMBER

Identify the essay questions for all your applications and write them down on the adMISSION POSSIBLE essay grid or a system that you have devised on your own. Go to the Checklists section of admissionpossible .com for the essay grid.

★ **Decide on a focus for your applications and topics for the essay questions.**
★ **Brainstorm content for your essays.**
★ **Write, edit, and complete essays for early applications.**

NOVEMBER/DECEMBER

★ **Write (or recycle), edit, and complete essays for November, December, and January** 1, 2, and 3 deadlines.

JANUARY

★ **Complete or recycle all remaining essays.**

CHAPTER 13

LETTERS OF RECOMMENDATION
Getting Others to Sing Your Praises

DEFINITION of LETTERS OF RECOMMENDATION: *Sometimes required, other times not, admission recommendation letters are usually written by high school counselors, teachers, and others who have firsthand knowledge about a student, including his or her academic background, personality characteristics, skills, talents, and potential to succeed in college.*

Virtually every private college and a few public schools require one or more of the following recommendation forms:

- **Secondary School Report/School Counselor form** *(Usually completed by a high school counselor, but on occasion filled out by a principal/headmaster, vice principal, or upper school director)*
- **Teacher Evaluation/Instructor Recommendation form** *(Completed by an academic teacher who has taught a student in a regular high school class)*
- **Optional Recommendation form** *(Usually completed by deans, other teachers, coaches; employers; community service supervisors; or family friends who know a student very well)*
- **Peer Recommendation form** *(Usually completed by a good friend; only a few colleges require this kind of recommendation)*

{ **THE BOTTOM LINE** } Many college admissions applications include recommendation forms, but some don't require or want any recommendations. For example, the University of California application flatly states, "Do not submit recommendations unless they are specifically requested by a UC campus."

Over 450 colleges utilize The Common Application that offers Secondary School Report and Teacher Evaluation forms. Information is available on the website that notes which and how many forms are required by each school. You can access these forms at www.commonapp.org. More than fifty colleges utilize the Universal College Application (UCA) also offers School Report and Instructor Recommendation forms. The UCA website notes which and how many forms are required by each school. You can access these forms at www.universalcollegeapp.com. A few private colleges, such as Georgetown University, and many public universities have their own applications and sometimes their own recommendation forms.

While it is unwise to brag about yourself on applications, it is totally appropriate, if not essential, for other people to sing your praises as persuasively and with as much detail as they can.

HIGH SCHOOL COUNSELOR, SECONDARY SCHOOL REPORT FORM, AND SCHOOL PROFILE

A student's high school counselor usually fills out the **Secondary School Report and/or the Counselor Recommendation forms and provides colleges with a School Profile.**

DEFINITION of SCHOOL PROFILE: The School Profile is a document that provides the following: a brief overview of a school, its location and contact information, the number of students and at what grade levels, grading and ranking systems, the number of faculty, the focus and breadth of the curriculum, whether Honors, AP, and IB courses are offered, if it is a coed or single-sex school or has a religious affiliation, and past years' college admissions results with test scores of students.

Your counselor is a very important person in the college admissions process because colleges often rely on him or her to offer a comprehensive, overall take on you as a person and student, including comments about your

* **Accomplishments and honors**
* **Any extracurricular activities, community service and sports involvements, and particular leadership roles**
* **Special talents, interests, and skills in and out of school**
* **Transcript regarding anything that needs explaining, e.g., upward or downward trend in grades and why**

With your and your parents' permission, the counselor can also describe and explain how such issues as learning disabilities, medical issues, or a family illness or tragedy have impacted your high school experience.

The college counselor needs to help admissions officers understand what is different, special, and appealing about you and how those qualities will contribute to their college.

Counselors are also the people admissions offices call if they have any questions about you, want feedback about how you would fit in at a particular college, or need clarification about inconsistencies in your application.

OTHER PEOPLE WHO MIGHT COMPLETE THE SCHOOL REPORT FORM

On a rare occasion, outstanding students or students with special circumstances ask high school principals, headmasters, vice-principals, or upper school directors to complete their Secondary School/ Counselor forms. This usually happens at smaller schools or when students get to know a school official through their activities on campus. It goes without saying that colleges are impressed when people of stature take the time to thoughtfully complete a student's Secondary School Report form.

HELPING THE COUNSELOR DO A GOOD JOB FOR YOU

In fall of every school year, school counselors (particularly those in public high schools) are overwhelmed by all that they must do for seniors and other students. Therefore, one of your roles as a senior is to make the counselor's job of helping you easy. You have nothing to lose by doing this, and often a lot to gain.

> **adMISSION POSSIBLE TIP!**
>
> Because handwritten materials can be difficult to read, ideally all information that goes to the counselor and teachers should be typed.

> **Little Known Fact**
>
> Parents: Do not ignore the counselor request for information. Counselors are known to take some—if not a lot—of what parents write (sometimes word for word) and make it a part of their own letter or report.

WHAT TO PROVIDE THE SCHOOL COUNSELOR

1. **High school counseling office materials:** Some high school counseling offices ask students and/or parents to fill out informational questionnaires during the summer or the first month of senior year. Some counselors even ask parents to write draft letters of recommendation for their sons and daughters. As you complete the counselor's questionnaire, try to differentiate yourself from the rest of the seniors in your class. Help the counselor explain who you are as a student and person and how you are unique and different.

2. **An up-to-date Activities Résumé:** Nothing provides a counselor with more information about who you are than an Activities Résumé. Make sure that you provide one that is filled with detail and totally up to date. See sample résumés in chapter 8.

3. **Your college list organized by application due dates:** It's very important to provide your college counselor with an up-to-date college list, organized by the dates when college applications are due. Due dates are critical because in order for the colleges to process and evaluate your application, every

piece of the application, including the counselor's remarks, must arrive at the college on time. You need to make sure that your counselor meets those deadlines. See college list form in the Checklist section of www.admissionpossible.com. **On your list, be sure to note if you are applying to any colleges early (action or decision) or to a college offering Rolling Admission.**

Optional for students: One way of helping the counselor (and perhaps guiding what he or she says) is to give specific reasons why you are interested in each college on your list. Ask the counselor if he or she would like to have this information.

4. **College Secondary School Report/School Counselor forms:** Most private college applications include Secondary School Report/School Counselor forms for counselors to complete. You must fill out the top portion of this form for each school and give it to your counselor. Very neatly provide your name, Social Security number, and all other required information on the forms.

5. **Copies of your college applications and/or essays:** Some private and public school counselors want to see students' application essay answers. Other counselors, particularly at private schools, want to see students' entire applications. Find out what your counselor wants in terms of applications and essays.

6. **List of teachers and other people who are writing letters of recommendation for you:** Some college counselors also want to know the names of teachers and other people who are writing letters of recommendation for you. It's a simple thing to do, so do it.

7. **Stamped, college-addressed envelopes:** Many high schools now use online recommendation forms. Check to see what your school policy is. A few ask students to provide a stamped envelope addressed for every college to which a hard copy form or letter is sent. Don't forget to put the counselor's return address in the lefthand corner of the envelope. Before you do that, find out what kind of envelope the counselor wants—a standard, small envelope or a larger, 8 1/2 x 11 one—and how much postage should be affixed.

8. **Other information, stories, and anecdotes for the counselor to use:** Some counselors love having lots of information and materials from students. They say this helps them to do their job. On the other hand, other counselors totally resist offers of extra materials because they want their comments to be totally their own. You're going to have to find out which kind of person your counselor is.

Depending on what your counselor wants, here are some items that you might include in your recommendation packet: copies of letters applauding your work or accomplishments or awards for different activities; small portfolios of your art, music, or writing; descriptions of special interests or projects in and outside of school (e.g., you have collected reptiles since the first grade, you're a prize-winning cook, you help take care of a grandparent who has Alzheimer's).

Recommendations come alive when writers integrate colorful stories or anecdotes about a student to illustrate a point. Ask your counselor if he or she would like to have some of these. (See chapter 9, "Collecting Personal Stories and Anecdotes," for examples of stories and anecdotes that have been used by students.)

Optional for parents: Again, depending on a counselor's preferences, you can provide a lot of useful information about your child, including a list of positive adjectives or adjective phrases that describe who your child is and his or her strengths, personal stories, obstacles or significant family events that have impacted your son or daughter, and interesting family background details.

9. **Cover sheet identifying exactly what you have given the counselor:** Not only is a cover sheet useful to let the counselor know what you have given him or her, it is also proof that you provided the material.

10. **Transcript request:** A number of counselors assume responsibility for including a high school transcript in their school report package; however, most high schools require that you make separate transcript requests to the registrar of the school. Find out what procedures you need to follow and associated fees, as well as how long it takes to get transcripts sent out.

adMISSION POSSIBLE TIP!

Always affirmatively sign the waiver on the Secondary School Report or Teacher Evaluation forms that gives away your right to see the evaluations written by the counselor. Colleges may be suspicious of students who do not waive their rights.

DOS AND DON'TS IN WORKING WITH THE SCHOOL COUNSELOR

DO	DON'T
1. Be proactive	1. Wait for the counselor to contact you
2. Have a positive, upbeat attitude	2. Whine, complain, be negative, have a bad attitude
3. Listen and be respectful to the counselor, even if you disagree with his or her advice or dislike the individual as a person	3. Argue with, challenge the authority of, or offend the counselor, even if he or she acts like a jerk
4. Be sensitive to the counselor's workload	4. Make unnecessary requests or demands
5. Supplement the counselor's advice with your own research	5. Take the counselor's words as the one and only truth
6. Be organized and neat	6. Give the counselor stacks of disorganized forms and papers that he or she will have to organize
7. Get everything to the counselor on time, if not early	7. Turn in forms and information in dribs and drabs, late or incomplete
8. Be forthcoming with information; make sure the counselor feels a real part of your application process	8. Be withholding and secretive

Much of the above can also be applied to your relationships with teachers and other recommenders.

FAQ #1: What if I get a new college counselor at the beginning of my senior year?

ANSWER: First, as soon as you can, stop by the counselor's office to introduce yourself and say hello. Second, make an appointment with the counselor and do everything to help him or her get to know you. Without becoming a bother, on a regular basis continue to stop by (with a smile on your face) so that you and your name become familiar.

Provide the counselor with as much organized information about you and your applications as you can. To do that, simply follow the directions in the previous section, "What to Provide the School Counselor."

If you are worried that the new counselor won't be able to provide the kind of School Report you desire and your old counselor is still at the school, ask the latter to fill out the School Report forms. Depending on the relationship you had with the old counselor, your request might be granted. If the old counselor simply cannot complete the school report forms for you, then talk with him or her about ways the two of you can help the new counselor.

Finally, remember to thank the counselor for whatever he or she does for you. By your attitude and actions, you can turn an overworked, reluctant counselor into an enthusiastic advocate who supports your case and spends the time and energy necessary to help you realize your admissions goals.

HIGH SCHOOL TEACHER EVALUATION AND INSTRUCTOR RECOMMENDATION FORMS

While counselor recommendations are general "takes" on students, teacher evaluations and recommendations usually focus specifically on students' academic background. Teacher recommendations usually include these topics:

* A student's work in a particular subject
* A student's qualities (e.G., Dependability, motivation, initiative, resourcefulness, maturity, perseverance, independence, respect for others) as relates to the academic world and college
* An identification of and comments about a student's different abilities and skills (e.g., writing or verbal skills, language, mathematical, musical, artistic)
* Remarks about performance or potential that distinguishes a student from others (e.g., a student's thoroughness, organizational skills, participation in class discussions, research capabilities, analytical prowess, etc.)
* Unique knowledge about how a student fits in or what he or she will offer a particular college
* How a student's work in a class relates to a future major

WHOM TO ASK TO COMPLETE THE TEACHER EVALUATION OR RECOMMENDATION FORMS

As for whom to choose for teacher evaluations/recommendations, think about the teachers with whom you have developed the best relationships. Here are some clues as to whom that might be:

★ In whose classes have you received the best grades, performed in some unique or outstanding way, or been seen as "the star pupil"?

★ Which of your teachers from freshman year on has been particularly complimentary of you and your work?

★ Have you been asked by one of your teachers to be a teaching assistant?

★ Has any teacher sponsored you for a special program or award?

★ Is there a teacher with whom you love to talk, discuss, or debate, both in and out of class?

★ Is there a teacher for whom you have completed an especially good paper, independent project, or demonstrated great curiosity or imagination?

★ Can you think of a teacher for whom you have performed particularly well in a class that is related to your future major in college?

FORMULA TO DETERMINE WHOM TO ASK

To begin with, check each application carefully to see if it has directions for what kinds of teachers they want to complete your Teacher Recommendation forms. After that, a good way to decide which teachers to ask is to brainstorm the names of potential recommenders with a parent. After you have come up with a few names, based on what kind of recommendation you think a teacher will write, assign each a number from 1 (terrible) to 10 (the best!). Once you have numbers for each teacher, then circle the ones with the two highest scores. They then become your choices.

FAQ #2: One of my applications says that I need teacher recommendations from different disciplines. What if my strongest ties are with teachers who are both in the sciences?

ANSWER: College admissions staffs want students to follow their directions as closely as they can. If you have a number of quality people from a variety of disciplines (e.g., sciences, social sciences, humanities, arts) who are available to write letters, by all means ask a science teacher for one and an English, Spanish, or history teacher for another. **The recommendation rule of thumb, however, is always to go with the strongest recommenders, regardless of their discipline.** If you don't follow college directions regarding a recommendation, be sure to send an email or note explaining why.

adMISSION POSSIBLE TIP!

Save special papers and projects for which you have received A's and good comments to give to teachers who complete your teacher recommendations.

HELPING TEACHERS DO A GOOD JOB FOR YOU

It's important to recognize that when teachers write letters of recommendation or fill out college evaluation forms for you, they are doing this in addition to their regular teaching responsibilities (in addition to all the other things they do as a professional and family person).

1. One of the first things you can do is ask your teachers early. The old saying, "The early bird gets the worm," is particularly appropriate for teacher recommendations. Because teachers usually write letters for many students, the earlier you ask, the better the letter probably will be.

2. It doesn't hurt to gauge a teacher's enthusiasm as he or she responds to your request for a recommendation. You could say something such as, "Mr. X, I'm thinking ahead to college applications in the fall and was wondering if you would be willing to write a letter of recommendation for me?" If there is real positive energy in his response, then you know you have one teacher on your team. However, if you hear hesitancy or a lack of enthusiasm, you can ask further or clarify: "Mr. X, from your response I sense that you may not be up for writing an admissions recommendation for me. Is that right?" Depending on his response, you can say thank you and suggest that you will ask another teacher or say thank you for being willing to do it.

Once you know that a teacher will be completing a teacher evaluation form for you, make sure that you are:

* Neat and organized
* On schedule getting everything to him or her or, even better, early
* Appreciative of whatever is done

WHAT TO PROVIDE TEACHERS

1. **High school counseling office materials**: Make sure that your counselor is planning to share all of the counseling office materials with the teachers you have asked to write recommendations. If he or she is not, then make a copy yourself and give it to the teachers.

2. **An up-to-date Activities Résumé:** Nothing gives teachers better ammunition to use in their comments than a very detailed Activities Résumé.

3. **Your college list organized by application due dates:** Don't forget to let teachers know if you plan to apply early to any colleges. As with the counselor, give specific reasons why you are interested in each college on your list.

4. **Teacher Evaluation and Instructor Recommendation Forms:** Fill in the top student portion of each form and waive your right to see what the teacher has written.

5. **Stamped, college-addressed envelopes:** If your teachers plan on using hard copy forms, find out what kind of envelope each teacher prefers: a standard envelope or a larger 8 1/2 x 11 envelope and how much postage to affix.

6. **Any other information or material that will be helpful to the teachers:** Again, if you have letters that laud your accomplishments or work, an art or musical portfolio or tapes, and/or special interests or projects outside of school, provide teachers with a neat, organized package of whatever you have.

   Optional for parents: Again, depending on a teacher's preferences, you can provide a lot of useful information about your child, including a list of positive adjectives or adjective phrases that describe who your child is and his or her strengths, personal stories, obstacles or significant family events that have impacted your son or daughter, and interesting family background details.

7. **Cover sheet identifying exactly what you have given the teacher:** See the Checklists section of www .admissionpossible.com for a sample cover sheet.

Finally, remember to thank the teachers for whatever they do for you. AND… don't forget to make photocopies of everything you give to them.

OTHER RECOMMENDERS

A few college applications will ask for an optional recommendation, beyond the school counselor and teacher forms, while others discourage additional recommendations. However, most applications say nothing about additional recommendations; they leave that up to the individual student.

Often it is useful for a student to ask one or two people who have special knowledge about them (or their accomplishments, talents, or activities) to write a letter of recommendation. The people to ask might include **1) a special art or drama teacher, 2) a music, chess, or athletic coach, 3) someone for whom you have worked, 4) a teacher or professor you had in a summer program, 5) a religious leader, or 6) the head of a community service agency** for whom you have volunteered.

When it comes to extra letters of recommendation, colleges often say that "less is more." Additional letters of recommendation should come from people who know you very, very well and provide a unique, in-depth perspective of you, some work you have done, some talent you have, life challenges you have faced, or an unusual experience you have had.

WHAT TO PROVIDE OTHER RECOMMENDERS

1. Activities Résumé
2. Your college list organized by the dates when the applications are due
3. Any information that you provided your counselor or teachers that will help the person write a very positive, revealing letter about you
4. Stamped, college-addressed envelopes

As with the counselor and teachers, be sure to thank the recommenders and let them know how much you appreciate their taking the time to write on your behalf.

FAQ #3: Who should I NOT ask to write an extra letter of recommendation for me?

ANSWER: A simple answer to this question is anyone who doesn't really know you or who is not going to rave about you.

Anyone who writes an extra letter of recommendation for you must know you very, very well and like you a lot. Many parents are under the impression that if they ask their prestigious, high visibility, famous, or college-connected friend—a senator, governor, CEO, NFL football player, movie star, or well-connected college alumni or trustee—to write a letter on your behalf, this will impress the admissions staff. Unless one of those people knows you very well, IT WON'T. In fact, it could even work against you.

KEEPING TRACK OF FORMS AND LETTERS

It would be such a shame if you filled in all of the forms, wrote your essays, paid your fees, sent the application packages in, and asked all the appropriate people to write letters on your behalf, and then found out after the college selections have been made that you were turned down because the college did not receive a required recommendation or form. Believe it or not, this does happen.

To make sure that it doesn't, a couple of weeks after you send in your application, call each college to which you sent an application to see if anything is missing from your file, including letters of recommendation. If everything has been received, relax and enjoy the feeling that all is done.

If, however, the college indicates that a recommendation is missing, act quickly to get them what they need. Immediately inform the counselor or teacher whose form is missing and ask him or her to fax or FEDEX the form. Check back with the college in a day or two to make sure that it has been received.

---

adMISSION POSSIBLE TIP!

Because counselors handle hundreds of college forms, and perhaps thousands of pieces of paper, sometimes things get misplaced or lost. Therefore, it is absolutely critical that you make photocopies of everything you give to the counselor and teachers.

ENDNOTE

Many letters of recommendation end up being generic, bland letters filled with clichés. What you want is positive, spirited recommendations that are filled with details and special knowledge about you. They must also be believable, realistic, and honest. You can do a lot to make that happen by wisely choosing whom you ask to write recommendations and also by providing these people with excellent information that will help them do a great job for you.

Timeline for Asking for Recommendations

» END OF JUNIOR YEAR

For both public and private school students, the end of your junior year is a good time to ask favorite teachers to write letters of recommendation for your college applications. Popular teachers often get overwhelmed with recommendation requests and, therefore, sometimes limit the number of recs they write. For this reason alone, it's smart to ask people about recommendations before school ends, ahead of the rest of the pack.

Know that some teachers like to use their summer vacation to write letters of recommendation.

» SENIOR YEAR

AUGUST/SEPTEMBER

If you haven't already, ask teachers to write your letters of recommendation by the end of the first week of school. Also ask other people you want to write extra, "unofficial" letters of recommendation. Don't forget to touch base with your high school counselor.

OCTOBER

Provide each teacher, the counselor, and others with a package of recommendation materials. Tactfully remind the counselor, teachers, and others a week before different applications are due.

NOVEMBER

Contact the colleges to which you are applying early to make sure that they have received your recommendation letters.

JANUARY

Contact all the colleges to which you have applied regular decision to make sure that they have received your recommendation letters.

adMISSION POSSIBLE TIP!

Admissions officers pay a lot of attention to the teacher and counselor evaluation/recommendation forms; they are important parts of the application package. This is even more the case in two circumstances:

1) Among Ivy League and other highly competitive schools, recommendation letters are one of the few distinguishing factors separating one outstanding applicant from another.

2) For applicants whose grades and test scores are less than optimal, very strong recommendation letters can sometimes make the difference between getting accepted or being put on a wait list or denied.

adMISSION POSSIBLE TIP!

Sometimes students find that a favorite teacher will be taking a sabbatical year, maternity leave, moving to another school, or retiring. This doesn't mean that they can't write a recommendation for you; but you do need to ask them to do this before the school year ends. Critical to your request is getting the teacher's email address, personal phone number, and home mailing address.

» PARENTS

Common wisdom says that students whose parents take a real interest in their education usually get better recommendations than students whose parents keep their distance. Starting your child's freshman year, make sure to go to teacher and counselor meetings and attend school open houses. It will help your child if you go out of your way to be friendly and develop relationships with teachers, the counselor, and others.

Remember that how you behave—positively and negatively—with school officials can affect your child. When you bring a request or complaint to someone, always be respectful and polite regardless of how you might be feeling. Negativism and anger rarely get you what you want and may provoke negative reactions toward your child.

CHAPTER 14

ADMISSIONS INTERVIEWS
Knowing Exactly What to Say and Do

DEFINITION of COLLEGE ADMISSIONS INTERVIEW: *Usually lasting between fifteen minutes to an hour, a college admissions interview is a meeting between an admissions representative from a college and a prospective student (or students) for the purpose of exchanging information, asking and answering questions, and evaluating a student's qualifications. Generally, there are two kinds of interviews:*

1. **The On-Campus Individual Interview** *can be with any number of people: a student who works in the admissions office, a faculty member, a part-time admissions counselor, an assistant or associate admissions dean, even the dean him- or herself.*
2. **The Off-Campus Individual Interview** *is an interview with an alumnus or alumna from a student's hometown, held any day, usually in the alum's office, or his or her home, or at a restaurant or coffee shop. These interviews often take place in the fall, and even into January and February of your senior year.*

{ **THE BOTTOM LINE** } Very few colleges require interviews; some colleges recommend them. Still others offer them only to legacies. (In case you don't know, a legacy is the son or daughter of a graduate of the college.) Many colleges, especially the large, public universities and a few of the private ones, don't offer interviews at all. The truth is that it is very difficult to "blow" an interview. Students have only to gain from doing them; if nothing else, to get information about the college and also develop an admissions contact.

FAQ #1: Is one kind of interview better than another?

ANSWER: Individual on-campus interviews will likely benefit you more than an alumni interview. However, a few colleges, notably Yale University, pay a lot of attention to alumni interview reports during their selection process. To determine which colleges you should set up interviews with, check individual college websites or call the different admissions offices on your college list to find out if they offer interviews, and which kind they prefer.

THE POINT OF AN INTERVIEW FOR YOU

A strong interview can create a friend and advocate for you in the final selection process. At the very least, you will become a real person to one individual in the admissions office.

THE POINT OF AN INTERVIEW FOR THE ADMISSIONS OFFICE

Many admissions people say that interviews are a good way to get to know students, as well as answer student questions. In general, the interview is a mechanism for admissions people to find out how interested a student is in their university, what makes an applicant a good match with their school, and the extent to which a student understands what their college is all about.

For college admissions people, an interview is an opportunity to check out an applicant's

* Academic background
* Extracurricular activities
* Personal style
* Potential for contributing to the university
* Strengths and weaknesses
* Ability to deal with life challenges

More than anything, though, admissions people want to find out what is special and unique about an applicant. The Ivies and other very competitive colleges also say that they look for students with intellectual curiosity and evidence of academic prowess.

adMISSION POSSIBLE TIP

Schedule your most important interviews after less important ones so that you can gain some interviewing experience.

SETTING UP AN INTERVIEW

Either you or one of your parents can call an admissions office for an interview appointment. While you have an admissions person on the phone, you might also ask about other things you can do while on campus, e.g., take a campus tour, attend a class or two, spend the night in a dorm, etc. If you don't have the name of the college's admissions representative assigned to your high school, this is a good time to ask for the name, and also get his or her email address. See the Checklists section of www.admissionpossible.com for an admissions appointment form.

PREPARING FOR AN INTERVIEW

Preparing for an interview will make a college visit more interesting, and the interview easier and more effective.

1. BRING AN ACTIVITIES RÉSUMÉ

Since admissions interviewers want to find out who you are, before you go to an interview you need to think about what you want them to "get" about you. Do you want them to see that you're a great student or a leader? That you are a musician who has been taking lessons since you were five years old? That you are the person to whom classmates come for counsel?

One of the best ways for gaining this kind of self-knowledge is to put together an Activities Résumé. (See chapter 8, "Your Activities Résumé," for model résumés.)

Be sure to take a copy of your résumé to each interview. You can't imagine how wonderful it will be to have all the information you need about your grades, test scores, and activities in front of you, rather than trying to dredge them out of your memory!

A résumé is also useful because in giving it to the interviewer, you give him or her something to talk about. And you never know—the interviewer might pass your résumé along to fellow committee members when your name comes up during the selection process.

2. IDENTIFYING WHAT YOU'RE LOOKING FOR IN A COLLEGE

Another way of preparing for an interview is to identify a list of characteristics you want in a college campus in general (e.g., a small campus, a good study abroad program, a reputation for having supportive professors, location on the East Coast, etc.).

Admissions officers want you to have done some research about their college, especially why it is of particular interest. Therefore, come up with at least three to five reasons why a school interests you. For example, you might note

- *The warm, friendly atmosphere of the college*
- *The kinds and variety of students who are there*
- *Specific departments that attract you*
- *Specific professors from whom you would like to take classes*
- *Specific classes that turn you on*
- *Specific activities you would love to get involved with*
- *Anything else that identifies why a specific college is a good match for you*

Be prepared to describe how you will take advantage of and contribute to some particular aspect of each college. Colleges want students who make full use of their resources and also add to their campus in some way.

3. WHERE TO GET INFORMATION ABOUT COLLEGES

Guidebooks

One way of getting information about colleges is to read books such as *The Fiske Guide to Colleges* and *The Insider's Guide to Colleges*. As you go through the individual descriptions, **highlight what you like in one color and what you don't like in another color.** Before an interview, either rip out (or photocopy) the pages you have highlighted or summarize the information in a notebook so that you can refer to it during an interview.

adMISSION POSSIBLE TIP!

Many interviewers take offense if a student comes to an interview knowing little about their college. If you don't say what aspects of a college attract you, it is very easy for an interviewer to assume you aren't interested. This perception—that you don't care enough about the interview or the college to do a little homework—is not what you want to leave with the interviewer.

Friends or Relatives Who Now Attend or Who Have Attended the College

This may be one of your best sources of information. Current and former students know colleges inside and out. One word of caution, though: they also bring personal biases, both positive and negative. Don't base your total assessment of a college on just one person's view of it (except maybe your own).

College Websites

College websites are often a good source of information, particularly in locating such things as departments that you're interested in, professors from whom you'd like to take classes, courses you'd love to take, and activities in which you would like to be involved. Unigo.com and collegeprowler.com are useful websites.

College Admissions Booklets and Other Materials

Colleges' own admissions booklets and other descriptive materials are also a good source of information; but don't forget that they are marketing materials, and only present the most positive sides of a school.

See the College Interview Cheat Sheet at the end of this chapter for a model of what information and questions to bring with you to an interview.

PRACTICING FOR AN ON-CAMPUS INTERVIEW

One of the best ways of ensuring that you have a good interview is to practice interviewing beforehand. To do this, schedule at least one mock interview session with someone whose judgment you trust, and with whom you feel comfortable. It probably makes sense for you to ask an adult because most adults have had some experience with interviewing. Some of the more obvious choices for you to consider are one or both of your parents (or grandparents), your high school counselor, a trusted teacher, an independent counselor, or anyone else (aunt, uncle, family friend) with whom you think you will have an instructive, positive experience.

This latter point is very important: do not role-play your college interview with someone who is going to criticize your answers or put you down. It's fine if your role-play partner gives you suggestions and constructive feedback, but you should avoid practicing with someone who is likely to be disparaging of you or judgmental. You want this to be a confidence and skill-building experience, not an attack session.

To help you role-play an interview, at the end of this chapter is a list of questions that admissions interviewers frequently ask students, as well as sample questions you can ask.

Practice Answering Questions

* **Obviously, interviewers won't ask you every one of these questions and some interviewers will no doubt have questions that are not on this list.**
* **During a mock interview session, practice answering each of these questions.**

Also, you might come up with some personal stories, examples, and/or anecdotes to illustrate your answers.

* **If an interviewer asks what your favorite activity is, tell him or her the answer, and then have an example ready to demonstrate your point.**

Not only should you be ready to answer questions, but also be sure to ask some of your own.

Practice Asking Questions

* **Before an interview, write down three to four questions to ask an interviewer specific to his or her college.**
* **The best questions are about things that you really want to know about, and that demonstrate knowledge of a particular campus.**
* **Avoid asking simplistic questions that can be easily found by looking at the college's handbook or application or silly questions.**
* **Ask questions that reflect whether and avoid not a college is a good match for you.**

The goal in practicing for a college interview is to be as relaxed (or appear as relaxed) and confident as you can be at the real interview. Practice interviews also help you to be the natural, "real you." You want to come across as an intelligent, interesting, well-prepared applicant. Finally, **you want the interviewer to know that this college is a top choice and a really good match for you.**

WHAT TO BRING TO AN INTERVIEW

Before you leave for an interview, make sure that you have the following:

Basics

1. A copy of your Activities Résumé that includes your cumulative GPA over four years, your besr SAT/ACT and Subject Test socres, activities, and other involvements

2. The number of AP classses you will have taken by the time you graduate

3. Class rank, if available

4. A map with directions to the campus, instructions about where to park, and specific directions from where the admissions office is

5. Notes and questions (your Cheat Sheet)

6. Notebook and pen to write down interesting things you hear that you might use when you're filling out the application

Under special circumstances, you may also need to bring:

Special Items

1. Portfolio if you are applying to an art program that requests it

2. Sports tapes if you will be speaking with a coach

3. Music and instrument, drama piece if you will be applying to a music or drama program and other audition materials

Just to be safe, it is also useful to bring along the following:

Emergency Supplies

1. An umbrella (should it be raining)

2. Aspirin or Tylenol should you arrive with a headache

3. Comb or hairbrush

4. A piece of fruit or a granola bar in case you miss a meal

5. Cosmetics, if you use them, for a quick touch-up

6. A bottle of water

FAQ #2: What should I wear to the interview?

ANSWER: The most important thing to know about what to wear is finding something that you feel really comfortable and good in. Colleges don't expect you to come all dressed up in a coat and tie or a fancy dress or suit. But if that's what you're really comfortable in, then go for it! Remember, though, what you wear leaves a lasting impression, positive or negative. Therefore, you don't want to wear anything that is provocative, unprofessional, or sloppy. Leave your T-shirts, cut-offs, shorts, and halter-tops back in the hotel room. Also, visible bra straps are not cool.

For guys, wear something like a favorite shirt and khaki pants, perhaps with a sweater if the weather is cool. For girls, wear whatever clothes make you feel like a million bucks. Consider a nice dress, a skirt, or nice pants and a blouse, perhaps a sweater. Also, because you're likely to be doing a lot of walking, don't forget to wear comfortable shoes.

FAQ #3: **What should I do when I arrive at the interview place?**

ANSWER: To begin with, be sure to arrive at the interview place on time, if not ten to fifteen minutes early. Nothing gives a worse impression than showing up late for an appointment. Before you walk into the office, turn off your cell phone, take out your chewing gum, and look in a mirror to make sure nothing is awry. Stand up straight, take a deep breath, and walk into the admissions office with a smile on your face.

Walk up to the receptionist, smile, and tell him or her your name and that you have an appointment for an interview at the time you have been given. If your parents are with you, they should either find a place to sit or leave the office once they know you are settled. You will probably be told to sit down in the reception area. It's important for you to make a good impression from the moment you enter until the time you leave. Smile; nod to people when they come into the room; if someone speaks to you, respond. If people in the waiting area speak to you, respond. Taking deep breaths will help relax you.

WHAT HAPPENS AT AN INTERVIEW?

When your interviewer comes out to meet you, stand up and; offer your hand for a good, firm handshake. If your parents are in the room, say, "I'd like to introduce you to my parents" (or mother or father), and identify their first and last names. It's almost unheard of for parents to be invited in for an interview. Occasionally an interviewer will ask if they have any questions. It's perfectly appropriate to ask one, maybe two. (Parents: don't go on and on because that will take time away from your student.) Once the introductions have been made, the interviewer will then lead you to the appointed interview office.

As you sit down in the interview office, give him or her a copy of your Activities Résumé and say, "I brought along a copy of my Activities Résumé so that you can know something about me, my academic background, and my activities." Sit up straight, and take deep breaths.

Remember, the first three or four minutes of any interview are the most important! This is the time when the interviewer forms his or her first impression.

The interviewer will probably start things off by commenting on the weather, or asking you how your trip was (if you have come a long way). Simply reply, but with more than just a word such as "OK." Say a few words about the weather or the trip. After the niceties are over, he or she will start the more formal part of the interview and begin asking you questions.

> *adMISSION POSSIBLE TIP*
>
> If an interviewer asks you a question and you don't know what to say, you can always say, "Gee, I'm not sure how to answer that question. Can I get back to you by email after I've had a chance to think about it?" Then follow up when you get home.

Throughout the interview, keep reminding yourself to relax and be as natural as you can. Keep focused on the questions, answering them with details and in the most conversational way you can. Don't forget to look the interviewer in the eye. If a question comes up for which you have prepared information, don't hesitate to refer to your notes. Remember to ask questions yourself from time to time.

Here are a few reminders about what not to do:

★ Don't tap your fingers or a pen on a table next to you.
★ Don't tap your foot on the floor.
★ Don't twirl your hair or chew your nails.
★ Don't slouch in your chair or stare into space.
★ Don't use profanity.
★ Try not to use too many slang words or phrases, such as "I'm all, like," "sweet," "dude," and "um" or "ah."

Most students report that interviews last from twenty minutes to an hour. Before leaving, let the interviewer know that this college is a top (if not THE top) choice for you. When the interview is over, stand up and thank him or her for taking the time to talk with you.

CREATING A FRIENDLY, CONVERSATIONAL ATMOSPHERE AT AN INTERVIEW

The more you can do to create a conversational atmosphere during an interview, the more comfortable you and the interviewer will be. If there is any way to find out who your interviewer will be in advance, do it. Also, try to find out something about the person before you meet him or her. Your high school counselor may be one source. The college's website may be another; they often post photos and short bios of their admissions staff. Find out whatever you can: where the person is from or where he or she went to college, and what his or her interests are. Any tidbit of information can be useful and offer you the opportunity to relate more personally to the interviewer.

> **adMISSION POSSIBLE TIP**
>
> Good conversationalists know that the key to making other people comfortable is to get them to talk about themselves. The college interview situation is no exception.

If information about the interviewer isn't available before the interview, then try to pick up cues from the person and/or his or her office when you first walk into the interview room. Are there photos on the desk that would indicate that the interviewer has children or pets? What are the books in the bookcase? Can you find one or more that you have read? What does the room say about the person's interests? Is he or she into sports or traveling? Is there art on the walls or desk? What do they say about the person?

As the interview progresses, try to tie your answers and questions into something personal about the interviewer. Use the cues that you observe about the interviewer to ask relevant questions or make appropriate comments. One of your goals is to find and create a common bond with the person.

WHAT IF YOU ARE SHY?

If you are a shy or nervous person, the best advice is to prepare, prepare, prepare; then practice, practice, and practice before you have an actual interview. Students who "freeze" usually do so when they are asked questions for which they don't have answers. If you have thoroughly prepared and practiced, it's unlikely that you'll freeze.

Spend some time preparing information for your interviews, both written answers for questions as well questions you can ask the interviewers. Don't try too hard to impress the interviewer; rather, try to be the way you are with your parents, favorite teachers, or older good friends. Act calm even if you don't feel it.

DO'S AND DON'TS ABOUT COLLEGE INTERVIEWS

Here are some quick do's and don'ts to remember while you're practicing (and for the interview itself):

DO	DON'T
1. Be specific in your answers, give details, always try to SHOW why	1. Give one- or two-word answers such as "yes," "no," or "golf," "math," or "video games"
2. Relate questions back to your activities and involvements	2. Miss opportunities to give examples from your personal experience
3. Be interested in the interviewer's questions and what he or she has to say	3. Appear to be bored or uninterested in the interprocess (even if you are)
4. Talk about what you are interested in and about what you feel passionate	4. In any way brag, boast, or appear to be a know-it-all, or arrogant
5. Be positive	5. Be negative, complaining, or put down others, yourself, your school, or other colleges
6. Tell the truth	6. Lie or exaggerate
7. Show real interest and knowledge about the college	7. Say or intimate that you are more interested in other colleges
8. Smile and look the interviewer in the eye	8. Avoid eye contact, scowl, or look unpleasant
9. Focus on your strengths, even when asked about weaknesses (E.g., "While one of my major weaknesses is taking on too many activities at one time, I am at least aware of that propensity now, and I've made major strides in getting it under control.")	9. Make excuses for or be defensive about a weakness or blemish on your record (E.g., "Well, yes, I got a D in English last year, but I was sick and then I had a teacher who really had it in for me.")

FAQ #4: During an interview, is there anything else I should deal with?

ANSWER: Yes, the interview is a perfect forum for you to deal with a variety of touchy or difficult issues, such as having any kind of **physical disability** such as a hearing impairment or an **illness** such as diabetes, or a **learning disability** such as ADD, or a family problem such as a death or divorce, or an aberration on your school record such as a difficult freshman year, or a **suspension from school.**

Colleges want to know about the challenges you have faced. If you have experienced any kind of difficulty, this is part of you as a person and your history. Briefly talking with the interviewer about it will offer him or her a chance to understand what you have gone through, and ask questions about it. How you have handled a life or academic challenge is important information for colleges. They really want to know.

In as descriptive a way as you can, simply explain what the situation is, how it affected your academics or activities, **what you have done to overcome it,** and, if it is ongoing, **how you intend to positively deal with it in college.** Whatever the situation is, try to avoid going on and on about it, as if you are trying to elicit sympathy from the interviewer.

If the challenge you bring up is a bad grade or two, or low SAT scores, or a disciplinary action at school, avoid making excuses, or blaming others, or anything that sounds like whining and moaning. This won't help you at all, and defeats the reason for your bringing up the subject in the first place. You want to explain the situation sufficiently enough that the interviewer can accept it and move on to the more positive aspects of your academic record, interests, activities, and life.

FAQ #5: What if my interviewer is a real jerk?

ANSWER: Every once in a while, a student will have an interview with someone who is simply a jerk. This is more likely to happen with unpracticed alumni interviewers, but it can also happen with an admissions rep. In the long run, this is more of a problem for the college than it is for you. But should it happen to you, try not to get rattled. Smile, be polite, answer the interviewer's questions, and be done with it. Remember, interviews themselves rarely determine one's admission result.

When you get back to school, you might let your high school counselor know about what you experienced, giving specific examples of what was said and done that seemed inappropriate. He or she may be able to help.

INTERVIEW FOLLOW-UP

Before you leave the interviewer, be sure to get his or her business card. As soon as you can, drop the person a short thank-you note. Take a look at a sample thank-you note in the Checklists section of www .admissionpossible.com for what that note might say.

ENDNOTE

In summary, the college interview is a wonderful opportunity for you to develop a personal relationship with someone on the college admissions staff. That connection is worth the time and trouble alone. Rarely does an interview negatively affect a student's chances of being admitted; usually it helps.

Timeline for On-Campus Interviews

» JUNIOR YEAR

SPRING

Most colleges don't offer formal interviews to students until the summer before and fall of their senior year. However, a few colleges are open to interviewing applicants during the spring of their junior year. If during Spring Break you and your family take a college trip and you know a lot about the schools already and are prepared for interviews, call ahead to the various admissions offices to see if you can schedule interview appointments. If you are unfamiliar with a school, it is probably better to wait for an interview until you are knowledgeable about it and prepared.

SUMMER BEFORE SENIOR YEAR

While the summer may not be the best time to visit a college to see it at its best, this may actually be one of the better times to request an admissions interview. In general, fewer students ask for interviews during the summer. Moreover, summer is a "down" time for admissions staffs, so you might find them fresher and less hassled during this time than during the regular school year.

For colleges that only offer group interviews, summer might be a time when you end up with a small group, or even are the only person who shows up, thereby providing yourself an inadvertent one-on-one session with an admissions officer when none is usually offered.

★ **In order to assure an interview for the fall, summer is the best time to call admissions offices for appointments.**

» SENIOR YEAR

FALL

Most students go on the interview circuit during the fall of their senior year. Admissions offices generally offer appointments during working hours Monday through Friday, and sometimes on Saturdays. Virtually no colleges offer appointments during Thanksgiving weekend, or after school closes for the holidays in December. Since Winter Quarter/Semester through the beginning of Spring Quarter/Semester is the application reading and decision time, few if any colleges offer interviews during those months.

COLLEGE INTERVIEW CHEAT SHEET

NAME OF COLLEGE: _____

I have done a lot of research about colleges. I know what I want, I have (circle)

- ★ **Read the guidebooks**
- ★ **Looked at the websites**
- ★ **Talked to students and alumni**
- ★ **Visited different campuses**

QUALITIES I AM LOOKING FOR IN A COLLEGE

1. _____
2. _____
3. _____
4. _____
5. _____

QUALITIES I LIKE ABOUT _____COLLEGE

1. _____
2. _____
3. _____
4. _____
5. _____

QUESTIONS TO ASK

1. _____
2. _____
3. _____
4. _____
5. _____

WHAT I WANT THE INTERVIEWER TO KNOW ABOUT ME

1. _____
2. _____
3. _____
4. _____
5. _____

Reminder: This worksheet is for your own use, *not* to give to the interviewer.

SOME POSSIBLE QUESTIONS FROM INTERVIEWERS

YOUR THOUGHTS ABOUT COLLEGE

1. Why are you interested in this college? What makes you think this college and you are a good match?
2. What other schools do you think you will apply to?
3. What do you think you will major in and why?
4. How would you like to see yourself grow over the next four years?
5. What would you add to this college?

YOUR ACADEMIC BACKGROUND

1. Tell me about your high school.
2. What kind of student are you? Are your grades and SAT scores an accurate picture of who you are?
3. What courses are you taking? Which classes have you enjoyed the most? The least?
4. What has been the highlight of your high school experience?
5. Who is your favorite teacher? Why?
6. Are there any circumstances or events that have interfered with your academic performance?

HOW YOU SPEND YOUR TIME

1. What do you do with your time when you are not in class? What kinds of extracurricular activities are you involved in? What are your hobbies and special interests?
2. What events or activities have made you feel involved?
3. Do you have a passion?
4. What have you done with your summers?
5. Have you done any volunteering?
6. Have you ever worked for pay?
7. What do you do for fun?

PERSONAL STUFF ABOUT YOU

1. Tell me about yourself. (Have three things ready.)
2. What are your personal strengths and weaknesses?
3. Tell me about your family.
4. Who are your friends?
5. Do you have a hero, heroine? Who and why?
6. If given the opportunity to do something in your life differently, what would it be and what would you do?
7. Who are your two favorite authors? What are some of your favorite books? Why?

THE WORLD AND CURRENT EVENTS

Be prepared to talk about what is happening in the world. You can do that by reading newspapers and magazines, or even taking a daily look at an Internet site such as www.cnn.com.

1. What newspapers and magazines do you read regularly?
2. What do you think about
- the war in Afghanistan
- terrorism
- the Middle East situation, Egypt, Libya
- global warming
- drug and alcohol use
- tests such as the SAT, ACT?
- the presidential race
3. If you could meet anyone, present or past, who would it be? What would you like to talk with him or her about?
4. What political or social issues do you think college people should be interested in? What issues or topics concern you?

YOUR GOALS AND FUTURE PLANS

1. What are your plans after college?
2. What do you expect to be doing ten years from now?
3. What are your goals in life?

SOME QUESTIONS TO ASK INTERVIEWERS

THE INTERVIEWER, HIM- OR HERSELF

1. *Where did you go to collge?" Why?*
2. *What made you decide to work at this college?*
3. *If you could do your college experience all over, what would you do?*
4. *What do you like best about this college?*
5. *What do you think students like me should be looking for in a college?*
6. *What would you change about this school?*

THE COLLEGE

1. *I am very excited about getting involved with (a specific sport or activity). Is there someone you can reccomend that I talk to about this?*
2. *I want to major in (your major). Which faculty member do you recommend I speak with about my interest? I read about Professor (professor name) on your website. Do you think he would be open to my talking with him? Can you tell me something about how faculty are involved with students in and out of the classroom?*
3. *Who are the most popular professors on campus? What courses should I not miss?*
4. *Can you tell me something about your study abroad program?*
5. *Where do the students come from at X college? What are they like?*
6. *What happens here on campus during the weekends? Where is the center of the social scene? Do many students go off campus on the weekends? Where do they go? What do they do?*
7. *What kinds of activities are really popular on this campus?*
8. *How do I get to do research with a professor?*

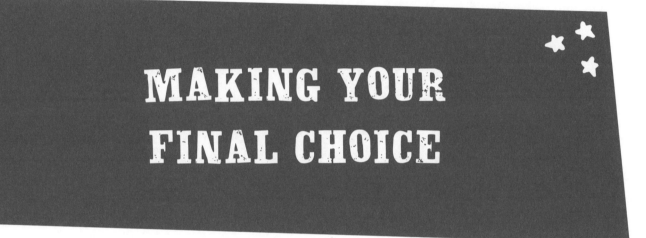

MAKING YOUR FINAL CHOICE

CHAPTER 15

THE END OF THE ADMISSIONS ROAD

A. Dealing with Deffered Admissions, Wait lists, and Denials
B. Choosing Your College

THE END OF THE ADMISSIONS ROAD

You have studied, tested, written essays, and filled out multiple applications. You've also read about and visited colleges, Internet-hopped college websites, consulted college-knowledgeable people, come down to a final list, and waited for the decisions. Finally, now is the time when all of that pays off.

★ If you are not an **Early Decision applicant** who was accepted in December or January, then March and April are the months most admission envelopes start appearing in your regular mail or email mailbox.

★ If letters from admissions offices say that you are **wait-listed, denied, or offered deferred** admission, then read Part A of this guide to find out what your options are.

★ If you have received letters of acceptance from admission offices and **are not sure which college you want to attend,** then read Part B of this guide to find out what to do.

★ If you know where you want to go to college and have been offered admission, congratulations! It's time to celebrate! There are just a few things left for you to do. Read the end of Part B of this guide.

> **DEFINITION of ACCEPTANCE:** *Sometimes arriving in the proverbial "big fat envelope," and other times arriving in a thin envelope or even by email, regardless of size or delivery mode, an admissions acceptance letter is the formal acknowledgment from a college or university that you have been admitted.*
>
> **DEFINITION of DEFERRED ADMISSIONS:** *Rather than putting applicants on a wait list, some colleges offer a few students deferred admission for a time later than the usual fall quarter. Some deferred students are given the option of enrolling second quarter/semester, freshman year. Another form of deferred admission offers applicants admission sophomore year, once the students academically prove they can handle a year of college at another college. Receiving a deferred admission is like being told, "Yes you can come, but under certain conditions and you have to wait a while."*

adMISSION POSSIBLE TIP!

In order to gain an edge on their competition and win over highly desirable applicants, some colleges sometimes send out "likely to get in," "early write," or "wink" letters to a selected group of students. While not official, these letters usually arrive weeks before regular admittance letters, offer heaps of praise, hints of future acceptance, and/or scholarship money to come. Students can usually consider these letters "admissions money in the bank."

DEFINITION of WAIT LIST: *In order for a college to ensure that it will have a full freshman class, the admissions office often creates a wait list; that is, a list of students to whom admittance might be offered should fewer students than predicted say yes to their admissions offers.*

Being wait-listed has the effect of saying to an applicant, "You're not admitted right now, but you may be a little later." The number of students admissions offices admit from their respective wait lists varies from year to year; some years it is zero and other years it can be as high as in the hundreds.

DEFINITION of DENIAL: *Sometimes called a letter of denial and also called a rejection letter, this is a college's formal notification that you have not gained admittance to the college.*

{ THE BOTTOM LINE #1 }

For most students, getting an acceptance letter is a joyous occasion, particularly if it is from one of their top-choice schools.

Receiving notice of deferred admissions is experienced variously by different students: some are happy just to have gotten in, while others are frustrated with having to sit out fall term (or wait a year) as other students attend their school of choice.

Receiving a wait-list letter puts students into a state of limbo; they're not out, but they're not in. Even more frustrating is the knowledge that there are no guarantees that they will get in.

Receiving a denial letter can feel like the end of the world. Rather than celebrate their acceptances, some students dwell on their rejections and often feel defined by them for many years to come. At the very least, this reaction is faulty thinking and serves only to diminish a student's ability to anticipate and enjoy his or her college experience. It's important for applicants to understand that, except for a very rare few, virtually every student going through the admissions process gets a wait-list or denial letter or a number of both.

A. CURVES AND ROADBLOCKS: DEALING WITH DEFERRED ADMISSIONS, WAIT LISTS, AND DENIALS

HANDLING A DEFERRED ADMISSION

Every year, a number of students are offered admittance to a college for some future time. There are both pros and cons for accepting this arrangement

PROS	CONS
1. You get to go to a college that might otherwise not be available to you.	1. You are not able to arrive on campus with the rest of the freshman class.
2. Even if you come a semester late, colleges often have special orientation programs to help second semester admits quickly integrate and adapt.	2. You have to develop your own plans for fall semester, a time when most of your friends will be off to their respective colleges.
3. After you arrive at your college, few will know that you were a second semester admit. Soon you will forget.	3. You may have to take extra classes or go to summer school to graduate with your class.
4. Having a summer and semester before you begin college can give you extra time to do something you've always wanted to do and/or perhaps earn a little money for college.	4. For a few students, an extra semester at home may test already tense relationships with parents or siblings.
5. If you have taken full advantage of a semester away from school, you may bring added maturity and a better sense of what you want from college or a future career.	5. Sometimes housing is a problem for second semester freshmen, but usually it is guaranteed.

In general, colleges that offer deferred admissions have specific expectations for students accepting this arrangement, including spending a semester in some kind of worthwhile involvement such as community service, education, or work.

Before students sign on for deferred admission, they should know exactly what the expectations are and feel good about accepting them. They should also discuss their plans with the college and get written confirmation that they approve the plan of action.

DEALING WITH A WAIT LIST

With growing numbers of students applying to increasingly larger numbers of colleges, coupled with difficult economic times, wait lists are more and more a fixture in the college admissions process.

adMISSION POSSIBLE TIP!

Sometimes it's easy to let your grades slide at the end of spring semester of your senior year. However, if you want to get off a wait list, this is not a smart thing to do. Acceptance slots might open up in May, after school ends, or even in the late summer, so a downturn in grades could severely compromise your chances of getting off a wait list.

WHAT TO DO

If you are on a college's wait list and would like to get onto their accepted list, here are some things to think about and do:

1. **If you are on a wait list of a top-choice school, then notifying them that you want to remain on their list is a good thing to do.** Each college usually gives students specific directions, ranging from mailing a reply postcard, to sending an email, to completing a questionnaire that updates your application or explains why you want to attend their school. **It is very important that you follow their directions, doing and not doing exactly as they say.** If they want a one-page letter, then write it. If they don't want any additional letters of recommendation, better not send them. Also, it is always better to do these things sooner rather than later.

2. **If there are no wait-list directions or vague directions, then call the admissions office (preferably the representative assigned to your high school) and tell an admissions officer how much you would like to attend their school.** Let them know that you will attend the college if you are taken off the wait list. Ask what additional information would be useful for them to have about you or your background. Most officers will suggest that you write a letter indicating your continued interest and an update of your application with any new information.

3. **Write a very positive, upbeat letter (not an email unless told to do so) to the college, indicating your continued, strong interest,** including the following:

   a. **Why you and the college are a perfect match.** Identify what you have been looking for in a college and very specific examples of courses, professors, activities, and programs at the college that meet those needs, wants and desires. Also, identify how you would contribute to the college community. If you have already done this or described the perfect match concept in your application, then do it again with new, more sophisticated material. Be as enthusiastic as you can be. Admissions officers like energetic applicants.

   b. **Update the college on what you anticipate your second semester grades will be (hopefully very good).** At the end of the year, don't forget to have a final transcript sent to the college.

   c. **Update the admissions office on any awards, honors, or successes you have achieved since you turned in your original application. Also, alert them to any accomplishments you have made in your academics, activities, work, volunteer efforts, or sports.** This can come in the form of a résumé or a list. Also, consider sending them any special work you have done, whether a paper, research project, art portfolio, or even a CD of a musical performance.

   d. If meaningful or impressive, let them know about your summer plans.

See the Checklists section of www.admissionpossible.com for a sample wait-list letter you can use to develop one of your own.

4. **Ask your high school counselor to go to bat for you with the college, remembering that it is best for you to make the first contact with the college.** At the very least, the counselor should call the admissions office on your behalf to confirm that you will attend the school if accepted and that you are a good match for them. Ask him or her to find out where you are on the wait list, and to get any information about what you can do to enhance your chances of being admitted. In addition, a letter from the counselor saying these things and extolling your virtues is a great move.

5. **Ask someone who is very credible (the principal, a well-known alum of the college, a highly respected teacher or friend) who thinks very highly of you to write a letter of recommendation.** An extra letter should be from someone who did not write a previous letter. Unless told otherwise, it never hurts to have a piece of true fan mail arrive at the admissions office.

6. **If you or your parents know a professor, administrator, or alum from the college,** see if one might call the admissions office on your behalf. If you have good college contacts, now is the time to use them.

7. **If time and finances permit, make a special visit to the college to plead your case face to face.** Before you drive/fly/take the train to a college, call the admissions office to make sure they are open to and would welcome your visit.

8. **Be in touch with the admissions office after you send your letter, but don't be obtrusive.** Keep admissions people informed about anything new, including your summer activities. Reiterate your very strong interest in the school. However, don't go overboard by calling them every week, sending them cookies or other gifts. You don't want to end up annoying them.

DON'T FORGET

By May 1, you must say yes to one school and send them their nonrefundable deposit. It is important for you to act as if you are going to attend that school, including attending events for pre-admit freshmen, registering for classes, completing forms that will help the college match you with a roommate, paying for room and board and tuition when it is due, and anything else that will get you ready to go off to college in the fall.

FAQ #1: If I let an admissions office know before May 1 that I want to attend their college and I send them my deposit, will they return the deposit if I get off a wait list and decide to go to another school?

ANSWER: No. Most admissions deposits are not refundable.

FAQ #2: I have two schools I am really interested in and can't seem to make up my mind. What if I say yes to both and send them deposits to give myself more time to make up my mind?

ANSWER: In the admissions world, putting down a deposit at more than one college, thereby accepting multiple invitations for admission, is called double depositing. According to the National Association for College Admissions Counseling (NACAC), double depositing violates ethical standards set by their association. You need to know that double depositing carries with it the risk of one or more colleges finding out that you have double deposited and, as a result, rescinding their offers of admission to you. In a nutshell: saying yes to more than one college is not a good idea.

APPEALING ADMISSIONS DENIALS

College applicants rarely appeal admissions denials, and for good reason. The chances of turning denials around are very, very slim. There are questionable reasons for appealing a denial, which will surely be turned down, but there are also a few plausible reasons that might turn the tide for some students.

QUESTIONABLE REASONS FOR APPEALING A DENIAL

These are two reasons that are not going to fly with admissions offices:

a. That you reeeeallly want to go to the school!
b. That your academic record, grades, and test scores are just as good as friends of yours who got into the school.

PLAUSIBLE REASONS FOR APPEALING A DENIAL

Those who appeal denials usually do so because somehow the denial doesn't make sense or because some new, compelling information has become available that was not on a student's original application. Some examples include the following:

REASON

a. The college did not receive your application, College Board or ACT test score reports, high school transcript, and/or other forms or recommendation(s).

ACTION

You need to provide documentation to the contrary for each of the above circumstances. Written proof includes a photocopy of any of the above missing pieces or written requests with dates.

REASON

b. Because of new educational testing, you have data to explain less than stellar grades or test scores and are now getting educational training, therapy, or tutoring to better handle your learning issues.

ACTION

Send the admissions office a copy of the new testing report, as well as a summary of the results by the educational psychologist who did the testing, including his or her educated projections about how well you will perform at the college.

REASON

c. Your academic performance has been affected by

- ★ A personal serious illness or injury
- ★ The death or serious illness of a parent or family member
- ★ An act of nature (hurricane, wild fire, flood, earthquake, etc.)
- ★ A crime, accident, or other tragedy
- ★ A traumatic family crisis

ACTION

Each of the above should be covered in a letter you send the admissions office, as well as documented by appropriate experts such as physicians, psychologists, social workers, newspaper accounts, etc.

If you are considering appealing a denial, here are some suggestions for how to do it:

> **adMISSION POSSIBLE TIP!**
>
> The different campuses of University of California, the University of Southern California, and very occasionally other colleges will accept denial appeals. Each UC campus has their own process that is identified on their respective admissions websites. Each appeal is dealt with on a case-by-case basis.

WHAT TO DO

1. **Call the college admissions office.**

   First, see if you can find out why you were denied. Politely ask if your application was received, and if there is anything missing or some specific reasons for this denial. Often there aren't any real answers, but every once in a while something substantive, such as a clerical or computer error, comes out. For example, you might find out that a piece of your application or SAT scores or a recommendation was never received, thereby eliminating you from consideration.

   If any of the above is the case, and you have proof to the contrary, then appealing a denial makes real sense. If you find something that needs to be corrected or sent, then do it pronto! Also, ask what the college needs from you to file an appeal, e.g., a formal appeal letter. Some colleges have their own specific appeal processes and forms for students to complete, usually available online on the college admissions website.

2. **Or ask your high school counselor to call the college admissions office.**

   If you are perfectly qualified (perhaps more than qualified) in meeting a college's SAT, GPA, and other requirements, ask your college counselor to call the college to find out why you were denied.

   If something is missing from, or in error on, your application, then immediately take whatever corrective action is necessary to fill the gap. Ask the counselor to find out how to have your application reconsidered!

3. **Send an appeal letter to the admissions office.**

Write a very positive, upbeat letter to the college indicating your continued, strong interest in the college, including information about any omissions or errors about which you have become aware. If there are none, but you still want to appeal, then you need to present your case as to why you want to have your application reconsidered. Use the same format as noted above in the wait-list letter.

4. **Be realistic about your chances.**

The chances of getting a denial turned around are slim to none. No matter how hard you work at an appeal, it simply may not work out.

FAQ #3: What can I do if I don't get accepted to any college?

ANSWER: It is rare for students not to get into any of the schools to which they have applied. However, it does occur: sometimes because a student has applied to schools that are all reaches, or has put together sloppy applications, or has applied to too few schools, or simply because of dumb luck.

There are a number of things you can do if you should find yourself in this situation. To begin **with, talk with your high school counselor to see what he or she suggests. Here are a few options you'll probably hear:**

a) You can always go to a community college and then transfer to a private college after as little time as a semester, but usually after a year.

b) After a couple of years and meeting their transfer requirements, you can transfer to one of a number of public universities.

c) There are a number of colleges and universities that offer Rolling Admissions to which you can apply, even in April, May, or later.

d) Every May, in a section called the "Space Availability Survey Results," the National Association of College Admissions Counseling website offers a list of colleges throughout the United States that are still accepting applications.

Remember, there is always something you can do, some college where you can go.

ENDNOTE TO PART A

Most students receive acceptances to a number of schools, in addition to wait lists and denials. If you have followed the suggestions of *adMISSION POSSIBLE*, you have not set your sights on just one college, but have applied to a number of colleges, any one of which you would be happy to attend. As mentioned before, **resist the temptation to dwell on where you have NOT been accepted.**

It is both useful and healthy to focus on choosing the best possible college from among your acceptance options. Having done that, then look forward to your new college life, and enthusiastically throw yourself into all that the college has to offer. Most students end up having wonderful college experiences, whether or not they have gotten into their first-choice school.

B. FINAL DESTINATION: CHOOSING YOUR COLLEGE
DECIDING ON ONE COLLEGE FROM MANY CHOICES

It is April, and all of your acceptances are in. If you are like many students, you now have a number of choices. From this point on, the tables are turned. No longer are you trying to dazzle colleges with your credentials and qualifications; rather, it is the colleges who are doing the dazzling, trying to convince you that they are "the one."

If you have been accepted to your one favorite college, then the decision is easy. Sometimes that doesn't happen, though, and then you must choose one college from a number of other choices. Here are some thoughts on how to do that.

If you are unsure about which college to choose, perhaps you don't have enough information to make a good choice, or the information you have is incomplete or disorganized. Here are some steps to take to get on top of the information you need:

Little Known Fact

At some colleges, it is easier to get in as a transfer student than it is as a freshman. On the other hand, some schools such as Princeton almost never take transfer students.

INFORMATION NEEDED FOR DECISION-MAKING

1. **Identify what you want in a college.**

    If you haven't done this before, put together a list of characteristics you want in a college. Go to the College Selection Questionnaire at www.admissionpossible.com for ideas about what to identify.

    Write down everything you want on a piece of paper and then circle the top 3-5 in terms of their importance to you. Your list might look like this:

    - Location in West, Pacific Northwest, and Midwest
    - Small to medium city or college town, rural area
    - Small, liberal arts college, with no more than five thousand students
    - An intellectually oriented, tight-knit community of students
    - A college that offers cooperative rather than competitive environment
    - Accessible, supportive professors, small classes, focus on undergraduate rather than graduate students
    - A good record for undergraduates getting into graduate school
    - Ethnically diverse students from all over the United States
    - Students who are active in social and political causes
    - Classmates who are lovers of ideas and good discussions
    - Beautiful, safe campus where most students live on campus

2. **Examine the financial aid packages.**

If financial aid is an important consideration, compare the financial packages offered by each college. If one college's package is better than the others, call the other financial aid offices and use the larger offer as leverage to ask them to match the better offer. Don't get your hopes up, though; some will negotiate and others will not.

Take into consideration what the total cost of attending each college will be, what the colleges are offering you, what your parents are able to contribute, and what you can contribute through working during the school year and in the summer.

3. **Re-read the highlighted descriptions of the colleges in your college guidebooks.**

If you have highlighted the things you like and don't like about each college in a college guidebook (e.g., *The Fiske Guide*, *The Insider's Guide*, etc.), go back to these highlights to reacquaint yourself with what you found. If you haven't gone through this process before, buy or borrow a guidebook and do the highlighting now. Compare the highlights with the list of desired characteristics you have noted down.

4. **Talk with students, teachers, counselors, family, and friends about the different colleges:**

adMISSION POSSIBLE TIP!

Students from low-income backgrounds should contact admissions offices to see if they have funds to help them with travel and other expenses to admit events.

Students

Graduates from your high school who are current students, other current students at colleges, and recent young alumni who live in your area (names and contact information should be available from the admissions office) all are excellent resources for finding out the "real skinny" about individual colleges.

Teachers and college counselors

Your teachers, as well as high school and independent counselors, can be valuable sources of insight and information about colleges. Over the years, they have taught and/or counseled scores of students. As a result, they probably have a sense for different colleges and what kinds of students usually do well at them.

Parents, older siblings, and other family members

No one knows you better than your family. Even though it might be hard to do, hear what your family's impressions are of different colleges. It's important to remember that they will be taking partial or total responsibility for paying for your college expenses, but it is also imperative that you make up your own mind.

5. **Pre-admit days and other college visits**

Many colleges offer pre-admit days in which admitted students are invited to spend a couple of days touring the campus, living in a dorm, participating in special activities, talking with professors and current students, attending lectures, and, of course, eating dorm food. If you can't attend one of these events, then visit a campus on your own. Some students prefer to see a campus under more normal circumstances.

Even if you have visited a college before, do it again. There is a big difference between seeing a college when you are an applicant and when you are an accepted student. A post-admit visit usually has a very different feel to it. You are now in the driver's seat, a place from which you can look at a college more realistically. Rather than gaining specific information about a college campus, what is most important about a pre-admit visit is experiencing how that campus feels to you.

THE ACTUAL DECISION-MAKING PROCESS

As you approach making your final decision, try to keep calm. Say to yourself, "I don't have to hurry or rush; I have until May 1. Everything is going to be just fine."

By getting involved with the above information-gathering exercises, you are performing your "due diligence" in terms of final choice decision-making. No one can expect more than that. After you have gathered all of the information you can about colleges, here are some techniques you can use to come up with your final decision.

1. **Pros (what I like) and Cons (what I don't like)**

   Students often find it useful to create a grid in which they identify the pros and cons of attending each college. It might look something like this:

COLLEGE	PROS	CONS
College A		
College B		
College C		
College D		

Remember that not all pros and cons are going to be equal.

* One pro, healthy good food, might be more important to you than another pro, being close to ski slopes.
* Likewise, one con, the school NOT offering a business major, might be more important to you than another con, NOT receiving a good financial aid package.
   - Compare your pros with the list of characteristics you identified as being important to you at the beginning of this section.
   - See if you can't come up with possible solutions or ways to ameliorate the cons on the list. This may lead you to crossing off a con or two.
   - After you have done that, circle the college(s) that have the most pros and least cons. This may provide you with the insight you need to make a decision.

2. **Rating colleges on a scale from 1–10**

   If identifying the pros and cons for each of the colleges doesn't give you a final answer, then list all of the colleges that you are considering and rate them on a scale from 1 (no interest at all) to 10 (love the school!). Once you have done this, order the colleges according to their numbers, highest first, followed by lower-scoring schools. One or two colleges should emerge with highest scores, getting you one step closer to knowing to whom you're going to say yes.

3. **If you still don't have the answer to which college you want to attend, ask yourself these questions:**

★ Picture yourself at different campuses walking around, living in a dorm, going to a football game, or sitting in a classroom. Which college(s) bring up positive thoughts and feelings? Do any make me feel anxious or concerned?

★ What does my heart tell me?

★ On which campus do I feel the happiest?

★ At what college do I feel most at "home?"

★ Which campus has students that seem most like me?

Keep in mind that no college is going to be perfect, and there are probably any number of colleges that will work very, very well for you.

4. **Ask for consultation.**

If you're still feeling uncertain, then sit down with someone you trust and who cares about you, and discuss where you are in the process and what information and conclusions you have come to so far. Ask them to help you sort through the information and feelings you have.

After that, it is up to you. REMEMBER

• Take care not to choose a college only for its prestige factor or high ranking in *U.S. News & World Report*, as opposed to one that feels best for you.

• Also, try to ignore whether the colleges you are considering are Reaches, Good Chances, and Pretty Sure Things. In many cases, students find that a Good Chance or Pretty Sure Thing school fits them better academically and personally than a Reach school.

• Finally, resist the temptation to accept admittance to a college to please someone else, even if that person is important in your life, such as a parent, grandparent, girlfriend, or boyfriend.

Only you can make the final decision. After all, you are the person who will be living with the choice. This is going to be your education.

Finally, remember that even if you happen to make a decision that turns out not to be right, it's not fatal. You can always transfer to another college.

One can begin the process of transferring from one college to another as soon as the first semester of your freshman year.

FAQ #4: **What if I want to take a gap year between high school and college?**

ANSWER: Most colleges are very sympathetic to students who want to take a gap year, provided that they do something productive with it.

The best approach is to go through the entire admissions process, accept admission to the school of your choice, and then ask them what you would need to do if you decided to take a gap year.

It is not a good idea to let colleges know in the middle of the admissions process that you are thinking of taking a gap year. This information alone might be a reason for them to turn you down in favor of another student who is sure to enroll in the fall.

You should also know that it is a lot easier to get counselor and teacher recommendations, as well as transcripts sent from your school, when you are a student rather than an alumni.

ENDNOTE TO PART B

So that's it! If you have read this and the other *adMISSION POSSIBLE* chapters, you probably know more about admissions than most people, maybe even your teachers and counselors. We wish you well and lots of fun and good luck. No matter what, you're about to begin four years of the best time in your life!

Timeline for End of Admissions Road

» SENIOR YEAR

MID-MARCH TO MID-APRIL

★ A few colleges begin notifying students about their admission decisions as early as late February and some send notices in March. The Ivies and other very competitive schools notify their applicants around April 1 or shortly after.

APRIL

★ April is the month during which many colleges offer accepted students on-campus and local pre-admit programs and receptions. Many accepted students take advantage of these college-sponsored events, as well as visit campuses on their own.

★ April is also the month that students should send in their wait-list or denial appeals.

Let your college counselor, teachers, and other recommenders know about your college admissions results. Be sure to thank them for their help.

MAY

★ By May 1, you must notify the school you have decided to attend of your decision to enroll and send in the deposit.

★ May 1 is also the date by which deferred admissions must be accepted.

★ Usually, there are housing and scholarship forms that must be returned.

★ Early May is also the time for students to inform all other colleges that they will not attend their schools.

JUNE

★ Make sure that your final transcript is sent to the college you plan to attend.

★ If you want to get college credit for high school AP courses, have College Board send an AP transcript to your college.

★ Note on your parents' calendar when tuition, and room and board are due at your college.

SUMMER

★ Have a great time!

RECOMMENDED RESOURCES

WEB RESOURCES

For the best, most up-to-date Internet resources, go to www.admissionpossible.com and the Cool Web Links section. On a regular basis, we make sure that the links are available and working.

CHECKLISTS, TO-DO LISTS, SAMPLE RÉSUMÉS, SAMPLE EMAILS TO ADMISSIONS REPS, APPLICATION GRIDS, QUESTIONS TO ASK, ETC.

All of the above and more are available in the Admissions Tool Chest section of www.admissionpossible.com. The site also provides a very comprehensive Admissions Glossary that defines A–Z, all of the major admissions terms and many other ready-to-use resources.

BOOKS

Here are some book resources; many others are identified by different content areas (such as Athletes, International Students, Learning Disabled, and Underserved Students, etc.) in Books People Rave About in the Other Resources section of www.admissionpossible.com.

Antonoff, Steven, PhD. *The College Finder: Choosing the School That's Right for You.* Westford: Wintergreen Orchard House, 3rd edition, 2008.

> Antonoff provides lists and lists of very useful information ranging from which colleges and universities offer the best majors in a range of subjects, to what kinds of learning environments different schools offer, to what kinds of students attend different colleges, etc. Very useful.

Asher, Donald. *Cool Colleges: For the Hyper-Intelligent, Self-Directed, Late Blooming, and Just Plain Different.* Berkeley: Ten Speed Press, 2007.

> Asher provides the inside scoop on what different kinds of colleges have to offer, including Prep Colleges, the Ivy Leagues, schools where scholarship is honored, the "Great Books" colleges, colleges that have an ecological focus, colleges that emphasize entrepreneurial studies, engineering, flying, sailing and the military, as well as men's, women's, and minority-focused colleges. This is a one of a kind, witty, useful book for students who are looking for any of the above mentioned categories.

The College Board. *Book of Majors 2012, 6th Edition.* **New York; The College Board, 2011.**

The most comprehensive list of academic majors and programs that exists. Identifies 900+ majors at 3,600 colleges in the categories of Associate of Arts, Bachelors, Masters, and Doctorate.

The College Board. *College Handbook 2012, 49th Edition.* **New York: The College Board, 2011.**

The most comprehensive, up-to-date demographic information about every accredited college and community college in the United States.

Fiske, Edward B. *Fiske Guide to Colleges 2012, 28th Edition.* **Naperville: Sourcebooks, Inc., 2011.**

Brought up to date every year, this book provides descriptions from the point of view of students of more than three hundred colleges and universities in the United States. The comments are usually "right-on" and are very useful for students as they develop their college lists. Also available as an app.

Goldberg, Natalie. *Writing Down the Bones: Freeing the Writer Within.* **Boston: Shambhala Publications, 2010.**

No writer knows better how to describe how to free yourself up to write well than Natalie Goldberg. She is the best!

Mathews, Jay. *Harvard Schmarvard: Getting Beyond the Ivy League to the College That Is Best for You.* **New York: Three Rivers Press, 2003.**

Well-known *Washington Post* education writer, Jay Mathews, uses his enormous treasure chest of knowledge and wonderful wit to explain what the myriad of college admissions elements are all about.

Pope, Loren. *Colleges that Change Lives: 40 Schools that Will Change the Way You Think About Colleges.* **New York: Penguin Books, 2006.**

Pope offers detailed information and descriptions of forty small, liberal arts colleges in the United States, many of which most people have never heard about. By the time you finish reading this book, you'll want to go to one yourself. This is a must-read for any student, whether they are an A or a C student.

Springer, Sally P., Jon Reider, Marion R. Franck. *Admission Matters: What Students and Parents Need to Know About Getting into College* **(paperback). San Francisco: Jossey-Bass, 2nd edition, 2009.**

A most reliable, comprehensive book about college admissions by people who really know.

Steinberg, Jacques. *The Gatekeepers: Inside the Admissions Process of a Premier College.* **New York: The Penguin Group (Non-Classics), 2003.**

New York Times education writer, Jacques Steinberg, gives a fascinating behind-the-scenes look at admissions from the perspective of Ralph Figueroa, an admissions officer at Wesleyan University. In many ways, this is what takes place at many private universities in the United States.

Strunk, William, Jr. , E.B. White *The Elements of Style, 4th Edition.* **Salt Lake City: Waking Luri Press, 2009.**

This is a fifty-year-old, timeless book on how to write, especially for people who have trouble with grammar.

U.S. News & World Report. *U.S. News & World Report's Best Colleges, 2012 Edition.* Washington, D.C.: U.S. News.

While many college admissions professionals eschew the rankings that *America's Best Colleges* offers, many others appreciate the up-to-date information it provides re median 25th–75th percentile scores for all the colleges in the United States, as well as current information on application deadlines, most popular majors, and expenses for tuition, room, and board.

Yale Daily News Staff. *The Insider's Guide to the Colleges, 2012, 38th Edition.* New York: St. Martin's Griffin, 2010.

Similar to the *Fiske Guide*, this book offers very useful information about colleges from students' points of view.

For other book recommendations, go to www.admissionpossible.com and check out the Books that People Rave About section.

ACKNOWLEDGMENTS

First of all, more thanks go to KellyAnne Hanrahan than I can ever begin to say. Without her help and advice, this book would never have become a reality. I am so lucky to have found her.

A special thanks goes to my family, all of whom were involved in one way or another with the book or the admissionpossible.com website. Thank you to my husband, Mort, who tirelessly offered ideas, gave feedback, and provided editing throughout the process. Many thanks to Marejka Shaevitz and her husband, Chris Esparza, who for years helped me counsel students, provided exceptional insights into such areas as students with disabilities and first-generation/minority students, wrote and edited special pieces, and were always there for a helping hand. Thanks to Jonathon Shaevitz, who helped with the development of the website. Geoff Shaevitz was always on hand to provide his wit and ideas to whatever I happened to be doing. And Erica Shaevitz Huggins also provided her own distinctive insights into the writing and media world.

A particular thank-you goes to Jon Reider, former associate dean of admissions at Stanford University and current director of college counseling at San Francisco High School, for line-by-line editing of an early version of the book and his much appreciated words of advice. Each in her and his own way, Donna Sevilla, Alan Sorkin, and David Brown have been amazing contributors to the web side of the book. On many occasions, Dann Parks provided his astute thoughts about the presentation and look of the book and website. Thanks, also, goes to Amy Ahlfeld for her special help.

A great big thank-you goes to Sourcebooks, Inc., especially Peter Lynch, for taking this book on and making it one of their own. No author could ask for a more supportive, imaginative publishing company. Merci to my literary agent and friend, Sandra Dijkstia, for introducing me to Sourcebooks, Inc.

Over the years, many friends not only provided comments but generous support for the work I do, including Stephen and Susan Polis Schutz, Christine Forester, Spencer Johnson, Marshall Goldsmith, Peter and Arlene Sacks. Harry Melkonian, Elisabeth Eisner and Danica Ray provided invaluable legal counsel. Dora Cruz has always been there with the care and help that only she can provide. Michael Diehl, Debbie Graves, Lisa Barton, and Adrienne Lane also know how much they contribute to my personal and work life. Thank you all.

ABOUT THE AUTHOR

Marjorie Hansen Shaevitz is Founder and Director of adMISSION POSSIBLE, a college admissions counseling program that began in 1996 and a website that was launched in 2007 (and re-launched in 2010). She is an award-winning author, speaker, and professional counselor who has successfully helped thousands of students select and get admitted to colleges. Over the years, Hansen Shaevitz has worked with both public- and private-school students throughout the United States, Canada, Mexico, Europe, Israel, and India. On a pro bono basis, she has also counseled students from disadvantaged family backgrounds.

After completing a master's degree in Counseling Psychology at Stanford University, Marjorie was Orientation Officer at the East West Center in Honolulu, Hawaii, an education/research association that strengthens relations among peoples of Asia, the Pacific, and the United States. She then returned to Stanford as a member of the Dean of Students Office. Later, she directed the Re-entry Program at the University of California, San Diego, and co-authored the McGraw-Hill book *So You Want to Go Back to School*. She also spent twelve years as a trustee for LaJolla Country Day School. Marjorie is a member of the National Association for College Admission Counseling (NACAC) and the Independent Educational Consultants Association (IECA).

A licensed Marriage and Family Therapist, Hansen Shaevitz is a former member of the Stanford University's Parents' Board and Chair of the Institute for Women & Gender's Advisory Council for which she received the Outstanding Achievement Award for her work on behalf of the university. Author of the bestselling books, *The Confident Woman* (Harmony/Random House) and *The Superwoman Syndrome* (Warner Books), Marjorie has appeared on many national radio and television programs, including *The Oprah Winfrey Show* and the "NBC White Paper on Women, Work, and Babies." Articles about her work have appeared in such publications as the *Wall Street Journal*, *USA Today*, the *New York Times*, *Vogue*, *Prevention*, and *Self*. She is also a contributor to the Unigo.com Expert Network.

As author of *adMISSION POSSIBLE: Everything You Need to Know about Finding, Applying, and Getting into the BEST COLLEGE for You*, Marjorie says that one of the most important credentials she brings to her admissions work is that she is a parent of two children and two step-children with whom she has gone through the admissions process.

INDEX

C

W

NOTES

NOTES

NOTES

NOTES

NOTES

Mokena Community
Public Library District